DIFFERENTIAL TREATMENT IN INTERNATIONAL ENVIRONMENTAL LAW

Differential Treatment in International Environmental Law

PHILIPPE CULLET

School of Oriental and African Studies – University of London
and
International Environmental Law Research Centre, Geneva

Routledge
Taylor & Francis Group

LONDON AND NEW YORK

First published 2003 by Ashgate Publishing

Published 2016 by Routledge
2 Park Square, Milton Park, Abingdon, Oxfordshire OX14 4RN
711 Third Avenue, New York, NY 10017, USA

First issued in paperback 2016

Routledge is an imprint of the Taylor & Francis Group, an informa business

British Library Cataloguing in Publication Data
Cullet, Philippe
     Differential treatment in international environmental law
     1.Environmental law, International 2.Equity (International
     law) 3.Sustainable development - Law and legislation
     I. Title
     341.7'62

Library of Congress Cataloging-in-Publication Data
Cullet, Philippe.
     Differential treatment in international environmental law / Philippe Cullet.
         p. cm.
     Originally presented as the author's thesis (doctoral)–Stanford Law School.
     Includes bibliographical references and index.
     ISBN 0-7546-2314-9
      1. Environmental law, International. 2.Equity (International law) I.Title.

     K3585.C85 2003
     341.7'62–dc21

                                                                    2002043895

ISBN 13: 978-1-138-25088-8 (pbk)
ISBN 13: 978-0-7546-2314-4 (hbk)

Contents

Contents

Acknowledgments

This book constitutes an updated and substantially modified version of a doctoral dissertation submitted to Stanford Law School. The dissertation owes a lot to the careful and attentive guidance of Professor John Barton, my supervisor. Professor Thomas Heller also supervized part of the research and was notably always available for discussing theoretical issues. Other Stanford Law School professors, in particular Lawrence Friedman, Linda Mabry, Margaret Radin and Buzz Thompson were always very supportive.

The conceptual framework for this study benefited considerably from the sustained interactions with Dr Patricia Kameri-Mbote who read several drafts with great perseverance. I am also grateful to Michael Anderson and Professor Laurence Boisson de Chazournes for their long-standing guidance and support which goes much beyond this study.

The research for this study was carried out mostly in the libraries of Stanford University. Special thanks are due to all the staff of the Robert Crown Law Library who provided the best possible working conditions I could have hoped for. I would like to thank in particular David Bridgman, Lois Drews, Andy Eisenberg, Andrew Gurthet, Kelly Kuehl, Paul Lomio and Erika Wayne. A number of other libraries also provided significant help. Thanks are due to the staff of the United Nations library in Geneva, and the staff of the library of the Institute of Advanced Legal Studies in London.

The final revisions and updates to the manuscript significantly benefited from the research assistance and inputs of Radhika Kolluru whose contribution is gratefully acknowledged.

Finally, the Swiss National Science Foundation (SNF) and the Swiss Agency for Development and Cooperation (SDC) are thanked for their generous financial support.

Geneva/London, September 2002

List of Abbreviations

ACP	Africa - Caribbean - Pacific
AIJ	Activities Implemented Jointly
CBDR	Common But Differentiated Responsibility
CDM	Clean Development Mechanism
CFC	Chlorofluorocarbon
CGIAR	Consultative Group on International Agricultural Research
COP	Conference of the Parties
ECOSOC	Economic and Social Council (United Nations)
EEZ	Exclusive Economic Zone
EPW	Economic and Political Weekly
EU	European Union
FAO	Food and Agricultural Organization of the United Nations
GATT	General Agreement on Tariffs and Trade
GDP	Gross Domestic Product
GEF	Global Environment Facility
GNP	Gross National Product
HDI	Human Development Index
IARC	International Agricultural Research Centre
ICJ	International Court of Justice
ILM	International Legal Materials
JI	Joint Implementation
Montreal Protocol	Protocol on Substances that Deplete the Ozone Layer

NGO	Non-governmental Organization
NIEO	New International Economic Order
ODS	Ozone Depleting Substances
OECD	Organization for Economic Cooperation and Development
PBRs	Plant Breeders' Rights
PCIJ	Permanent Court of International Justice
PGRFA Treaty	International Treaty on Plant Genetic Resources for Food and Agriculture
R&D	Research and Development
RCADI	Recueil des cours – Académie de droit international
Res.	Resolution
TRIPS Agreement	Agreement on Trade-Related Aspects of Intellectual Property Rights
UN	United Nations
UNCED	United Nations Conference on Environment and Development
UNCTAD	United Nations Conference on Trade and Development
UNDP	United Nations Development Programme
UNEP	United Nations Environment Programme
UNFCCC	United Nations Framework Convention on Climate Change
UNGA	United Nations General Assembly
UNIDO	United Nations Industrial Development Organization
UNRISD	United Nations Research Institute for Social Development
UNTS	United Nations Treaty Series
UPOV	International Convention for the Protection of New Varieties of Plants
WTO	World Trade Organization

Chapter 1

International Environmental Law, Sustainable Development and Differential Treatment: An Introduction

This book focuses on differential treatment in international environmental law. In other words, it studies situations where the principle of reciprocity of obligations gives way to differentiated commitments, for the purpose of fostering substantively more equal results than what is achieved through the principle of formal equality, in situations where actors are not equal.

A study of differential treatment is in fact a study about equity in international environmental law with a focus on development issues. While the relevance of equity in general international law is not questioned, its specific application beyond the judicial field remains controversial, especially in fields like trade law. From a broader perspective, differential treatment is closely related to the notions of partnership and solidarity. In fact, through differential legal arrangements, the international community provides an indication of its commitment to foster the development of new relations based on solidarity and partnership.

International law is fundamentally premised on the principle of sovereign equality and the concomitant principle of legal equality of all states. Over time, international law has progressively developed principles and tools to take into account existing inequalities between states, such as differences in levels of economic development. In fact, it has developed up to a point where it has been argued that states have a collective duty 'to take responsible action to create reasonable living standards both for their own peoples and for those of other states'.[1] The conceptual bases and practical implications of such a duty have not been given much attention, particularly in relation to recent international environmental issues. This book attempts to provide a response to some of these issues by focusing on recent developments in international environmental law, an area of international law which has developed very rapidly over the past few decades but whose importance from the point of view of the development of general international law has, perhaps, not yet been fully recognized.

Over the past few decades, the scope of international environmental law has steadily increased. It now covers not only issues related to the protection of the

---

[1]   Ian Brownlie, *Principles of Public International Law* 256 (Oxford: Clarendon, 5th ed. 1998).

environment, nature conservation and pollution abatement but also encompasses a number of issues related to the use of natural resources, energy policies and the impact of trade on environmental management. In other words, there is a close connection between international environmental law and what is referred to as the international law of sustainable development. In this book, a specific distinction between the two is not operated.

This book is organized along the following lines. The present chapter provides a general background to the study and an introduction to the notion of differential treatment in international law. Chapter 2 analyzes the conceptual framework with respect to differential treatment and its justifications. It starts by examining the notions of formal equality and equity which constitute fundamental legal concepts in many jurisdictions. It then outlines the contours of the notion of differential treatment, its justifications and identifies the various potential beneficiaries. This analysis is undertaken partly with a view to elaborate on the foundations of differential treatment which have received little attention in the literature till date and partly to examine whether the principle of differential treatment could be applied beyond the field of international environmental law.

Chapter 3 maps out the development of differential treatment in international law. It concentrates in particular on a comparison between the international law of development and recent trends in international environmental law. It further analyzes a number of specific differential treatment techniques with a view to ascertaining the practice and the legal status of differential treatment in international law. Chapter 4 analyzes differential treatment as an instrument to further the implementation of international environmental norms. Applying differential treatment to foster effective implementation in developing countries has had significant impacts in practice.[2] Interestingly, differential implementation, often in the form of technology transfer or implementation aid, is significant not only at the conceptual level in the context of a study of differential treatment but also constitutes one of the ways in which the international community seeks to develop effective tools in the pursuit of sustainable development at the local and international levels. This analysis provides the basis for conclusions concerning the effectiveness of differential treatment in practice and reflections on some of the missing dimensions of current differential treatment. Chapter 5 goes beyond the field of strict environmental law to examine how differentiation has been applied in the field of plant variety protection. This example highlights the relevance of differential treatment in other areas of international law and the need for broadening the range of actors involved to make differential treatment more effective in practice. Finally, Chapter 6 sets out the broad conclusions of the study and highlights some of the ways in which differentiation is slowly (re)gaining acceptability even in areas like international trade law where the Uruguay Round

---

2   In this study, the terms developing countries or South, and developed countries or North are used interchangeably.

agreements had indicated a clear shift away from differentiation in favour of common rules.

International Law in a Globalized World

The Emergence of Community Interests in a World of Sovereign States

International law has long been mainly concerned with the co-existence of sovereign entities.[3] This system was not based on the existence of common interests but rather sought to contain antagonistic forces and the main obligations of states were to respect other states' sovereignty.[4]

The significant transformation of the international community brought about by the accession to statehood of many nations following decolonization and the emergence of issues of global concern have had a profound impact on inter-state relations in recent decades. It has become apparent that the sustainable management of the environment or a solution to the economic development problems of developing countries cannot be brought about exclusively through bilateral arrangements. The protection of human rights also constituted a major area where community interests developed. All this has led to significant changes in the nature of international law.[5] In recent decades, common interests have been given higher prominence with the progressive internationalization of the world economy and the realization that there exist environmental problems which are global in scope. In turn, globalization implies that states have become more interdependent.[6] In recent years, this has been most clearly marked by the collapse of communist regimes with the ensuing consolidation of a unified 'world economy' and by technological developments such as the information technology revolution.[7]

For the time being, there still exists a tension between the recognition of interdependence and the current organizational structure of the international society, where the latter remains based on the principle of decentralization through reliance on separate sovereign entities.[8] However, while the assertion of

---

3   Case of the S.S. 'Lotus', Permanent Court of International Justice, Collection of Judgments, Series A – N° 10, 1927, at 18. See also, Philip Allott, *Eunomia – New Order for a New World* 324 (Oxford: Oxford University Press, 1990).

4   Georges Abi-Saab, 'Whither the International Community?', 9 *Eur. J. Int'l L.* 248 (1998).

5   Bruno Simma, 'From Bilateralism to Community Interest in International Law', 250 *RCADI* 217 (1994).

6   Cf. Jost Delbruck, 'The Role of the United Nations in Dealing with Global Problems', 4 *Indiana J. Global Legal Studies* 277 (1997).

7   Harry G. Gelber, *Sovereignty through Interdependence* (London: Kluwer Law International, 1997).

8   Juan-Antonio Carrillo-Salcedo, 'Droit international et souveraineté des Etats', 257 *RCADI* 35 (1996).

sovereignty is blocking the emergence of stronger relations of solidarity, there is little doubt that most states seek to cooperate at the international level to solve an array of problems whose solution cannot be found domestically.[9] The existence of issues that must be solved collectively, in an international society organized on principles which favour egocentric attitudes, has tended to create tensions among states negotiating specific issues. This has contributed, among other things, to the emergence of country groupings with polarized views.[10] While sovereignty remains the cornerstone of international law, the process of globalization is having serious repercussions on its practical significance.[11] Indeed, a number of non-state actors, whether from the civil society or the private sector are challenging the current structures inherited from the past.

The Internationalization of Environmental Issues

As noted, the emergence of community interests has been bolstered by the realization that there are environmental problems which can only be solved internationally. While international environmental problems seemed to be largely confined to bilateral or at most regional issues until the late 1960s, the UN Conference on the Human Environment held in 1972 constituted a turning point in the perception of environmental problems.[12] Since then, the international community has acknowledged, and in some cases addressed, a number of problems that are truly global in scope, such as the depletion of the ozone layer, climate change, the management and protection of biodiversity or land degradation. Indeed, current international environmental law focuses to a large extent on the protection of the common interests of all states.[13]

Even though a number of environmental problems can be said to be global in scope, only a fraction is currently addressed and recognized as such. Cooperation on problems that affect global commons such as the atmosphere or the high seas has proven feasible to a certain extent. However, one important exception can be

9   Cf. Robert O. Keohane et al., 'The Effectiveness of International Environmental Institutions', in Peter M. Haas et al. eds, *Institutions for the Earth – Sources of Effective International Environmental Protection* 3 (Cambridge, Mass: MIT Press, 1993).
10   René-Jean Dupuy, *La communauté internationale entre le mythe et l'histoire* 105 (Paris: Economica, 1986) and Carrillo-Salcedo, supra note 8 at 53.
11   Cf. Tony Evans, 'International Environmental Law and the Challenge of Globalization', in Tim Jewell and Jenny Steele eds, *Law in Environmental Decision-Making – National, European, and International Perspectives* 207 (Oxford: Clarendon, 1998).
12   See generally Report of the United Nations Conference on the Human Environment, Stockholm, 5-16 June 1972, UN Doc. A/CONF.48/14/Rev.1.
13   Pierre-Marie Dupuy, 'Où en est le droit international de l'environnement à la fin du siècle?', 101 *Revue générale de droit international public* 873 (1997) and Eva Kornicker, *Ius Cogens und Umweltvölkerrecht* 157 (Basel: Helbing, 1997).

noted at this juncture. It has been extremely difficult to find a consensus on the question of the conservation and management of forests. This is due in part to strong concerns from some states that the international community should not interfere with the management of resources that are under their sovereign jurisdiction. As a result, no forest treaty could be adopted at Rio.[14] Since then, several forest-related institutional initiatives have only resulted in the establishment of a United Nations Forum on Forests whose mandate includes in the medium-term to examine the question of developing an international forest convention.[15]

Cooperation on most international environmental issues is generally required since by definition no single country has the capacity to protect the global environment over time exclusively through its own efforts. It is now recognized that long-term threats to the global environment are of 'common concern' to all states.[16] The need for cooperation constitutes a positive incentive for all countries to reach a consensus on an equitable and effective basis for allocating responsibility for conservation.[17] Cooperation has however been marred by dissensions amongst different groups of countries. The existence of entrenched positions on these issues can be explained via the links between environmental degradation and economic development. In fact, most global environmental problems must be seen in a context which goes beyond strict environmental management. In some cases such as air pollution, there is a direct link with industrialization. Here, given historical patterns of economic development, the responsibility of developed countries in creating these problems is more important.[18] In other cases, such as environmental problems related to nature conservation and the exploitation of natural resources, an indirect link with patterns of economic development can sometimes be seen. Thus, developing countries today hold the majority of the remaining biological resources partly because of historical patterns of development and partly because of climatic factors.[19]

---

[14] Non-Legally Binding Authoritative Statement of Principles for a Global Consensus on the Management, Conservation and Sustainable Development of all Types of Forests, Rio de Janeiro, 14 June 1992, reprinted in 31 *ILM* 881 (1992).

[15] ECOSOC Res. 2000/35, Report on the Fourth Session of the Intergovernmental Forum on Forests, 18 Oct. 2000, in Resolutions and Decisions of the ECOSOC, UN Doc. E/2000/99.

[16] Programme of Action for the Least Developed Countries, Third United Nations Conference on the Least Developed Countries, Brussels, Belgium, 20 May 2001, UN Doc. A/CONF.191/11, §73. On the notion of common concern, see infra text at note 37.

[17] Edith Brown Weiss, 'Environmental Equity and International Law', in Sun Lin ed., *UNEP's New Way Forward: Environmental Law and Sustainable Development* 7 (Nairobi: UNEP, 1995).

[18] Tariq Banuri, John Weyant et al., 'Setting the Stage: Climate Change and Sustainable Development', in Bert Metz et al. eds, *Climate change 2001 – Mitigation* 73 (Cambridge: Cambridge University Press, 2001).

[19] Cf. Layashi Yaker, 'Joint Implementation from a Southern Perspective', in Catrinus J. Jepma ed., *The Feasibility of Joint Implementation* 87 (Dordrecht: Kluwer, 1995)

Since global environmental problems cover much more than pure environmental issues, tackling them also requires measures which take into account a number of other dimensions. Firstly, the marked differences between countries' contributions to global environmental problems has led the international community to recognize the 'common but differentiated responsibilities' of states with regard to global environmental problems.[20] Secondly, solving global environmental problems must take into account the fundamental development needs of developing countries. In other words, it is, for instance, not possible to address the conservation and use of biodiversity without taking into account the links with agricultural production needs, itself a function of population growth. The issue of population growth is closely linked to the more general question of the carrying capacity of the earth.[21] The concept of carrying capacity as developed by the Club of Rome suggests that population and economic growth are limited by the capacity of the planet to accommodate them in terms of food, mineral and energy resources, and pollution.[22] There have been significant debates over the relevance of the concept for long-term policy making. However, whether the earth's carrying capacity is finite or not in the long term, the question of the availability of resources on a day-to-day basis is relevant from the point of view of differential treatment. Even if the earth can yield enough food for the whole of humankind today, there are a number of reasons, ranging from technological to socio-economic issues which ensure that resources are in fact finite in specific contexts or localities.

State Sovereignty

State sovereignty is one of the most important principles around which international legal relations are organized.[23] In fact, the development of modern international law has been predicated on the common consent of states acting as sovereign, and equal entities.[24] Even though States have never been perfectly equal in power, the understanding that international law is a law among nations and not above them has

---

        stating that the environments of developed and developing countries are more
        complementary than replicative.
[20]   Programme of Action for the Least Developed Countries, supra note 16 at §7 and §73.
[21]   See generally, Donella H. Meadows/Club of Rome, *The Limits to Growth* (London:
        Earth Island, 1972).
[22]   Malcolm Waters, *Globalization* 141 (London: Routledge, 2nd ed. 2001) and Paul R.
        Ehrlich et al., *The Stork and the Plow – The Equity Answer to the Human Dilemma* 3
        (New York: Putman's Sons, 1995).
[23]   Brownlie, supra note 1 at 289 noting that sovereignty and equality of states represent
        the basic constitutional doctrine of the law of nations.
[24]   Antonio Cassese, *International Law in a Divided World* 351 (Oxford: Clarendon,
        1986) stating that '[t]raditional law was geared to States' freedom and formal equality
        and no attention whatsoever was paid to factual inequalities'.

necessitated the fiction of equality.[25] In other words, the international legal system has been based on juridical equality coupled with political independence.[26] However, there is no necessary connection between the recognition of sovereignty at the international level and states' ability to exercise the associated authority and control domestically.[27]

In present day international law, Article 2.1 of the UN Charter recognizes sovereign equality of States as one of the most fundamental principles of international law.[28] This principle of legal equality is translated into rules which apply to all states equally. While formal equality has been at the root of most modern international law, there have been different attempts to change the conceptual bases of the international legal system.

The existence of inequalities between states has been acknowledged for a long time.[29] However, before the Second World War, this was within a predominantly European context where countries had a shared political, historical and cultural background. This commonality of interests was reinforced by the reliance on the notion of civilized nations which excluded many non-European nations from the international community.[30]

The accession to statehood of a number of nations in the decades following the end of the Second World War led to a number of attempts at going beyond the principle of formal equality. The solution advocated by new states was the adoption of preferential treatment measures in the economic field to wipe out the consequences of colonialism. A whole body of legal norms known as the international law of development developed along these lines. Politically, it culminated in the call for a new international economic order (NIEO). The international law of development was sometimes characterized by acrimonious confrontation between developing and developed countries. While the lack of

---

25   L. Oppenheim, *International Law – A Treatise* 18 (Ronald F. Roxburgh ed., 3rd ed. vol. 1, London: Longmans, 1920).

26   Surya Prakash Sinha, *Legal Polycentricity and International Law* 15 (Durham, North Carolina: Carolina Academic Press, 1996).

27   Marian A.L. Miller, 'Sovereignty Reconfigured: Environmental Regimes and Third World States', in Karen T. Litfin ed., *The Greening of Sovereignty in World Politics* 173 (Cambridge, Mass: MIT Press, 1998).

28   One of the consequences is that States are juridically equal. UNGA Res. 2625 (XXV), Declaration on Principles of International Law Concerning Friendly Relations and Co-operation Among States in Accordance with the Charter of the United Nations, 24 Oct. 1970, reprinted in 9 *ILM* 1292 (1970). See also, Abi-Saab, supra note 4 at 252.

29   Cassese, supra note 24 at 43.

30   James Lorimer, *The Institutes of the Law of Nations* (Edinburgh: William Blackwood and Sons, 1883) distinguishing clearly between civilised men and savages and John Westlake, *Chapters on the Principles of International Law* (Cambridge: University Press, 1894). See also Nagendra Singh, 'The Distinguishable Characteristics of the Concept of Law as it Developed in Ancient India', in Marten Bos and Ian Brownlie eds, *Liber Amicorum for the Rt. Hon. Lord Wilberforce* 91 (Oxford: Clarendon, 1987).

agreement between these two groups hampered its development, it led, for instance, to the recognition of the principle of permanent sovereignty over natural resources.[31] Overall, one of the causes of the failure of the international law of development to push through substantive reforms was its focus on a classical conception of international law based on competing sovereignties. This contributed to shaping the issues as a confrontation between developed and developing countries.

The new era of economic and environmental globalization have marked the end of the international law of development and have posed new challenges to the international legal order.[32] From a political perspective, the confrontational approach has given way to a much more cooperative outlook. The collapse of the main alternative economic model to the market economy and the increasing number of transboundary problems have forced most countries to change their attitude towards the development of international legal regimes. This has fostered a new willingness to reconsider the classical bases of international law and to take into consideration factors which cannot be accounted for in a framework of strict legal equality of all states. Thus, opposition to the establishment of a different set of rules in international environmental law for developing countries which was often seen as undesirable has receded and there is today a much broader consensus around the notion of differentiation.[33]

While the principle of permanent sovereignty over natural resources remains at the centre of current international environmental law, it has been qualified both at the conceptual and practical levels.[34] Firstly, states' sovereign rights to exploit their resources according to their own environment and development policies – one of the few generally accepted principles of customary international environmental law – is limited by their 'responsibility to ensure that activities within their jurisdiction or control do not cause damage to the environment of other States or of areas beyond the limits of national jurisdiction'.[35] Secondly, the increasing recognition of the need to cooperate with regard to global environmental problems has led to the

---

[31]   UNGA Res. 1803 (XVII), Permanent Sovereignty over Natural Resources, 14 Dec. 1962, reprinted in 2 *ILM* 223 (1963). See generally Nico Schrijver, *Sovereignty over Natural Resources – Balancing Rights and Duties* (Cambridge: Cambridge University Press, 1997).

[32]   Philippe Sands, *Principles of International Environmental Law I – Frameworks, Standards and Implementation* 14 (Manchester: Manchester University Press, 1995).

[33]   For the view opposed to differentiation, G.E. Do Nascimento E Silva, 'Pending Problems on International Law of the Environment', in René-Jean Dupuy ed., *The Future of the International Law of the Environment* 217 (Dordrecht: Nijhoff, 1985).

[34]   Christopher R. Rossi, *Equity and International Law – A Legal Realist Approach to the Legal Process of International Decisionmaking* 255 (Irvington, NY: Transnational Publishers, 1993).

[35]   Principle 2 of the Rio Declaration on Environment and Development, 14 June 1992, Rio de Janeiro, reprinted in 31 *ILM* 874 (1992). See also Principle 21 of the Declaration of the United Nations Conference on the Human Environment, Stockholm, 16 June 1972, reprinted in 11 *ILM* 1416 (1972).

development of the notion of 'common concern'.[36] The recognition that some issues, like the conservation of biodiversity, are a common concern of humankind represents a compromise which maintains the assertion of permanent sovereignty while recognizing that all states have an interest in the conservation of biodiversity and a duty to cooperate in this regard.[37] In other words, while sovereignty remains the central principle of international environmental law, the preoccupation with new issues, such as global environmental problems, or the increasing importance of non-state actors in environmental management participate of a progressive redefinition of the notion of sovereignty.[38]

Theory and Practice of Development

As noted, the scope of international environmental law has steadily grown over time and it is today impossible to study it without generally analyzing the notion of sustainable development. In the context of differential treatment, it is therefore essential to discuss at the outset the material and political aspects of development which influence and inform international environmental law and policy making.

Evolving Development Discourses

The development of differential treatment has happened largely alongside the various phases of the evolution of history of development discourses at the international level. A cursory glance at debates in the field of development theory is therefore in order at this juncture. Development has traditionally been equated with a linear process through which less economically advanced countries would catch up with industrialized countries.[39] The economically advanced countries thus constitute the point of reference that other countries must emulate. In the decades following the Second World War, the belief was that state-led development constituted the best avenue to allow the South to catch up. States were seen as the only agent having the capacity to bring about development. This emphasis on states coincided well with the traditional emphasis of international law on sovereign equality. By the 1970s, at the domestic and international levels, there was a

---

36   Jutta Brunnée and André Nollkaemper, 'Between the Forests and the Trees – An Emerging International Forest Law', 23 *Envtl. Conservation* 307 (1996).

37   Preamble to the Convention on Biological Diversity, Rio de Janeiro, 5 June 1992, reprinted in 31 *ILM* 818 (1992). See also, Frank Biermann, '"Common Concern of Humankind": The Emergence of a New Concept of International Environmental Law', 34 *Archiv des Völkerrechts* 426 (1996).

38   Concerning the increasing role of non-governmental organizations, Jessica T. Mathews, 'Power Shift (Changing Role of Central Government)', 76 *Foreign Aff.* 50 (1997).

39   Thus, the Concise Oxford Dictionary (9th ed.) defines development as 'industrialization or economic advancement of a country or an area'.

realization that state-led development had not been as successful as had been anticipated. This led to the progressive recognition of the role of NGOs and other non-state actors in development. Concurrently, there was a shift away from macro-level strategies and the emphasis on the well being of the state at large to a focus on basic needs and the condition of individuals.[40]

The last two decades have also witnessed a much greater emphasis on the private sector as an agent for fostering economic growth. This shift has been premised on the perceived advantages of private enterprises in bringing about improved use of public resources, improved operating efficiency and more willingness to innovate and take risks.[41] In fact, the framework within which development takes place has changed dramatically in recent years. The collapse of the non-capitalist model has broadly led to the adoption of a single dominant model of development. This is most clearly illustrated by the establishment of the WTO whose membership has steadily increased since 1995.[42] One of the consequences of the spread of a development model fostering privatization and liberalization is the decreasing importance of states in economic affairs, which is slowly affecting international legal structures as well. In other words, the role of the state in international legal affairs is slowly being redefined.[43]

Another major change has been the increasing importance given to environmental management in development discourses, a shift which is broadly captured under the concept of sustainable development. From the point of view of economic development, the notion of sustainability represents an attempt to limit environmental damage caused by the process of industrialization.[44] In other words, sustainable development implies changes in human material activities which lessen the depletion of non-renewable resources and the pollution of the environment.[45] More recently, sustainable development has been linked more closely to human development. The resulting concept of 'sustainable human development' links the right to development, human rights and good governance. It focuses both on fostering material factors such as meeting basic needs and non-material factors such as rights and participation. Generally, it seeks to achieve a number of related goals

---

40   International Labour Office, *Employment, Growth and Basic Needs* (New York: Praeger, 1976).

41   Mary M. Shirley, 'The What, Why, and How of Privatization: A World Bank Perspective', 26 *Fordham L. Rev.* S23 (1992).

42   Agreement Establishing the World Trade Organization, Marrakesh, 15 Apr. 1994, reprinted in 33 *ILM* 1144 (1994). While 114 states signed the final act of the Uruguay Round in Marrakesh, membership of the WTO was 144 countries as of 1 Jan. 2002.

43   Boaventura De Sousa Santos, *Towards a New Common Sense* 254 (New York: Routledge, 1995).

44   See generally World Commission on Environment and Development, *Our Common Future* (Oxford: Oxford University Press, 1987).

45   Bob Sutcliffe, 'Development after Ecology', in V. Bhaskar and Andrew Glyn eds, *The North, the South and the Environment – Ecological Constraints and the Global Environment* 232 (London: Earthscan, 1995).

at the same time: these include the elimination of poverty, the promotion of human rights, the provision of equitable opportunities through good governance, together with a focus on the conservation of environmental resources and full environmental and social assessment of the impacts of development activities.[46]

In recent years, the notion of sustainable development has come to link not only economic development and environmental management but also social policies. In other words, sustainable development implies the realization that economic goals cannot be reached without also achieving environmental and social goals such as universal education, employment opportunity, universal health and reproductive care, equitable access to and distribution of resources, stable populations, and a sustained natural resource base.

World Development Patterns

Economic and social development across the world is characterized by marked divergences amongst regions and countries. Countries remain, to a large extent, the basis for policy decisions at the international level even though data at the country level does not necessarily give an accurate picture of divergences in the level of development in different regions.[47] The practice is to make distinctions between 'developed' and 'developing' countries, with the addition of sub-groupings, such as 'least developed countries'.[48]

The classification of developed and developing countries has generally been made on the basis of economic development indicators. The World Bank captures, for instance, differences in development through a measure of GNP per capita before separating countries into those which are eligible for borrowing and those which are ineligible.[49] The limits of GNP per capita as an indicator of development has led to the search for alternatives which take into account the fact that development is a multifaceted process encompassing economic, but also social,

---

[46] UNDP, Integrating human rights with sustainable human development (1998), *available at* http://magnet.undp.org/Docs/policy5.html.

[47] As illustrated, for instance, by the marked differences in levels of human development between different states in India. Planning Commission-Government of India, *National Human Development Report 2001* (New Delhi: Oxford University Press, 2002).

[48] 'Least developed countries' are countries that are structurally handicapped in their development process, have low per capita income (less than $900); have a human resource weakness in the areas of health, nutrition, education and adult literacy; and are economically vulnerable. UNCTAD, Statistical Profile of the Least Developed Countries 2001, UN Doc. UNCTAD/LDC/Misc.72 (2001).

[49] Eligible countries are moreover separated into three sub-categories, starting with countries eligible for IBRD funds only, countries in the IDA category only, and countries receiving a blend of the two. Countries eligible for IDA funds are usually the poorest and the ones lacking creditworthiness. World Bank, *The World Bank Annual Report 2001 – Volume 1 – Year in Review* (Washington, DC: World Bank, 2001).

political and cultural aspects.[50] One standard measure of an extended notion of development is the Human Development Index (HDI).[51] GDP per capita still constitutes one of the components of the HDI but it is combined with literacy and life expectancy indices that are more likely to capture some of the social dimensions of development. Out of a maximum value of 1, OECD countries score 0.905, all developing countries score 0.654, while least developed countries only reach 0.445.[52] It is noteworthy that amongst the three indicators considered, the most significant gap between developed and developing, and even more so between developed and least developed countries, is at the level of the measure of income per capita.[53]

While several indicators of development show a narrowing of the gap between developed and developing countries over the last few decades, such as in life expectancy or literacy, some show marked discrepancies between developing and least developed countries. Thus, while the daily calorie supply per capita increased from 71 per cent of the average of developed countries in 1970 to 79 per cent by 1997 for all developing countries, it fell from 70 per cent to 62 per cent in least developed countries.[54] Indicators in the trade sector, show a general worsening of the terms of trade for developing countries in the low and medium human development categories over the past two decades.[55] ACP countries have fared particularly badly. Thus, while they accounted for 7.6 per cent of total EU imports in 1975, their share had dropped to 2.8 per cent by 1999 despite the existence of preferential arrangements within the context of the Lomé conventions.[56] They have also seen their share of world exports fall from 3.4 per cent in 1976 to 1.1 per cent in 1999.[57]

[50]   World Commission on Environment and Development, supra note 44.
[51]   UNDP, *Human Development Report 2002* (New York: Oxford University Press, 2002).
[52]   UNDP 2002, supra note 51.
[53]   While developing countries score 0.66 on life expectancy and 0.69 on literacy, OECD countries score respectively 0.86 and 0.94. On the GNP per capita measure, OECD countries score 0.91, all developing countries 0.61 and least developed countries 0.41. UNDP 2002, supra note 51.
[54]   UNDP, *Human Development Report 2000* (New York: Oxford University Press, 2000).
[55]   UNDP, *Human Development Report 2001* (New York: Oxford University Press, 2001).
[56]   Peter Gakunu, 'ACP-EU Trade: Past, Present and Future', 167 *ACP-EU Courier* 16 (1998) and European Commission, 'ACP/trade: Commission unveils new Economic Partnership Agreements', *Development: Weekly News Archives*, 15 Apr. 2002.
[57]   European Commission, supra note 56.

Economic Development and Environmental Management

The link between environmental management and development has become more and more apparent over time. First, industrialization has been the cause of some significant environmental problems, such as local and global air pollution, ozone depletion or the generation of hazardous wastes. While some of these problems may only affect areas where actual industrialization is taking or has taken place, other have broader impacts. In many cases, the linkages are even more complex. The case of the contribution of vehicle emissions to climate change exemplifies this. Greenhouse gases are emitted in large part by vehicles in the North,[58] while the petrol burnt comes in large part from other source countries. The resulting climate change is, however, spread across the globe without any relation to the source of emissions.

At the other end of the scale, the relationship between economic poverty and environmental degradation has also been the object of significant attention. Ever since Indira Gandhi's speech at the Stockholm Conference in which she suggested that poverty and need were the greatest polluters,[59] the poor have routinely been accused of doing serious harm to the environment.[60] In reality, while the progression of poverty sometimes contributes to certain environmental problems, the poor are usually the worst hit by environmental degradation without being responsible for it.[61]

The nexus between development and environment can be addressed at various levels. At the policy level, the linkage between the two is reflected in the concept of sustainable development.[62] In fact, it has become increasingly difficult to separate 'international environmental law' from the 'international law of sustainable development' as illustrated by the decision to organize a world summit on sustainable development as a follow-up to the Rio conference on environment and

[58] Laurie Michaelis et al., 'Mitigating Options in the Transportation Sector', in Robert T. Watson et al. eds, *Climate Change 1995 – Impacts, Adaptations and Mitigation of Climate Change: Scientific-Technical Analyses* 679 (Cambridge: Cambridge University Press, 1996) noting that in 1990, in twenty countries including all the major economies, road traffic accounted for 80% of total transport final energy consumption.

[59] Speeches by delegations, United Nations Conference on the Human Environment, Stockholm, 5-16 June 1972, UN Doc. A/CONF.48/.

[60] World Commission on Environment and Development, supra note 44 at 49 stating that '[p]overty reduces people's capacity to use resources in a sustainable manner; it intensifies pressure on the environment'.

[61] UNDP, *Human Development Report 1998* at 74 (New York: Oxford University Press, 1998).

[62] On the legal status of sustainable development, Gabčíkovo-Nagymaros Project (Hungary/Slovakia), Judgment – Separate Opinion of Vice-President Weeramantry, *ICJ Reports 1997*, p. 7, 88.

development.[63] The twin focus on environmental protection and economic development has been instrumental in the development of new concepts and principles, from the notion of inter-generational equity to the principle of common but differentiated responsibility.[64]

In practice, one of the levels at which the environmental consequences of economic development can be addressed is that of technology. The development of environmentally sound technologies probably constitutes one of the main vehicles for fostering less environmentally damaging economic growth. These include production technologies and waste management technologies which must both be adaptable to the various conditions met in different countries and regions.[65]

An Introduction to Differential Treatment

International law is founded upon the notion that states are juridically equal. One of the consequences of this legal equality is the principle of reciprocity whereby each state party to a treaty has the same rights and obligations.[66] In practice, however, states vary greatly in wealth, resource endowment, military strength, size and population.[67] These differences or inequalities influence, for instance, political clout in the international arena or the capacity to implement certain treaties.

The concept of judicial equity has been known to different legal systems for a long time.[68] This constitutes an acknowledgment that formal equality may lead in some cases to results which are undesirable according to broader conceptions of justice. This is an excellent tool to address situations which are inherently unusual. Where the results brought about by the application of formally equal rules do not appear to bring about substantively just outcomes on a regular basis, it becomes necessary to devise different schemes which, however, fulfil the same goals as judicial equity.

---

[63]   UNGA Res. 55/199, 10-year Review of Progress Achieved in the Implementation of the Outcome of the UN Conference on Environment and Development, 20 Dec. 2000, UN Doc. A/RES/55/199.

[64]   See generally Philippe Sands, 'International Law in the Field of Sustainable Development', 65 *British Yb. Int'l L.* 303 (1994) and Pemmaraju Sreenivasa Rao, 'Environment as a Common Heritage of Mankind: A Policy Perspective', in *International Law on the Eve of the 21st Century – Views from the International Law Commission* 201 (New York: UN, 1997).

[65]   UNDP 1998, supra note 61.

[66]   Michael Byers, *Custom, Power, and the Power of Rules – International Relations and Customary International Law* 88 (Cambridge: Cambridge University Press, 1999).

[67]   Edith Brown Weiss, 'The Emerging Structure of International Environmental Law', in Norman J. Vig and Regna S. Axelrod eds, *The Global Environment: Institutions, Law And Policy* 98 (Washington, DC: Congressional Quarterly, 1999).

[68]   Michael Akehurst, 'Equity and General Principles of Law', 25 *Int'l and Comp. L.Q.* 801 (1976).

Differential treatment refers to instances where, because of pervasive differences or inequalities among states, the principle of sovereign equality is sidelined to accommodate extraneous factors, such as divergences in levels of economic development or unequal capacities to tackle a given problem. Differential treatment has strong affinities with preferential treatment as conceived in the international law of development era and, in practice, preferential or differential treatment leads to broadly similar results. Differential treatment is, however, predicated on a different conceptual basis which emphasizes solidarity and partnership. It does not require the establishment of a 'new' legal order but seeks to achieve more equitable and effective results within the existing system.

It is also noteworthy that the various affirmative action programmes which have been implemented at the national level in a number of countries share interesting conceptual premises with differential treatment. Indeed, the basis for affirmative action is often the existence of persistent differences in achievement between different groups which can be attributed to past and present discrimination, structural factors and other causes beyond the control of the disadvantaged group or its members.[69]

Differential treatment does not encompass every deviation from the principle of sovereign equality. It refers to non-reciprocal arrangements which seek to foster substantive equality in the international community. In practice, this mainly includes deviations which seek to favour least favoured states. The latter can often be equated with developing and least developed countries. This categorization is relevant in a number of cases because economic development is of prime importance in a number of fields covered by international cooperation, such as trade, and because it is often correlated with levels of political or military power. However, the level of economic development is not the only way to categorize states for purposes of differentiation and this has been acknowledged in the practice of international institutions. Environmental agreements have also gone beyond the simple division between developed and developing countries in some instances. Thus, the Climate Change Convention singles out, among others, the situation and needs of countries with low-lying coastal areas and small island countries.[70]

Differential treatment does not include non-reciprocal arrangements which tend to increase disparities and inequalities. One example of this is found in the current set-up of the UN Security Council which is biased in favour of a handful of the most powerful states. It is also noteworthy that a given non-reciprocal technique may be seen as differential or not depending on the context. Granting different groups of countries different implementation timetables to implement their commitments constitute one such case. Longer implementation periods in the case of environmental agreements, such as the Protocol on Substances that Deplete the

---

69   Devanesan Nesiah, *Discrimination with Reason – The Policy of Reservations in the United States, India and Malaysia* 7 (New Delhi: Oxford University Press, 1999).

70   Article 4.8 of the Framework Convention on Climate Change, New York, 9 May 1992, reprinted in 31 *ILM* 849 (1992) [hereafter Climate Change Convention].

Ozone Layer, definitely favour the group of countries for which compliance with the instrument is relatively more cumbersome.[71]

Differential treatment is expressed in different ways in international environmental law. Firstly, differential treatment refers to situations where treaties provide different commitments for different states. Treaties often provide a general framework applicable to all member states and differentiate at the level of specific commitments. In some cases, however, a whole legal regime can be governed by differential considerations as in the case of the legal regime regarding the exploitation of deep seabed resources.[72] The underlying practical rationale for differential treatment in such situations is to foster more effective action on issues of common concern, such as climate change, which requires the cooperation of all states. Secondly, differentiation has increasingly been used as a way to foster more effective implementation of existing norms – whether differential or reciprocal – adopted in international environmental treaties. Differential mechanisms include, for instance, technology transfer or aid mechanisms which are meant to encourage the implementation of a treaty by countries with comparatively less ability to implement it. Thirdly, the same principles that provide the rationale for differentiation among states can also be applied to other actors. In fact, there are a number of situations where the predominance of states in international legal relations may not foster the best possible outcome. 'Decentralization' or the recognition of the importance of non-state actors in bringing about effective and fair environmental regimes is thus also of great significance.

Differential treatment has often been granted in favour of a group of countries, most often developing or least developed countries. While these categorizations have the advantage of highlighting the existence of significant differences between states in these different groups of countries, they tend to be reductionist. Disparities and inequalities within the developing country group are immense and it is hardly feasible to amalgamate all these countries together even when the least developed ones are separated. Given the relatively low number of states in the international community, an alternative differential framework is to take into account the situation of each and every state to determine their actual capacity to respond to a given problem. This would not be feasible in the case of individuals in domestic law but does not present significant difficulties in a community comprising about 200 members. This has already been experimented with in practice and the UN has, for instance, since inception sought contributions from member states according to a scale of assessment where each state is classified mainly according to its capacity to pay.[73]

---

[71]   Article 5.1 of the of the Protocol on Substances that Deplete the Ozone Layer, Montreal, 16 Sept. 1987, reprinted in Ozone Secretariat – UNEP, *Handbook for the International Treaties for the Protection of the Ozone Layer* (5th ed. 2000).

[72]   See infra Chapter 3 at pp. 80 ff.

[73]   See infra Chapter 3 at p. 72.

One of the consequences of differentiation is to make the legal system more complex than in the case of strict reliance on sovereign equality. This may be seen as negative to a certain extent but is probably only a reflection of the actual growing complexity of international relations in a more globalized world. Thus, the so-called 'flexibility mechanisms' of the climate change regime may appear on the surface to provide for the relaxation of normal international law concerning the implementation of international commitments. In reality, they reflect mainly the growing importance of non-state actors both domestically and internationally and the necessity to incorporate them more directly into the international legal process.[74]

Development of Differentiation

Differential treatment emerges from a long process aimed at providing a new foundational basis to international law in order to reflect its more diverse membership and new international challenges. As noted, the rapid increase in the number of member states in the UN in the decades following the end of the Second World War triggered the first series of attempts at reforming the international legal system. The confrontational approach in place until the late 1970s resulted, for instance, in some strongly worded political declarations calling for a new international economic order but failed to win the full backing of developed states. The envisaged reforms eventually collapsed with the end of the cold war. This failure can be partly attributed to the fact that the notion of solidarity promoted by NIEO advocates was conceived as an obligation on the part of developed countries to grant preferences to developing countries.[75] This 'one-sided' obligation of solidarity was not fully accepted by developed countries which refused to recognize a general legal obligation arising from this notion of sovereignty.[76] However, the internationalization of environmental problems has triggered new debates concerning the structure of international law.[77] States have progressively acknowledged that traditional reciprocal international norms are not well suited to demands for the protection of the environment.[78]

---

74   See infra Chapter 4 at pp. 113 ff.
75   Michel Virally, 'Panorama du droit international contemporain', 183 *RCADI* 9, 326 (1983/V).
76   R.St.J. McDonald, 'Solidarity in the Practice and Discourse of Public International Law', 8 *Pace Int'l L. Rev.* 259 (1996).
77   Cf. Bharat Desai, 'Global Accords and Quest for a New International Ecological Order: From Law of Indifference to Common Concern', 9 *Business and Contemporary World* 545 (1997).
78   Mohamed Abdelwahab Bekhechi, 'Une nouvelle étape dans le développement du droit international de l'environnement: La Convention sur la désertification', 101 *Revue générale de droit international public* 5, 37 (1997).

The development of differentiation in international environmental law has firstly been guided by the principle of common but differentiated responsibilities.[79] The notion of differentiated responsibilities reflects the idea that states' responsibility to address global environmental problems should be shared on the basis of their respective historical and current contributions to the creation of the problems, as well as their capacity to address existing problems.[80] It is useful to note at this juncture that differential treatment as conceived in this study is intrinsically linked, but not equivalent to, the principle of common but differentiated responsibility. This is due to the fact that the scope of differential treatment is broader and the focus is not merely on states' responsibilities to protect the environment.[81] Secondly, recent environmental law has also been influenced by the need to establish partnerships to deal with global environmental problems. This is, for instance, reflected in Agenda 21 which states that no nation can achieve the integration of environment and development on its own and that the realization of sustainable development will only be brought about through a global partnership.[82] The notion of partnership is particularly interesting because it goes beyond mere cooperation between states and encompasses other actors as well, an important dimension of differential treatment covered in chapter 5.

Differentiation and Solidarity

Differential treatment is closely linked to the concept of solidarity. Solidarity based on commonalities of interest and differentiated responsibilities is more widely accepted than the solidarity promoted in the NIEO era and implies a stronger partnership amongst states to solve common problems. In this sense, solidarity can be defined as 'an understanding among formal equals that they will refrain from actions that would significantly interfere with the realization and maintenance of common goals or interests'.[83]

In the field of international environmental law, the principle of common but differentiated responsibility best captures the essence of this new trend. The partnership envisaged implies, for instance, the need to take into account existing differences amongst states. The recognition that economic development or natural resource endowments can constrain the ability of a state to respond to a global environmental problem – and acknowledgment of differing historical and present contributions to the problem – has led the international community to take

[79]   Cf. Brussels Declaration, Third United Nations Conference on the Least Developed Countries, 20 May 2001, UN Doc. A/CONF.191/12, at § 3 and 5.
[80]   Article 3.1 of the Climate Change Convention, supra note 70.
[81]   Anita Halvorssen, *Equality Among Unequals in International Environmental Law – Differential Treatment for Developing Countries* 4 (Colorado: Westview Press, 1999).
[82]   Agenda 21, Report of the United Nations Conference on Environment and Development, Rio de Janeiro, 3-14 June 1992, UN Doc. A/CONF.151/26/Rev.1 (Vol. 1), Annex II, at §1.
[83]   McDonald, supra note 76.

unprecedented measures to ensure the full and effective implementation of the standards adopted. These include, for instance, longer implementation periods for some countries or mechanisms to ensure that the necessary technologies are effectively transferred.

The willingness of most countries to cooperate regarding international environmental issues can be ascribed to a number of factors, as illustrated in the case of climate change. While climate change has historically been caused mainly by industrial countries in the course of their industrialization, developing countries are expected to become the major greenhouse gas emitters within the next few decades. Further, climate change has been put on the international agenda by developed countries while developing countries tend to be reluctant to divert scarce resources to tackle long-term problems which do not alleviate more immediate problems such as water scarcity, water borne diseases or food security.[84] Consequently, through a process whereby each group of countries sought concessions from the other parties, an agreement was reached taking into account the diverse responsibilities and capabilities of states, but ultimately based on the principle of sovereign equality. In the Kyoto Protocol, for instance, developed countries accepted that developing countries would not take on emission reduction commitments. In turn, developing countries accepted the establishment of a Clean Development Mechanism allowing developed countries to meet their obligations at a lesser cost by fulfilling part of the agreed emission reduction commitments in developing countries.[85]

Differentiation, Decentralization and Participation

Differential treatment is intrinsically linked to the search for substantive equality. The central theme of differentiation refers to norms and regimes seeking to achieve results that generally favour weaker parties. Further, differentiation is also increasingly used as a tool to foster more effective implementation of international environmental treaties, in particular through the provision of implementation aid. Beyond these two main functions, differentiation also provides the framework for other changes in international law. The attempt at going beyond the veil of formal equality provides, in a number of cases, an incentive for cooperation amongst states that may not have any direct interest in addressing specific environmental issues, as in the case of climate change which is not an immediate priority for most developing countries. Similarly, differentiation can provide the basis for measures which take into account the needs and specificities of different countries. The recognition of the existence of varying situations in the face of a given problem is at the same time a powerful incentive for cooperation and an instrument of decentralization. Finally, differentiation also provides the conceptual background

---

[84] Joyeeta Gupta, *The Climate Change Convention and Developing Countries: From Conflict to Consensus?* (Dordrecht: Kluwer, 1997).
[85] On the Clean Development Mechanism, see infra Chapter 4 at pp. 118 ff.

for a broader rethinking of the place of different actors in international law. Attempts at developing international legal regimes in the field of the environment have clearly demonstrated the importance of a range of non-state actors in the management of the environment. The need to involve much more directly organizations of the civil society or private businesses is being felt more and more. The climate change regime is, for instance, the first to so closely involve the private sector in the implementation of an international treaty. Differential treatment, though not directly concerned with the position of non-state actors in international law, constitutes an interesting point of departure to rethink traditional categories with a view to foster more relevant and more effective environmental regimes.

Chapter 2

A Conceptual Framework for Differential Treatment

Differential treatment is today a common feature in international environmental law. While there are sound conceptual grounds for granting differential treatment in international environmental law, it is still debated whether differentiation could be used more systematically and in other areas of international law. Given the paucity of studies examining the conceptual bases of differential treatment, this chapter provides an overview of some general theoretical issues concerning differentiation.

It starts by examining justifications for formal and substantive equality and concludes that substantive equality has a lot to offer in situations where members of a community are not perfectly equal in all respects. The realization of substantive equality requires distributive justice measures, differential treatment being one of them. In the following analysis, a strict separation between justice at the state and individual levels is not operated for two reasons. Firstly, the principles of justice upon which differential treatment relies are broadly similar in both cases.[1] Secondly, distributive justice at the international level cannot be fully realized without taking into account justice at the individual level. This is due to the fact that states are not necessarily successful in passing on the benefits of differential treatment to other actors and also because international law ought to ultimately benefit human beings and not states. The rest of the chapter focuses on general definitions and issues relating to differential treatment in international law, with special emphasis on international environmental law and examines the aims, forms and instruments of differentiation. Further, it considers the grounds upon which differential treatment can be based and the ways in which the benefits of differentiation can be allocated. Finally, it explores which entities should benefit from differential treatment.

Equality and Equity in Theory and in Practice

Formal Equality as Justice

Human societies usually seek to achieve an 'equitable' distribution of goods within the society and the rules established for this purpose are based on an agreed notion

---

[1]   John Rawls, *A Theory of Justice* 378 (Oxford: Clarendon, 1972).

of equity.[2] Equality is an elusive concept and different versions of equality yield extremely different substantive outcomes. Formal equality posits that all subjects of the law should be treated in a similar fashion. Rules are usually deemed to be just if they apply to all without discrimination. No attempt is made to correct, for instance existing economic or other inequalities in the society. The aim is to foster a system in which goods are distributed so as to maximize the total welfare of the claimants.[3]

The entitlement theory is representative of a strict application of this principle.[4] In this case, a right is justly acquired as long as it was acquired according to the rules in force at the time of acquisition. The distribution of wealth is thus deemed to be fair as long as everyone is entitled to the holding they possess under this scheme. In other words, the entitlement theory upholds the existing distribution of goods.[5] However, it has been contended that even by utilitarian standards such inequalities are counterproductive because they give the few who own wealth too high a reward to encourage productivity while at the same time denying essential commodities to the majority.[6]

The Rawlsian theory of justice is also broadly based on formal equality but in a much milder form. While it accepts the inevitability of inequalities in the basic structure of any society,[7] it provides that inequalities in access or distribution must have advantages for the beneficiaries as well as for everyone else. Further, while it does not seek to guarantee the realization of minimum basic needs to all,[8] it provides that the poorest must not become relatively poorer.[9]

At the international level, the principle of formal equality has been translated into the notion of sovereign equality of states, which constitutes a cornerstone of international law.[10] Historically, the neutrality of the law has been premised on the legal equality of all states with the consequence that treaties were traditionally deemed to be 'just' if they provided for reciprocity of obligations amongst

---

[2]   H. Peyton Young, *Equity in Theory and Practice* (Princeton, NJ: Princeton University Press, 1994).

[3]   *Id.*

[4]   R. Nozick, *Anarchy, State and Utopia* (New York: Basic Books, 1974).

[5]   Justice in holdings is historical and a fair distribution results as long as the goods were acquired or transferred according to rules in force at the time. Nozick, supra note 4 at 152.

[6]   Thomas M. Franck, *Fairness in International Law and Institutions* 151 (Oxford: Clarendon, 1995).

[7]   Rawls, supra note 1 at 7 states that inequalities are inevitable in the basic structure of any society. See also, Andrew Dobson, *Justice and the Environment* 81 (Oxford: Oxford University Press, 1998).

[8]   Cf. Henry Shue, *Basic rights – Subsistence, Affluence, and U.S. Foreign Policy* (Princeton: Princeton University Press, 2nd ed. 1996).

[9]   Rawls, supra note 1 at 151.

[10]   UNGA Res. 2625 (XXV), Declaration on Principles of International Law Concerning Friendly Relations and Co-operation Among States in Accordance with the Charter of the United Nations, 24 Oct. 1970, reprinted in 9 *ILM* 1292 (1970). See also I. A. Shearer, *Starke's International Law* 99 (London: Butterworths, 11th ed. 1994).

contracting states. In other words, traditional international law sought to provide to all states equal opportunities to participate in the system even though all of them were not exactly identical in power or size.[11]

At the individual and international levels, formal equality seeks to give every member of the community equal opportunities. Internationally, this conception is, for instance, translated into the notion that states have the right to take any amount of shared common resources on a first-come, first-served basis.[12] This is theoretically appealing but in practice tends to allow states having the most advanced technological capacity to appropriate de facto a disproportionate share of the resources while less technologically advanced states benefit less despite the status of such resources as *res communis*. In the case of deep seabed resources where high technology is required for the exploitation of these resources, formal equality privileges states which can make much better use of the opportunities offered.[13] Similarly, in a trade context, the standard national treatment clause, which requires that imported and locally produced goods should be treated equally, is difficult to justify in a situation where parties are economically and technically unequal.[14]

Substantive Equality as Justice

The provision of formal equality as an ultimate policy goal can produce an optimal aggregate outcome, such as a high rate of overall economic growth, but tends to overlook the welfare of disadvantaged individuals. Indeed, equality of rights or opportunities does not necessarily bring about equality of outcomes. This is especially relevant in a world characterized by disparities in resources and capabilities, both at the inter-individual and inter-state levels.[15] Accordingly, even if the international community adopts a system built on the rule of law, in which the weak and strong are treated equally and where all have a chance to benefit from an open, market-based, global economy, the least favoured will continue to be relatively disadvantaged.[16]

Legal systems are premised on the need to bring stability, coherence and foreseeability to human relations. One of the instruments used to regulate social

---

11   Georges Abi-Saab, 'Whither the International Community?', 9 *Eur. J. Int'l L.* 248 (1998).
12   Edith Brown Weiss, 'International Environmental Law: Contemporary Issues and the Emergence of a New World Order', 81 *Georgetown L.J.* 675 (1993).
13   R.R. Churchill and A.V. Lowe, *The Law of the Sea* 224 (Manchester: Manchester University Press, 3rd ed. 1999).
14   Cf. Michael Blakeney, *Legal Aspects of the Transfer of Technology to Developing Countries* 93 (Oxford: ESC Publishing, 1989).
15   Oscar Schachter, *Sharing the World's Resources* 7 (New York: Columbia University Press, 1977).
16   *Contra, e.g.,* Jeffrey Sachs, 'A New Blueprint: Beyond Bretton Woods', *Economist*, 1 Oct. 1994, at 31.

conduct in large groups is the enactment of rules and standards. As noted by Hart, 'the law must predominantly (...) refer to *classes* of person, and to *classes* of acts, things, and circumstances'.[17] It does not however follow that all rules should necessarily apply uniformly to all individuals. Different factors indicate why a strict reliance on the principle of fixed rules applying uniformly to all may not constitute the best solution in the face of significant inequalities. Firstly, the changing nature of society and human needs calls for progressive change in the legal system. There is thus a need for balance between the desire for certainty in legal results and the desire for modification and improvement.[18] The fulfilment of unmet basic needs may, for instance, push people to seek changes in the existing legal order.[19] Secondly, the application of a general rule to a particular case may necessitate the consideration of special factors and the balancing of the various interests at stake. There is thus a border area where enforcement agencies need to supplement gaps in existing rules.[20] Thirdly, the fact that rules emanate from competent organs and have been adopted using normal procedures does not guarantee that the rule is equitable. Even though law is usually based on the premise of a coincidence with justice, this is not necessarily realized in practice.[21]

The search for an alternative basis to the principle of fixed rules leads to the old principle that like cases be treated alike and that dissimilarly situated people should be treated dissimilarly.[22] In Aristotle's own words,

> if they are not equal, they will not have what is equal, but this is the origin of quarrels and complaints – when either equals have and are awarded unequal shares, or unequals equal shares. Further, this is plain from the fact that awards should be 'according to merit'; for all men agree that what is just in distribution must be according to merit in some sense.[23]

While stressing the importance of foreseeability, this principle of distributive justice implies that relevant dissimilarities between subjects of the law warrant special attention or special treatment.[24] Judge Tanaka in his dissenting opinion in

---

[17] H.L.A. Hart, *The Concept of Law* 124 (Oxford: Clarendon, 2nd ed. 1994).

[18] R. Neil Snyder, 'Natural Law and Equity', in Ralph A. Newman ed., *Equity in the World's Legal Systems* 34 (Brussels: Bruylant, 1973).

[19] Franck, supra note 6 at 7, noting that the different expectations of people may cause a tension between the search for change (for instance, meeting basic needs) and the search for stability in the legal order.

[20] Hart, supra note 17 at 135.

[21] René-Jean Dupuy, *La communauté internationale entre le mythe et l'histoire* 103 (Paris: Economica, 1986).

[22] Hart, supra note 17 at 159.

[23] Aristotle, *The Nicomachean Ethics* (trans. David Ross, revised by J.L Ackrill and J.O. Urmson, Oxford: Oxford University Press, 1991).

[24] Cf. Principle 10 of the Declaration on the Progressive Development of Principles of Public International Law relating to a New International Economic Order, in International Law Association, *Report of the Sixty-Second Conference* 2 (1987).

the South West Africa case adopts a similar conception of justice. He states that formal equality must remain the basic principle by which to abide and that proponents of differential treatment bear the onus of substantiating their claims. He further asserts, however, that once the case for differential treatment is established, it is then not only permissible but compulsory as a matter of justice to take remedial action: 'To treat unequal matters differently according to their inequality is not only permitted but required'.[25] This conception of distributive justice has, however, never been embraced by the ICJ.[26]

It is not sufficient to assert that like cases must be treated alike to determine which differences should be taken into account. Indeed, individuals in a given society will often have several common and several distinct characteristics. It is therefore important to determine whether height, gender, age, wealth or income constitute relevant factors. Thus, while discrimination on the basis of gender is banned in a number of countries, it is not uncommon for tax systems to tax more heavily people in higher income brackets.[27] This constitutes an acknowledgment that a strict reliance on formal equality may yield results which may not be 'just' if the existence of inequalities in society is not taken into account.[28] In other words, the fulfilment of formal equality may not necessarily bring about substantive equality.

The realization of substantive equality implies that existing inequalities, such as inequalities in wealth or natural endowments should be acknowledged and taken into account. In the context of the current international community, this may preclude reliance on the theory of the veil of ignorance advocated by Rawls.[29] Indeed, Rawls' veil of ignorance implies that members of the community do not know whether their society will be a developed or a developing country.[30] Given the existing distribution of resources and wealth across the world, the choice

---

25   South West Africa, Second Phase, Judgment – Dissenting Opinion of Judge Tanaka, *ICJ Reports 1966*, p. 6, 306.

26   Christopher R. Rossi, *Equity and International Law – A Legal Realist Approach to the Legal Process of International Decisionmaking* (Irvington, NY: Transnational Publishers, 1993).

27   Joel Slemrod ed., *Tax Progressivity and Income Inequality* (Cambridge: Cambridge University Press, 1994). See also, Young, supra note 2.

28   *Contra* Michael Akehurst, 'Equity and General Principles of Law', 25 *Int'l and Comp. L.Q.* 801 (1976) stating that it is more important to have certain rules than just rules.

29   In justice as fairness, Rawls envisages an original position of equality corresponding to the state of nature in traditional social contract theory. One of the essential features of this situation is that no one knows their place in society, class position or social status. Further, no one knows their fortune in the distribution of natural assets and abilities, their intelligence and strength. This 'veil of ignorance' provides the basis for choosing principles of justice that are deemed fair because no one can design principles that favour their particular condition. Rawls, supra note 1 at 12.

30   John Rawls, *The Law of Peoples* 33 (Cambridge, Mass: Harvard University Press, 1999).

between being born in a developed or a developing country may well be more significant than arrangements within a given society.[31] Contractarian principles may also prove misplaced at the international level because they are usually developed for national societies and do not imply redistributive obligations between persons situated in different societies.[32] In other words, an enquiry into matters of equality cannot be based exclusively on theoretical preferences but must relate to existing realities. Further, discrepancies which cannot be traced to individuals' choices should be taken into account and may constitute grounds for redistributive claims.[33] This is true both in the case of a country lacking primary natural resources and in the case of an individual born without wealth. The limits of the traditional notion of equity in law thus call for new approaches to the realization of substantive equality.

The measures called for to realize substantive equality are not meant to be permanent exceptions to the principle of formal equality but specifically to offset the problem areas that may have been identified. These may include gaps in economic development at the state level or the special vulnerability of cultural, linguistic or other minorities.[34] Further, the realization of substantive equality in the context of differential treatment does not imply the elimination of all inequalities but it is much more a question of eliminating existing gross inequalities.[35]

Equity in International Law: The Case of Judicial Equity

The harshness of strict reliance on positive law was realized early on in different countries and it is noteworthy that principles developed within Roman law still influence the notion of equity in many countries.[36] By the early twentieth century, most western states had developed a body of equitable principles which had become part of the law.[37] Due to this consensus, when the Permanent Court of International Justice (PCIJ) was established in the aftermath of the First World War, 'the general principles of law recognized by civilized nations' were included

---

[31]   Brian Barry, *The Liberal Theory of Justice: A Critical Examination of the Principal Doctrines in* A Theory of Justice *by John Rawls* 129 (Oxford: Clarendon, 1973).

[32]   Charles R. Beitz, 'Justice and International Relations', in Charles R. Beitz et al. eds, *International Ethics* 286 (Princeton, NJ: Princeton University Press, 1985).

[33]   On the contrary, as acknowledged by Eric Rakowski, *Equal Justice* 1 (Oxford: Clarendon, 1991), differences resulting from voluntary wagers cannot serve as a basis for redistributive claims.

[34]   Cf. S. James Anaya, 'On Justifying Special Ethnic Group Rights', in Will Kymlicka and Ian Shapiro eds, *Ethnicity and Group Rights – Nomos XXXIX* at 222 (New York: New York University Press, 1997).

[35]   For an argument against complete equality of wealth, Guido Calabresi and A. Douglas Melamed, 'Property Rules, Liability Rules, and Inalienability: One View of the Cathedral', 85 *Harvard L. Rev.* 1089, 1099 (1972).

[36]   Snyder, supra note 18 at 34 and Ralph A. Newman, 'The General Principles of Equity', in Ralph A. Newman ed., *Equity in the World's Legal Systems* 589 (Brussels: Bruylant, 1973).

[37]   Franck, supra note 6 at 48.

among the various sources of law laid down to govern the Court.[38] Both the PCIJ and the International Court of Justice (ICJ) which is governed by a similar provision have made frequent recourse to general principles of equity.[39]

In a judicial sense, equity appears as a form of individualization of justice and serves to temper gross unfairness which sometimes results from the strict application of the law. It represents the liberty offered to the judge to achieve material justice that a formal application of the norm at stake may not provide.[40] It can serve to fill gaps in the law, to provide a basis for a more just interpretation, to provide a moral basis for making an exception to the normal application of a rule of international law or to provide the basis for deciding a case in a way that disregards existing law.[41]

Reliance on the principles of equity has been particularly important in the various cases concerning the delimitation of continental shelves that have been submitted to the ICJ.[42] The Court has thus acknowledged that '[e]quity as a legal concept is a direct emanation of the idea of justice' and that it is bound to apply it as part of the process of administering justice.[43] It has even pointed out that it is more concerned with striking an equitable solution than with equitable principles as such because it considers the result to be of overwhelming importance.[44] It has, for instance, been willing to consider geographical factors as relevant indices in the application of the rule of law at stake. However, the Court has generally refused to take into consideration economic factors stating, for instance, that economic matters are extraneous to the delimitation of continental shelf areas, because of the cyclical and changing nature of economic development.[45] As per this view, the law must thus remain detached from the vagaries of development to favour solutions of

---

[38] Statute of the Permanent Court of International Justice. See also Sir Hersch Lauterpacht, *The Development of International Law by the International Court* (London: Stevens and Sons, 1958).

[39] Article 38.1.c of the Statute of the International Court of Justice. Note however that for some commentators, the recourse to equity illustrates the failure of the law to fulfil its task. M. Chemillier-Gendreau, 'La signification des principes équitables dans le droit international contemporain', 16 *Belgian Rev. Int'l L.* 509 (1981).

[40] M. W. Janis, 'The Ambiguity of Equity in International Law', 9 *Brooklyn J. Int'l L.* 7, 8 (1983) notes that since Grotius equity has been seen as the discretionary corrective element of a strict universal law.

[41] Edith Brown Weiss, 'Environmental Equity and International Law', in Sun Lin ed., *UNEP's New Way Forward: Environmental Law and Sustainable Development* 7 (Nairobi: UNEP, 1995).

[42] Barbara Kwiatkowska, 'Equitable Maritime Boundary Delimitation, as Exemplified in the Work of the International Court of Justice During the Presidency of Sir Robert Yewdall Jennings and Beyond', 28 *Ocean Development and Int'l L.* 91 (1997).

[43] Continental Shelf (Tunisia/Libyan Arab Jamahiriya), Judgment, *ICJ Reports 1982*, p.18, 60.

[44] *Id.*

[45] Maritime Delimitation in the Area between Greenland and Jan Mayen, Judgment, *ICJ Reports 1993*, p. 38, 74.

a permanent character.[46] The Court has nevertheless opened the door for the consideration of economic factors in situations where a decision would entail 'catastrophic repercussions for the livelihood and economic well-being of the population of the countries concerned'.[47]

Judicial equity has an important role to play in bringing about substantive equality. However, the role of courts in this regard is limited since judges operate at the level of the enforcement of legal rules whereas the creation of distributive rules or regimes does not usually fall within the domain of the courts.[48] Even though both legal doctrines work towards the same broad goal of fostering the material realization of a conception of justice, the use of equitable principles at the level of rule making and implementation is of much broader application than judicial equity. This broader conception of equity constitutes a much more direct challenge to the standard legal framework than the now well established judicial equity.[49] It constitutes the focus of the present study.

Differential Treatment: General Considerations

As noted, international law is founded on the concept of the legal equality of states. Reliance on formal equality cannot foster the realization of substantive equality in situations where all members of the community are not equal. This requires the introduction of corrective measures to remedy existing inequalities; measures which constitute the core of what is referred to as differential treatment in this study. Differentiation looks beyond the principle of juridical equality to take into account factors such as divergences in levels of economic development or unequal capacities to tackle a given problem.

Differential treatment can take several forms. The first type of differentiation refers to situations where treaties provide different obligations for different groups of states. Secondly, differential treatment also takes the form of measures to facilitate implementation in states which do not have the capacity to implement specific commitments. This is premised on equity and also the desire to foster the realization of results benefiting the whole international community such as in the case of global environmental problems. Thirdly, while differential treatment is primarily a concept applying to inter-state relations, it is also relevant to the issue of the broadening of the range of actors in international law and the role of non-state actors in addressing problems like climate change.

---

[46]   This approach is in stark contrast to the emphasis on socio-economic factors apparent, for instance, in the Climate Change Convention.

[47]   Delimitation of the Maritime Boundary in the Gulf of Maine Area, Judgment, *ICJ Reports 1984*, p. 246 at 342.

[48]   Cf. Lauterpacht, supra note 38 at 213 on *ex aequo et bono* adjudication.

[49]   Cf. Ian Brownlie, 'Legal Status of Natural Resources in International Law (Some Aspects)', 162 *RCADI* 245 (1979-I) arguing against the use of rule making to effect distributive justice.

Differential Treatment and Traditional International Law

Differential treatment constitutes a novel instrument which supplements the architecture of traditional international law. It builds upon the structure enshrined, for instance, in the UN Charter. It generally reflects one of the ways in which international law is adapting itself to the new realities facing the international community. Chief among these are the globalization of issues of common concern, the increasingly diverse nature of the states forming the international community and the increasingly important role played by non-state actors in various areas covered by international law.

Even though reciprocity constitutes a direct consequence of the cardinal principle of legal equality of states, examples of non-reciprocity abounded even in earlier times. To take but a few significant examples, non-reciprocity is at the core of the voting arrangements in the Security Council or at the World Bank. Thus, what is novel in the conceptualization of differential treatment is not non-reciprocity as such but the specific focus it adopts. Indeed, differential treatment only refers to legal arrangements which seek to foster substantive equality. The specific concern for differentiation in environmental law stems from the fact that it does not focus exclusively, or even primarily, on principles but on making international law more effective in practice. By and large, differential treatment does not imply that the basic principle of formal equality should be discarded. It simply gives recognition to the fact that in practice, legal equality does not always concur with economic, political or military equality and that these factors can be of direct relevance in the formulation and implementation of international agreements.

Aims of Differential Treatment

Differential treatment broadly seeks to foster the realization of substantive equality. This objective can, however, not be achieved in a vacuum. Thus, differentiation is specifically geared towards making the legal system more effective, for instance, by enhancing the prospects of full implementation of international commitments. Differentiation in its present form is not an instrument for the transformation of the current international legal order but only for adapting it in the face of new circumstances and challenges.

Differential treatment is intrinsically linked to the notion of equity. As traditionally conceived, equity seeks to influence results brought about by the application of a given rule of law which are deemed undesirable according to broader justice, moral or social concerns.[50] This approach thus excludes permanent exceptions but provides remedial measures to the harsh consequences of the application of a rule of law applying to all in a similar way. Rules which treat all partners in the same way, even if permitting divergence from the established pattern

---

50   Georges Pinson (France) v. United Mexican States, Decision of 19 Oct. 1928, 5 *Rep. Int'l Arbitral Awards* 327, 355.

in special circumstances, are suitable so long as the partners have the same capacity to benefit from the standards in place. In practice, there are many cases where inequalities among partners or countries influence their capacity to benefit from a given legal regime.

Since inequalities witnessed in the real world occur, in large part, independently of people or states' actions, the necessity arises to devise exceptions which take into account some existing inequalities so as to bring about substantively equal results. As Sen recalls, this is a difficult task since '[t]he demands of substantive equality can be particularly exacting and complex when there is a good deal of antecedent inequality to counter'.[51] The rationale is not to create permanent exceptions but a temporary legal inequality to wipe out an inequality in fact.[52] This implies that certain classes of actors need to be singled out on account of differences which affect their capacity to enjoy the rights established by the rules in force. Thus, while identical rules of access to resources constitute the fairest allocation among equal partners, this is not necessarily the case when people do not have the same economic capacity to acquire the resources. This constitutes the rationale for the establishment of rules which give disadvantaged members of the community the capacity to compete. In international law, political independence and legal equality do not suffice to explain the realities of the different members of the international community. Gaps in economic development among different countries influence, for instance, their capacity to realize their political independence and constitute one of the relevant factors in the search for substantive equality. It is noteworthy that differential treatment seeks to adapt the legal system to social and economic realities and is not akin to charity. While aid is motivated at least in part by charity and is based on the discretionary motives of the donor,[53] differential treatment seeks to find firmer bases for redistributive measures whose eventual aim is the empowerment of weaker actors.[54]

While differential treatment implies a necessity to identify groups of actors who tend to fare less well than others under existing legal systems, this is not to discount the importance of aggregate measures of welfare. On the contrary, especially in the field of natural resources, the global limited availability of resources calls for an all-encompassing strategy which recognizes the need to both allocate sufficient minimum amounts to all and to guarantee sustainability in the long term. Thus, it is necessary to consider both aggregate fairness which seeks to ensure overall

---

[51]   Amartya Sen, *Inequality Reexamined* 1 (Cambridge, Mass: Harvard University Press, 1992).
[52]   Emmanuel Decaux, *La réciprocité en droit international* (Paris: Librairie générale de droit et de jurisprudence, 1980).
[53]   Edward Kwakwa, 'Emerging International Development Law and Traditional International Law – Congruence or Cleavage?', in Anthony Carty ed., *Law and Development* 407 (Aldershot: Dartmouth, 1992).
[54]   Cf. Salman Khurshid, 'Justice and the New International Economic Order', in Kamal Hossain ed., *Legal Aspects of the New International Economic Order* 108 (London: Pinter, 1980) noting that reverse discrimination is not based on charity.

availability of the necessary resources and disaggregate fairness which seeks to allocate existing resources in such a way that individuals, or states, who need them most get a share.[55] The maximization of the welfare of a given individual may in fact be achieved more surely if the welfare of the group is taken care of at the same time.[56]

The difficulty in allocating shares is well exemplified by discussions concerning the allocation of carbon emission rights for the purposes of allowing trading in carbon rights to stem climate change. Many different allocation methods have been proposed.[57] Emissions can firstly be allocated on the basis of current emission levels. The consequences of this type of allocation – or grandfathering, as it is called – would be the promotion of stability in the international economic order by allowing current polluters to carry on and by limiting low polluters' rights to expand their polluting industries. This allocation scheme benefits neither the global environment nor the most disadvantaged countries and in practice tends to reward countries which industrialized first and those that have done the least to reduce their own emissions. Another allotment system focuses on the global good nature of the environment and the need to take action to mitigate climate change. A global burden which has to be shared according to specific criteria is thus recognized. Various standards have been proposed, ranging from the ability to pay of each nation to the idea of an equal per-capita entitlement.[58] They seek to establish a basis which recognizes the different contributions to the creation of the problem, the different capacities to respond to the problem and the link between economic development and environmental degradation in the form of carbon emissions. While these proposals are controversial because of their potentially immense impact on economic development in industrial countries, they are noteworthy in this context because they seek to go beyond the formal fairness of the first proposal which focuses on the single dimension of economic growth in developed countries. The case of carbon emissions clearly shows that environmental problems like climate change cannot easily be dissociated from underlying economic, social and historical realities. The role of differential treatment in this case is not limited to

---

55   On the link between aggregate and disaggregate fairness, Franck, supra note 6 at 30 distinguishing between aggregate fairness (at the community level) and disaggregate fairness that is fair to each person.

56   Mohammed Bedjaoui, 'Pour un nouveau droit social international', 39 *Yb. Association Attenders and Alumni* 17 (1969).

57   V. Bhaskar, 'Distributive Justice and the Control of Global Warming', in V. Bhaskar and Andrew Glyn eds, *The North, the South and the Environment – Ecological Constraints and the Global Environment* 102 (London: Earthscan, 1995) and P.R. Shukla, 'Justice, Equity and Efficiency in Climate Change: A Developing Country Perspective', in Ferenc L. Tóth ed., *Fair Weather? Equity Concerns in Climate Change* 145 (London: Earthscan 1999).

58   See generally Prodipto Ghosh and Jyotsna Puri eds, *Joint Implementation of Climate Change Commitments – Opportunities and Apprehensions* (New Delhi: Tata Energy Research Institute, 1994).

fostering rules which take into account the situation of countries most likely to be affected by the regime instituted but also to foster the recognition of the links between environmental protection and economic and social development, since the solution to the former cannot be dissociated from the latter.

Forms of Differential Treatment

Differential treatment measures can take two main forms. The first focuses on the allocation of rights and entitlements while the second is based on the redistribution of resources. These two categories are examined separately in the next few paragraphs but the distinction is artificial insofar as both are required simultaneously to ensure the realization of desired outcomes.[59] This is valid in the case of global environmental problems such as biological resource management where the realization of a differential solution at the international level requires not only financial aid but also a new perspective on the allocation of rights.

As far as the allocation of rights and entitlements is concerned, it is necessary to go back to the basic premise that legal rules apply to all subjects without distinction. From this starting point of a 'universal' rule, differential treatment leads to positive discrimination in favour of a given class or classes of subjects. Positive discrimination does not usually seek to bring about the complete elimination of inequality but to make sure that inequalities are only the result of individual differences, uncomplicated and unburdened by historical handicaps.

At the domestic level, policies seeking to redress existing inequalities have been used in different countries, for instance, under the heading of affirmative action, or reservation policies.[60] Affirmative action has been controversial in all the countries where it has been applied. Indeed, in California where a wide-ranging affirmative action programme had been previously put in operation, the acceptance of Proposition 209 in 1996 now prohibits the state from granting preferential treatment to any individual or group on the basis of race, sex, colour, ethnicity, or national origin with respect to public employment, public education, or public contracting.[61] This new provision was challenged in court on the grounds that it denied racial minorities and women the equal protection of the laws guaranteed under the Federal Constitution.[62] It is noteworthy that the two conceptions of equity at stake were weighed differently in different forums. The district court which granted a preliminary injunction relied on the notion that the equal protection

---

59   *Cf.* Philippe van Parijs, *Real Freedom for All* 30 (Oxford: Clarendon, 1995).

60   Reservation policies of India are particularly noteworthy because India is one of the few countries to have embodied such principles in its constitution. Bhikhu Parekh and Subrata Kumar Mitra, 'The Logic of Anti-Reservation Discourse in India', in Subrata Kumar Mitra ed., *Politics of Positive Discrimination – A Cross National Perspective* 91 (Bombay: Popular Prakashan, 1990). See generally Marc Galanter, *Competing Equalities – Law and the Backward Classes in India* (Berkeley: UC Press, 1984).

61   Article 1 §31, Constitution of the State of California.

62   Girardeau A. Spann, 'Proposition 209', 47 *Duke L.J.* 187 (1997).

clause guarantees racial minorities the right to full participation in the political life of the community.[63] On the other hand, the Court of Appeals found that Proposition 209 fitted within the framework of the equal protection clause insofar as it fundamentally seeks to eliminate all governmentally imposed discrimination based on race.[64]

Despite the controversies, even the opponents of affirmative action accept that there is a need for measures targeting the poorest and enhancing the status of disfavoured communities.[65] In most cases, affirmative action has been proposed to remedy current inequalities, but such measures also constitute a way to redress past injustices.[66] Despite the controversies and critiques, positive discrimination, wherever it has been used, has been successful in highlighting the extent of existing deprivation; in promoting specific schemes benefiting some, usually economically deprived sections of the society; and redressing inequalities in general. It can easily be transferred to the international sphere to deal with economic and other inequalities because the issues at stake are broadly similar.[67]

The attention given to positive discrimination at the national level has parallels in several areas of international law. Chapter 3 examines in more detail the development of positive discrimination in international environmental law. Other areas where a number of examples of positive discrimination can be found include human rights. Human rights instruments include flexibility clauses recognizing that levels of economic development can affect a state's capacity to implement its obligations in the field of socio-economic rights.[68] The UN Human Rights Committee has, for instance, recognized that the principle of equality may require states to take affirmative action to diminish or eliminate conditions which cause discrimination. Such affirmative action is deemed legitimate under the Covenant as

---

63   Coalition for Economic Equity et al. v. Pete Wilson, et al., United States District Court, N.D. California, 23 Dec. 1996, 946 F. Supp. 1480.

64   Coalition for Economic Equity et al. v. Pete Wilson et al., United States Court of Appeals, Ninth Circuit, 8 Apr. 1997, 122 F.3d 692. See also, Coalition for Economic Equity et al. v. Pete Wilson et al., Supreme Court of the United States, 3 Nov. 1997, 118 S. Ct. 397.

65   Julio Faundez, *Affirmative Action – International Perspectives* 7 (Geneva: International Labour Office, 1994) and Anaya, supra note 34. Cf. Thomas Sowell, *Preferential Policies – An International Perspective* (New York: W. Morrow, 1990) who takes a negative view of preferential treatment.

66   Brown v. Board of Education, 347 U.S. 483 (1953).

67   Khurshid, supra note 54 at 112.

68   Article 2 of the International Covenant on Economic, Social and Cultural Rights, New York, 16 Dec. 1966, reprinted in 6 *ILM* 360 (1967) and Article 3 of the Convention Concerning Minimum Standard of Social Security (Convention N° 102), 28 June 1952, reprinted in International Labour Organization, *International Labour Conventions and Recommendations – 1952-1976 – Volume II* (Geneva: International Labour Office, 1996).

long as it is required to correct discrimination in fact.[69] Some treaties have been more specific with regard to positive discrimination. The Convention on the Elimination of All Forms of Discrimination against Women recognizes, for instance, that differential measures to bring about de facto equality between men and women are legitimate and cannot be held to be discriminatory in nature.[70] More recently, Protocol 12 of the European Convention on Human Rights specifically reaffirmed that the principle of non-discrimination is not incompatible with positive discrimination as long such measures are based on 'objective and reasonable' grounds.[71]

The second form of differential measures concerns the direct redistribution of resources. This re-allocation is only necessary in situations where goods are available in finite quantities. Any mandated re-allocation of a given stream of benefits must, therefore, benefit some people and deprive others. In fact, it is often the case that '[p]rovision for the poor can be made only out of the goods of others'.[72] In practice, differential treatment may involve the redistribution of a measure of direct or indirect wealth or income redistribution. The allotment of burdens and benefits among the various actors in society implies the need for enactment of rules for this purpose.[73]

At the global level, it is clear that humanity has only access to a limited quantity of resources at any one point, due to climatic, technical and other constraints. Since basic needs have to be met immediately, part of the redistribution envisaged thus involves a static transfer of resources from the North to the South.[74]

Instruments of Differential Treatment

A number of differential instruments have developed over time in international law, ranging from non-reciprocal legal norms to implementation aid seeking to help certain groups of states implement their obligations.

Historically, there have been different types of non-reciprocal obligations. Before the Second World War, departures from reciprocity often signalled an 'unequal' treaty or more precisely a treaty imposed on a given state, such as a peace treaty.[75] After decolonization, the absence of reciprocity started to indicate a shift

---

[69]   General Comment N° 18, Non-discrimination (Thirty-seventh session, 1989), Human Rights Committee, UN Doc. E/C.12/2000/4 (2000), at §10.

[70]   Article 4 of the Convention on the Elimination of all Forms of Discrimination against Women, New York, 18 Dec. 1979, reprinted in 19 *ILM* 33 (1980).

[71]   Preamble of Protocol N° 12 to the Convention for the Protection of Human Rights and Fundamental Freedoms, Rome, 4 Nov. 2000, *European Treaty Series – N° 177*.

[72]   Hart, supra note 17 at 166.

[73]   Cf. Hart, supra note 17 at 163.

[74]   Brian Barry, 'Humanity and Justice in Global Perspective', in J. Roland Pennock and John W. Chapman eds, *Ethics, Economics and the Law – Nomos XXIV* 219 (New York: New York University Press, 1982).

[75]   See generally, Lucius Caflish, 'Unequal Treaties', 35 *German Yb Int'l L.* 52 (1992).

from reliance on formal equality to compensatory inequality taking into account that powerful states are favoured by a legal system focusing on the formal validity of legal rules.[76] This compensatory inequality also known as preferential treatment constituted the core of the international law of development and formed the basis of claims made by developing countries against developed countries. More recently, non-reciprocal norms known as differential treatment are based on mutually accepted non-reciprocity.

The distinction between reciprocal and differential norms requires elaboration. In many cases, rules which formally apply to all in the same way will provide for some type of flexibility, for instance, by stating that the special situation of a group of states should be taken into account.[77] This 'contextualization' can be found in either reciprocal or differential clauses and therefore defines neither. Differential treatment specifically refers to situations where norms providing for different obligations for different groups of actors are adopted. The term 'dual norms' was coined to describe these differentiated norms in the context of the international law of development to emphasize the distinction between the North and the South and the clash between classical international law and more recent legal developments.[78] It is noteworthy that differential treatment norms are no less obligatory than reciprocal rules. The only special feature of differentiation is to foster a different form of justice by, for instance, giving special implementation incentives to some parties less likely to have the capacity to fully comply with the rules adopted.[79]

Apart from differentiated standards, differential treatment also refers to various situations where equity, justice or moral considerations lead to the adoption of solutions which constitute a departure from normal legal arrangements.[80] The setting up of a regime for the exploitation of deep seabed resources which provides for the compensation of states affected by the exploitation of these common resources constitutes one such example.[81] Other instances include specific implementation mechanisms, such as aid mechanisms or technology transfer specifically geared towards fostering the implementation of a given set of norms by

---

[76]   Decaux, supra note 52 at 41.

[77]   Daniel Barstow Magraw, 'Legal Treatment of Developing Countries: Differential, Contextual and Absolute Norms', 1 *Colorado J. Int'l Envtl. L. and Pol'y* 69 (1990).

[78]   W. Benedek, 'The Lomé Convention and the International Law of Development: A Concretisation of the New International Economic Order?', 26 *J. African L.* 74 (1982).

[79]   Cf. Felipe Paolillo, 'Final Report', 67/1 *Yb. Institute Int'l L.* 437 (1997) noting that some critiques of differential treatment which argue that the adoption of economic incentives to ensure the broad acceptance of environmental rules seem preferable to the imposition of differentiated obligations.

[80]   *Cf.* T. Banuri et al., 'Equity and Social Considerations', in James P. Bruce et al. eds, *Climate Change 1995 – Economic and Social Dimensions of Climate Change – Contributions of Working Group III to the Second Assessment Report of the IPCC* (Cambridge: Cambridge University Press, 1996).

[81]   See also chapter 3 at pp. 80 ff.

countries which are willing to take on these obligations but probably do not have the necessary resources to carry them out.[82]

Rationale for Differential Treatment

Differential treatment has been justified in various ways at different times. The following cursory review of some of the main justifications for differentiation is necessary to understand its evolution and its present position in international law.

Principles of Justice

A number of arguments used to validate differentiation reflect a strong link with notions of justice and morality. These include concerns with regard to protection of the weak and disadvantaged, compensation for past injustices, and social justice.[83]

Needs of the weak The needs of the weakest individuals and states constitute an overwhelming concern at the national and international level. The main reason for this concern is the globally limited available supply of resources at any given point in time and the skewed distribution of these resources as a result of either natural causes, such as different endowments in primary resources, or human induced causes, such as different patterns of economic development. Thus, while food is globally available in sufficient quantities, it is estimated that 38 per cent of the population of least developed countries are undernourished and that in some regions of the world like South Asia, about half of the children under five years of age are malnourished.[84] This may seem close to Rawls' condition of 'moderate scarcity' that relates to a situation in which natural and other resources are not so abundant that schemes of cooperation are superfluous.[85] In practice, a situation of moderate scarcity does not obtain because this requires that at least everyone's basic needs are fulfilled, which is not the case for millions of people today.[86] This calls for much stronger principles than those advocated by Rawls and may necessitate the guarantee of minimum subsistence standards.[87] By extending the

[82]   On differential treatment at the implementation level, see infra chapter IV.
[83]   Cf. Devanesan Nesiah, *Discrimination with Reason – The Policy of Reservations in the United States, India and Malaysia* 71 (New Delhi: Oxford University Press, 1999) concerning India.
[84]   UNDP, *Human Development Report 2001* (New York: Oxford University Press, 2001) and World Bank, *World Development Report 2000/2001 – Attacking Poverty* (New York: Oxford University Press, 2000).
[85]   Rawls, supra note 1 at 126.
[86]   Shue, supra note 8 at 27.
[87]   S.C. Vasciannie, *Land-Locked and Geographically Disadvantaged States in the International Law of the Sea* 21 (Oxford: Clarendon, 1990) stating in the context of the law of the sea that landlocked States '[o]bjectively . . . have greater needs than

idea of justice further, the existence of inequalities constitutes the basis for an entitlement to a higher share of available resources.[88] In fact, it may be argued that when the total resources are sufficient to provide everyone with enough while still allowing some people to retain considerably more than others, an adequate minimum should be guaranteed to everyone.[89]

At the individual level, the reference to needs is closely associated with the concept of basic needs and human rights. Even though all human beings have similar fundamental requirements, the concept of needs is rather elusive because needs are not absolute or static.[90] Someone's basic needs may be someone else's luxury because in many cases this concept reflects more a socially determined minimum quality of life than 'vital' needs.[91] Thus, it is necessary to qualify the concept of basic needs so as to primarily focus on people at the lower end of the economic and social scales. Examples of such basic needs include the availability of safe drinking water, shelter or primary health care and measures for the reduction of life-threatening diseases such as malaria.[92] It is noteworthy that the focus on the most disadvantaged is also a general feature of human rights. International human rights are universal entitlements but their implementation is to be judged against the degree to which the most disadvantaged and marginalized benefit.[93]

The necessity to cater to basic needs is already firmly entrenched in international law. Human rights instruments have long recognized an array of economic and social rights such as the rights to food or to health.[94] The Brundtland report in its definition of sustainable development also emphasized that needs of the poor should be given overriding priority to foster the realization of the

---

    others, and for this reason it is considered unjust that they should be accorded the same treatment as their economically advanced counterparts'.

[88]   Subrata Ray Chowdhury, 'Common but Differentiated State Responsibility in International Environmental Law: From Stockholm (1972) to Rio (1992)', in Konrad Ginther et al. eds, *Sustainable Development and Good Governance* 322 (Dordrecht: Nijhoff, 1995).

[89]   Henry Shue, 'Global Environment and International Inequality', 75 *Int'l Aff.* 531, 541 (1999).

[90]   *Cf.* Mary Douglas et al., 'Human Needs and Wants', in Steve Rayner and Elizabeth L. Malone eds, *Human Choice and Climate Change – Volume One – The Societal Framework* 195 (Columbus, Ohio: Battelle Press, 1998).

[91]   Eric Dudley, *The Critical Villager – Beyond Community Participation* (London: Routledge, 1993).

[92]   Malaria is estimated to claim the lives of 1 to 3 million people each year. The World Resources Institute et al., *World Resources 1998-99* (New York: Oxford University Press, 1998).

[93]   Statement by the Committee on Economic, Social and Cultural Rights on Human Rights and Intellectual Property, in Committee on Economic, Social and Cultural Rights, Report on the Twenty-Fifth, Twenty-Sixth and Twenty-Seventh Sessions, UN Doc. E/2002/22-E/C.12/2001/17, Annex XIII, at § 8.

[94]   International Covenant on Economic, Social and Cultural Rights, supra note 68.

principles of sustainable development.[95] At the inter-state level, it has also been posited that needs of the least favoured states constitute a strong basis for special treatment.[96] It has thus been asserted that the right to development could be based upon the concept of needs or basic rights.[97] In turn, this constitutes the basis for claims that States should have a right to an equitable share of what belongs to all, because common goods should be used for the benefit of humankind as a whole without consideration of territorial borders.[98] While these claims have not been translated into binding legal principles, international instruments have made reference to these issues. Thus, the Rio Declaration recognizes, for instance, that States must cooperate to reduce poverty in order to more effectively meet the needs of the majority of the population of the world,[99] and Article 69.2 of the Law of the Sea Convention states that one of the criteria to be taken into account while determining the extent of the participation of landlocked countries in the exploitation of surplus resources in the Exclusive Economic Zone (EEZ) is 'the nutritional needs of the populations of the respective States'.[100]

Compensation The need to compensate individuals or states for past or present inequalities has been debated for a long time but remains contentious. Compensation for historical wrongs has been particularly controversial and does not figure prominently in present international law. Compensation for breaches of existing norms of international law has received much more support.

Compensation based on historical developments History provides a basis for differential claims insofar as a duty of moral reciprocity is recognized, whereby wealthier people or states acknowledge that they would not agree to be in the poorest's position.[101] Under this scheme, developed countries would accept

---

95   World Commission on Environment and Development, *Our Common Future* 43 (Oxford: Oxford University Press, 1987).
96   Inamul Haq, 'From Charity to Obligation: A Third World Perspective on Concessional Resource Transfers', 14 *Texas Int'l L.J.* 389 (1979). See also Schachter, supra note 15 at 6.
97   Mohammed Bedjaoui, 'Some Unorthodox Reflections on the "Right to Development"', in Francis Snyder and Peter Slinn eds, *International Law of Development: Comparative Approaches* 87 (Abingdon: Professional Books, 1987). See also Shue, supra note 8.
98   Thus, Bedjaoui, supra note 97 contends that the world food resources should be declared a common heritage of humankind.
99   Principle 5 of the Rio Declaration on Environment and Development, 14 June 1992, Rio de Janeiro, reprinted in 31 *ILM* 874 (1992).
100   Article 69.2 (d) of the United Nations Convention on the Law of the Sea, Montego Bay, 10 Dec. 1982, reprinted in 21 *ILM* 1261 (1982) [hereafter Law of the Sea Convention].
101   Kai Nielsen, 'Global Justice, Capitalism and the Third World', in Robin Attfield and Barry Wilkins eds, *International Justice and the Third World – Studies in the Philosophy of Development* 17 (London: Routledge, 1992).

resource redistribution, even if they were to become worse off, since this appears morally just. In fact, it can be argued that justice requires that the one who gains unequal and unilateral advantages should bear an unequal share of reversing the burden.[102]

Various historical contexts have provided the basis for numerous 'preferential' claims and have constituted, in particular, some of the fundamental tenets on which the international law of development was predicated. It was argued that developed countries had a duty to provide for the enhancement of living conditions in all parts of the world. The rationale lies in the advantages gained by developed countries that industrialized early and benefited in many cases from the existence of colonies whose economies were often severely disrupted.[103] In India, for instance, technological development may have been significantly hampered by colonialism and British technological imperatives.[104]

Similarly, the right to development can be construed from a historical perspective as a request for the reparation or compensation for past actions.[105] From this perspective, developed countries which often managed a successful path to industrialization through the consumption of a large share of their own natural resources, and in many cases exploitation of resources in territories formerly under their dominion, should agree to compensatory measures.[106] Arguments have also been put forward with respect to the claims of indigenous peoples to preferential treatment for remedying past suffering.[107] Domestic preferential policies are also sometimes based on compensation for past injustice.[108]

In practice, claims based on colonial history have been largely sidelined as a ground for 'preferential treatment'. Historical patterns of development have, however, again attained some degree of prominence in the context of differential treatment in recent international environmental law. The matter of states'

---

102 Shue *quoted in* Franck, supra note 6 at 390.
103 C. Clyde Ferguson, Jr., 'Redressing Global Injustices: The Role of Law', in Frederik E. Snyder and Surakiart Sathirathai eds, *Third World Attitudes Toward International Law: An Introduction* 365 (Dordrecht: Nijhoff, 1987) and Immanuel Wallerstein, 'The Present State of the Debate on World Inequality', in Mitchell A. Seligson and John T. Passé-Smith eds, *Development and Underdevelopment: The Political Economy of Inequality* 217 (Boulder, CO: L. Rienner, 1993).
104 Ian Inkster, 'Colonial and Neo-Colonial Transfers of Technology: Perspectives on India Before 1914', in Roy McLeod and Deepak Kumar eds, *Technology and the Raj – Western Technology and Technical Transfers to India 1700-1947* at 25 (New Delhi: Sage, 1995).
105 Bedjaoui, supra note 97 at 107.
106 In this respect, see also, Shue, supra note 89 at 535 arguing that even if developing countries benefited in some regard from the economic development of developed countries, they were usually charged for the benefits obtained.
107 Feisal Hussain Naqvi, 'People's Rights or Victim's Rights: Reexamining the Conceptualization of Indigenous Rights in International Law', 71 *Indiana L.J.* 673 (1996).
108 Nesiah, supra note 83 at 71.

differentiated responsibility for climate change is one of the most important global environmental issues where the question of historical responsibility for the creation of a current environmental problem comes to the fore. The broad coincidence between states' current levels of economic development and their historical contribution to climate change puts this issue at the centre of debates over differential treatment.[109]

State responsibility and liability The breach of international law is a much more widely accepted basis for compensation.[110] This is derived from the general principle of international law concerned with the incidence and consequences of illegal acts, and particularly with reparation for loss caused.[111] In the environmental field, the main ground for state responsibility is the classical principle that enjoins states not to act in a way that causes damage to the environment of other states or to the global commons.[112] This basic principle of responsibility was first articulated by the arbitrators of the Trail Smelter case who stated that

> under the principles of international law . . . no State has the right to use or permit the use of its territory in such a manner as to cause injury by fumes in or to the territory of another or the properties or persons therein, when the case is of serious consequence and the injury is established by clear and convincing evidence.[113]

This was further reinforced in the Corfu Channel case where the ICJ stated that every state has an obligation not to knowingly allow its territory to be used for acts contrary to the rights of other states.[114] While it has been argued that in case of environmental harm, states are liable irrespective of any fault, international law does not yet include any such principle.[115] A more fundamental limitation is that in most cases it is difficult to demonstrate that a particular damage has been caused to one state by actions of another state.[116]

---

109 For further details, see infra at p. 46.
110 Malcolm N. Shaw, *International Law* 541 (Cambridge: Cambridge University Press, 4th ed. 1997).
111 Ian Brownlie, *Principles of Public International Law* (Oxford: Clarendon, 5th ed. 1998).
112 Principle 2 of the Rio Declaration, supra note 99. See also Principle 21 of the Declaration of the United Nations Conference on the Human Environment, Stockholm, 16 June 1972, reprinted in 11 *ILM* 1416 (1972) [hereafter Stockholm Declaration].
113 Trail Smelter Case (United States v. Canada), 16 Apr. 1938 and 11 Mar. 1941, 3 *Rep. Int'l Arbitral Awards* 1905, 1965.
114 Corfu Channel Case, Judgment, *ICJ Reports 1949*, p. 4, 22.
115 Shaw, supra note 110 at 592.
116 An added difficulty is that in the case of transboundary environmental problems, enhancing the effectiveness of the state responsibility model may require allowing any member of the community of states to act on behalf of the whole community as in the case of some human rights treaties. On this point, Rüdiger Wolfrum, 'Means of

State responsibility in environmental matters has been the focus of renewed attention in recent years. Principle 7 of the Rio Declaration deals, for instance, with the issue of the international responsibility of developed states to pursue sustainable development.[117] In the context of the climate change regime, different propositions have been put forward though none have been tested. In the context of the negotiations for a Protocol to the Climate Change Convention, Brazil submitted a proposal which would have made countries making emission reduction commitments liable to pay a kind of fine to an international fund if they happened to emit more greenhouse gases than their allotted share.[118] There have also been talks of possible legal action that could be brought against some states for past or present omissions in preventing climate change.[119] The multitude of actors and factors involved in causing global warming would probably make it difficult under existing rules to sanction any given state. Indeed, the damage must normally be identifiable, traceable to a state of origin and reasonably foreseeable for that state. These conditions may be easy to satisfy in the case of oil spills or nuclear plant accidents but would be more difficult to ascertain in the case of greenhouse gas emissions. Another difficulty is that claimant states would have to assert that developed countries have engaged in acts constituting a breach of an international obligation, that the obligation was in force at the time the acts in question took place and that the breach is attributable to the developed countries.[120] However, it is still possible that the test of serious consequences laid down in the Trail Smelter arbitration would be sufficient to warrant state responsibility if low lying islands were to be wiped off by rising sea levels. Further, the types of remedies proposed under general international law could also be used in a different format to the same effect.[121]

On the whole, compensation, either based on moral considerations or legal principles, is worthy of attention because it highlights some elements which underlie current differential treatment mechanisms, in particular with regard to the question of common but differentiated responsibilities.

Ensuring Compliance with and Enforcement of International Environmental Law', 272 *RCADI* 9, 90 (1998).

[117] Rio Declaration, supra note 99.

[118] Implementation of the Berlin Mandate – Additional Proposals from Parties, UNFCCC Ad Hoc Group on the Berlin Mandate, 7th Session, 31 July – 7 Aug. 1997, UN Doc. FCCC/AGBM/1997/MISC.1/Add.3.

[119] Andrew L. Strauss, Suing the United States for Global Warming Emissions: Discussion Paper for In the Red Conference, London, 10 July 2001 (on file with the author). See also Michael Christie, 'Lawsuits may be next Weapon in Climate Change Fight', *Environmental News Network,* 6 March 2002, available at www.enn.com/news/index.asp.

[120] Frank Biermann, "'Common Concern of Humankind": The Emergence of a New Concept of International Environmental Law', 34 *Archiv des Völkerrechts* 426 (1996).

[121] Cf. Jacob Werksman, 'Compliance and the Kyoto Protocol: Building a Backbone into a 'Flexible' Regime', 9 *Yb. Int'l Envtl. L.* 48 (1998).

Solidarity and fairness At the broadest level, solidarity is an expression by members of a community that they have common interests and that they should collectively contribute to their realization and furtherance. It implies a sense of partnership among all actors in solving issues which are of interest or of concern to the community at large. These may include problems whose solution requires common action on the part of all members, such as environmental problems caused in varying degree by all, or problems faced by some members the disappearance of which constitute a gain to the community as a whole, such as poverty.

The principle of solidarity or partnership has been identified as a basic ethical principle in most cultures of the world.[122] It also constitutes one of the ethical bases for inter-state relations,[123] often seen as a prerequisite for the existence of the community of states and a basic unalterable feature of international law. In this sense, solidarity is an unenforceable, yet compulsory basic moral standard for peaceful relations among states.[124] The principle of solidarity reflects the interdependence of states and their responsibility to ensure that their economic, environmental or other policies do not harm other states while prohibiting interference with the interests of other states.[125]

Today, the existence of a principle of solidarity at the international level is widely accepted.[126] However, divergent views exist as to the precise content of the principle. While some commentators argue that solidarity does not imply any obligations beyond treaty obligations, others opine that solidarity implies extra legal obligations on the part of developed countries to assist developing countries and that this has become a principle informing the entire legal system. Taken in this sense, solidarity goes beyond levelling the 'playing field' and applies itself to the rules of the game.[127]

Solidarity is relevant at different levels. It is not limited to intra-generational equity but also extends to inter-generational equity. This concept is embodied in a number of international legal instruments, though mostly non-binding.[128] Both the

---

[122]   Raimund Schütz, *Solidarität im Wirtschaftsvölkerrecht – eine Bestandsaufnahme zentraler entwicklungsspezifischer Solidarrechte und Solidarpflichten im Völkerrecht* (Berlin: Duncker and Humblot, 1994).

[123]   Emer de Vattel, *Le droit des gens ou principes de la souveraineté* (1758, reprint Geneva 1958) at préliminaires ss.13.

[124]   Ronald St. John McDonald, 'The Principle of Solidarity in Public International Law', in Christian Dominicé et al. eds, *Etudes de droit international en l'honneur de Pierre Lalive* 275 (Basel: Helbing, 1993).

[125]   Jerzy Makarczyk, *Principles of a New International Economic Order* (Dordrecht: Nijhoff, 1988).

[126]   R.St.J. McDonald, 'Solidarity in the Practice and Discourse of Public International Law', 8 *Pace Int'l L. Rev.* 259 (1996). See also, Shue, supra note 89 at 532 arguing more generally that fairness is a universal concept.

[127]   McDonald, supra note 124 at 281.

[128]   Catherine Redgwell, *Intergenerational Trusts and Environmental Protection* 115 (Manchester: Manchester University Press, 1999).

Stockholm and Rio declarations include a reference to the present generation's duty to also meet developmental and environmental needs of future generations.[129] One of the most specific provisions on inter-generational equity is found in a treaty on the safety of nuclear waste. This treaty obligates states to take steps to avoid actions that impose reasonably predictable impacts on future generations greater than those permitted for the current generation and generally aim to avoid imposing undue burdens on future generations.[130] While inter-generational equity is included in a number of legal instruments, there is as yet only limited application of this principle in judicial decisions.[131] Generally speaking, the theory of inter-generational equity implies a broad duty of solidarity of the present generations with unborn ones. This includes, for instance, the need to conserve the diversity of natural resources to avoid restricting options available to future generations. From the point of view of differential treatment, the theory of inter-generational equity can be the basis of an argument that since some countries are not wealthy enough to take care of future generations, wealthier countries have a duty to help them in these efforts. Further, they ought to finance the efforts of poorer countries in gaining access to the planetary legacy left by previous generations, to which all members of the present generation are entitled, and also help protect them from environmental harm.[132]

Differential treatment builds upon these and other ideas of solidarity. The broad link with solidarity implies, for instance, that differential treatment acknowledges the possibility of placing positive duties on the part of the better off. This relates closely to the moral argument put forward by Singer who posits that if it is in our power to prevent something bad, like suffering and death from lack of food, shelter and medical care, we have moral duty to do it. More generally, if we can prevent something bad without sacrificing anything morally significant, we ought to do it.[133] Differential treatment is thus closely linked to the necessity of sharing existing resources. It would thus go against Hardin's metaphor of the tragedy of the commons which provides a moral basis for the wealthy not to share their resources

---

129   Principle 1 of the Stockholm Declaration, supra note 112 and Principle 3 of the Rio Declaration, supra note 99.

130   Article 4 of the Joint Convention on the Safety of Spent Fuel Management and on the Safety of Radioactive Waste Management, Vienna, 5 Sept. 1997, reprinted in 36 *ILM* 1436 (1997).

131   At the international level, Request for an Examination of the Situation in Accordance with Paragraph 63 of the Court's Judgment of 20 December 1974 in the Nuclear Tests (New Zealand v. France) Case – Dissenting Opinion of Judge Weeramantry, *ICJ Reports 1995*, p. 288, 341. At the national level, Minors Oposa v. Secretary of the Department of Environment and Natural Resources, Philippines Supreme Court, 30 July 1993, reprinted in 33 *ILM* 173, 185 (1994).

132   Edith Brown Weiss, *In Fairness to Future Generations: International Law, Common Patrimony and Intergenerational Equity* 27 (Tokyo: UN University, 1989).

133   Peter Singer, 'Famine, Affluence, and Morality', in Charles R. Beitz et al. eds, *International Ethics* 247 (Princeton, NJ: Princeton University Press, 1985).

with the rest of the world.[134] While solidarity is in large part a moral standard, differential treatment is a practical application, one whose direct impacts are more easily measurable.

The principle of solidarity finds its expression, for instance, in Article 55 of the UN Charter which recognizes the need for cooperation among nations to achieve the goals of economic and social development.[135] This conception of international law goes beyond the recognition of the factual existence of states and seeks to promote substantive cooperation, thereby acknowledging the transformation to a legal structure based upon the interdependence of all States.[136] The cooperation envisaged calls for the recognition of the need for positive discrimination in a world of politically and economically unequal states. More recent instruments have reiterated and given content to these principles. Thus, the preamble to the instrument establishing the WTO states that one of the objectives of the organization is to ensure that least developed countries secure a share in the growth of international trade that is commensurate with their economic development needs.[137]

At the level of the individual too, solidarity has informed the development of international law. In human rights instruments, the existence of a supportive national and international social framework has already been recognized as necessary for the realization of human rights.[138] Further, 'solidarity rights', such as the right to development or to environment, have been discussed for some time. They, however, remain extremely controversial because their existence implies the recognition of an international legal order not built exclusively upon the supremacy of the nation state but upon higher values of common interest to the international community.[139]

---

[134]   Hardin posits the world as a sea on which a small number of well-equipped ships are surrounded by a multitude of shabby boats whose passengers all want to board the better equipped ones. Since this will cause the well-equipped ships to sink with all their passengers, he argues against sharing. Garrett Hardin, 'Living on a Lifeboat', 24 *Bioscience* 561 (1974).

[135]   Article 55 of the UN Charter.

[136]   John O'Manique, 'Development, Human Rights and Law', 14 *Hum. Rts. Q.* 383 (1992).

[137]   Agreement Establishing the World Trade Organization, Marrakesh, 15 Apr. 1994, reprinted in 33 *ILM* 1125 (1994).

[138]   Article 28 of the Universal Declaration of Human Rights, in Human Rights – A Compilation of International Instruments, UN Doc. ST/HR/1/Rev.4 (Vol.I/Part 1, 1993) and Articles 2.2 and 3.1 of UNGA Res. 41/128, Declaration on the Right to Development, 4 Dec. 1986, in Resolutions and Decisions Adopted by the General Assembly During its 41st Session, 16 Sept.-19 Dec. 1986, UN Doc. A/41/53.

[139]   See generally Marlies Galenkamp, 'Collective Rights: Much Ado About Nothing? – A Review Essay', 9 *Netherlands Q. Hum. Rts.* 291 (1991). On the right to environment, Michael R. Anderson, 'Human Rights Approaches to Environmental Protection', in Alan E. Boyle and Michael R. Anderson eds, *Human Rights Approaches to Environmental Protection* 1 (Oxford: Clarendon, 1996).

The emergence of global environmental problems has given a new prominence to the notion of solidarity. This is linked to the recognition that cooperation of all nations and more generally, all concerned actors will be necessary to tackle most international environmental issues. This implies that solidarity cannot be conceived exclusively at the inter state level or as a human rights issue. Today, solidarity spans the whole range of actors engaged in environmental management. As later chapters of this study argue, while the consideration of differential treatment at the inter state level is a valid and useful endeavour, its current shortcomings may stem from the narrow definition of actors included within the scope of differential measures. This is because international environmental law still conceives states as the most prominent actors in all aspects of environmental management.

Inequalities in Economic Development

While principles of justice can be used as an ethical basis for differentiation, existing economic development disparities among countries and regions constitute another basis for differential treatment. Indeed, despite their legal equality, the two hundred states forming the international community are at widely differing levels of social and economic development. The gap in terms of economic development between countries is well illustrated by the existing gap between developed and developing countries. Developed countries which account for a total share of the world's population of less than 20 per cent command more than 80 per cent of the world's GDP.[140]

Furthermore, inequalities have vastly increased over time.[141] The ratio of the income of the richest decile to the poorest decile on a world level has, for instance, increased from 19.4 to 26.9 on a purchasing power parity basis and from 51.5 to 127.7 on an exchange rate basis between 1970 and 1997.[142] If the world economy has experienced positive growth in each of the last three decades, least developed countries have under performed and become relatively poorer.[143] This latter group

---

[140]   OECD countries accounted for 83% of the world's GDP and 60% on a purchasing power parity basis in 2000. They share of the world population was 19% in 2000. UNDP, *Human Development Report 2002* (New York: Oxford University Press, 2002).

[141]   The gap in per capita GDP has, for instance, increased even in relative terms between 1980 and 1999. Per capita GDP in 1999 dollars increased between these two dates from $284 to $288 in least developed countries, from $893 to $1,326 in all developing countries and from $18,491 to $26,692 in developed countries. UNCTAD, *The Least Developed Countries 2002 Report* (Geneva: UNCTAD, 2002).

[142]   UNDP 2001, supra note 84.

[143]   In relative terms, while the GDP per capita gap between developed and developing countries diminished slightly between 1960 and 1995, the gap between developed and least developed countries widened significantly. The GDP per capita of least developed countries in 1987 $US diminished from 245 to 233 between 1960 and 1995 while that of developed countries grew from 7097 to 12764 during the same

even experienced an absolute decline in GNP per capita in the 1980s.[144] The
relevance of economic inequalities in the differentiation debate does not require
further elaboration given the significant attention it has received for several
decades. A point concerning the Rawlsian theory is, however, in order. It is
unlikely that individuals would agree to be kept under a veil of ignorance if they are
to live in a system where 20 per cent of the population reaps 80 per cent of the total
income.[145] In such a situation, measures to correct the original position should be
adopted before society can be left to function according to Rawl's principles of
justice.[146]

Contribution to Environmental Problems and Capacity to Respond

While economic globalization has attracted a lot of attention in recent years, the
internationalization of environmental issues has been extremely wide-ranging and
rapid too. There is today a clear recognition that countries are linked by issues of
'common concern' which relate, for instance, to the protection of the ozone layer,
global climate change and the protection of biodiversity.[147]

The importance of global environmental problems in the context of differential
treatment stems in part from their relationship with economic development. Human
induced climate change has, for instance, primarily been caused by
industrialization. There is thus a good correlation between current levels of
development and emissions of greenhouse gases.[148] A temporal dimension must

---

period. UNDP, *Human Development Report 1998* (New York: Oxford University
        Press, 1998).
[144]   The growth rate of the GDP per capita for least developed countries was -1.1%
        between 1980 and 1992. UNDP, *Human Development Report 1995* (New York:
        Oxford University Press, 1995).
[145]   Barry, supra note 31.
[146]   Cf. John Rawls, 'The Law of Peoples', in Steven Shute and Susan Hurley eds, *On
        Human Rights – The Oxford Amnesty Lectures* 1993 at 41 (New York: Basic Books,
        1993). Rawls himself rejects the idea that rich states owe a redistributive moral
        obligation to the poor. He argues that the difference principle is not reasonable to deal
        with the general problem of unfavourable conditions among societies. See also
        Franck, supra note 6 at 19 who is unconvinced by Rawls' objections that some nations
        may prefer to be poorer if that spares them the direr consequences of urbanization and
        industrialization and that in the absence of a global community rich nations do not
        owe a redistributive moral obligation to the poor.
[147]   Interdependence had already become the subject of intense international discussions at
        the time of the successive oil price shocks in the 1970s which brought to the fore
        northern economies' dependence upon primary commodities. Georges Abi-Saab, 'The
        Legal Formulation of a Right to Development (Subjects and Content)', in René-Jean
        Dupuy ed., *The Right to Development at the International Level* 159 (Alphen aan den
        Rijn: Sijthoff and Noordhoff, 1980).
[148]   OECD countries account for 49.9% of all carbon dioxide emissions. UNDP 2001,
        supra note 84.

however be added since greenhouse gases remain in the atmosphere for significant periods of time. Looking back, countries which industrialized early have produced an overwhelming share of total emissions over the last two hundred years. At the same time, it is expected that the share of developed nations' emissions will substantially decrease over the coming decades as developing countries rapidly develop fossil fuel based industries.[149]

Since the effects of climate change will probably be felt the world over, the necessity for cooperation is acutely felt. While developed countries who still account for the largest share of emissions can take action to reduce their own emissions, this will probably not be sufficient in the long run. Whether the underlying motive is compensation for past action, solidarity in solving a global problem or the search for cheap solutions, special measures for developing countries are necessary if the development of substantial fossil fuel based industries is to be averted.[150] It would not be morally, legally, or economically feasible to expect developing countries to pay the supplemental costs associated with leap-frogging the fossil-fuel stage of industrialization through which all currently developed countries have passed.[151]

Differentiated measures can also be justified on the basis of past, current and expected future per capita emissions. Even if the overall share of developing countries' emissions is to rise substantially, their per capita emissions will remain much below that of developed countries in the foreseeable future. Also, the increased share of developing countries' emissions will not notably alter current disparities in standards of living. Transfers of technologies and other redistributive measures are thus called for because inaction may threaten not only the process of development in developing countries but also current standards of living in the North. At the same time, equalizing levels of development in developed and developing countries, where the latter follow the development path pursued by the former, would lead to an environmentally unsustainable situation.[152]

Further, inequality with regard to resources and capacities constitutes another important factor influencing the ability of states to take effective action to address specific environmental problems.[153] This constitutes another important rationale for differential treatment which has been acknowledged in some international instruments such as the FAO Code of Conduct for Responsible Fisheries which

---

149 Banuri et al., supra note 80 at 94.
150 Cf. Shue, supra note 89 at 531.
151 Cf. Paolillo, supra note 79 stating that the extent to which States have contributed to environmental degradation in a particular field constitutes one criterion on which differential treatment can be based.
152 Will Kymlicka, 'Concepts of Community and Social Justice', in Fen Osler Hampson and Judith Reppy eds, *Earthly Goods – Environmental Change and Social Justice* 30 (Ithaca, NY: Cornell University Press, 1996).
153 Lothar Gündling, 'Compliance Assistance in International Environmental Law: Capacity-Building Through Financial and Technology Transfer', 56 *Zeitschrift für ausländisches öffentliches Recht und Völkerrecht* 796 (1996).

recognizes that '[t]he capacity of developing countries to implement the recommendations of this Code should be duly taken into account'.[154]

Self-interest

As noted above, differential treatment is often put into practice through redistributive policies in a world of finite resources. In the context of international relations where there is no authority superior to states, the consent of states who give up certain benefits which traditionally accrue to them is usually necessary.[155] In the present world order, where developed countries command a dominant position in most spheres, there are different levels at which the protection of their own interests can contribute to the realization of differential treatment. Economic and financial integration at the global level constitutes a first example. The debt crisis of the early 1980s and the several financial crises hitting various developing countries in the past decade seem to show that developed countries cannot afford bankrupted developing countries.[156] The packages put together by the IMF and some developed countries in response to the collapse in some 'tiger economies' may imply a duty of solidarity but can largely be explained by the necessity to prevent the crisis from spreading further.[157] In economic terms, developed countries gain from a secure access to primary resources situated to a large extent in developing countries. Besides, they will also eventually gain from developing countries becoming richer and being more amenable to absorb part of the production of developed countries, be it in the form of manufactured goods or services. Some developing countries now constitute significant export markets for the North and cannot easily be abandoned.[158]

In the environmental field, it is apparent that among the numerous issues of international significance those of greater concern to developed countries, such as ozone depletion, have been addressed more thoroughly and rapidly than issues of lesser importance to them, such as desertification. Developed countries have specific interests that push them to provide more favourable treatment to the South

---

[154]   Article 5 of the Code of Conduct for Responsible Fisheries, Report of the Conference of FAO, 28th Sess., Rome 20-31 Oct. 1995, Doc. C 95/REP, Annex I.

[155]   Note however that this is not necessarily the case where there is effective interdependence among all states.

[156]   On the debt crisis of the 1980s, Bedjaoui, supra note 97.

[157]   Roman Terrill, '1998/1999 Update: The Asian Crisis Goes Global', 9 *Transnational L. and Contemporary Problems* 325 (1999). See also, Joseph Stiglitz, 'Must Financial Crises be this Frequent and this Painful', in Pierre-Richard Agénor et al. eds, *The Asian Financial Crisis – Causes, Contagion and Consequences* 386 (Cambridge: Cambridge University Press, 1999).

[158]   However, this is mainly true in the context of the already economically successful developing countries. Globalization tends to increase the gap between the poorest countries, especially those in sub-Saharan Africa, and the Newly Industrialised Countries.

to ensure that their current priorities are acted upon throughout the world.[159] Thus, in the case of the depletion of the ozone layer, it is a combination of economic and environmental interests which ensured the success of the Montreal Protocol. Developed countries went as far as enticing developing countries into ratifying the Protocol through the provision of financial incentives and technology transfer.[160] This was done to ensure that, even though the current per capita consumption and production of ozone depleting substances in developing countries was still comparatively very low, a projected surge in production and consumption of such substances in those countries would not thwart the aims of the Protocol.[161] There were also specific commercial interests linked to the accession of developing countries to this agreement since all the alternative, environmentally friendly technologies have originated in developed countries.

The predominance of developed countries' views in the granting of differential treatment is also apparent in the way global environmental and local priorities are apportioned. In most cases, differential treatment is granted primarily to achieve global environmental benefits.[162] This is reflected in the concept of incremental costs that is present in most global environmental agreements.[163] The Global Environment Facility was, for instance, specifically set up to meet the costs of measures that benefit the global environment but would not be otherwise undertaken because they entail an extra financial burden for developing countries that the latter have no incentive to shoulder. Thus, additional finance is provided to developing countries with a more limited aim of achieving global benefits, even though it is hoped that it offers benefits for individual recipient countries as well.

Beneficiaries of Differential Treatment

Differential treatment has habitually focused on the enhancement of the position of weaker groups of states. Categorizing states into groups has served as a tool to brush aside individual demands and focus on generic problems, such as inequalities between the broad categories of developed and developing countries. The need for more refined categorization has, however, surfaced in a number of contexts. Insofar as states are concerned, a more individualized version of differentiation is not too problematic since their number remains relatively low, even though this is more difficult to administer.

---

[159] Andrew Jordan and Jacob Werksman, 'Incrementality and Additionality: A New Dimension to North-South Resource Transfers?', 6 *World Resource Rev.* 178 (1994).
[160] Cf. Günther Handl, 'Environmental Security and Global Change: The Challenge to International Law', 1 *Yb Int'l Envtl. L.* 3 (1990).
[161] On the Montreal Protocol, see also *infra* chapter IV.
[162] Jordan and Werksman, supra note 159 at 179.
[163] On the concept of incremental costs, Ken King, *The Incremental Costs of Global Environmental Benefits* (Washington, DC: Global Environment Facility, 1993).

While states still play a predominant role in international law, the importance of non-state actors in environmental management necessitates a closer look at the ways in which differentiation is being extended to them in some cases. National policies relating to differential treatment are of special interest in this regard.

State-based Categories

Traditionally, the comparatively weaker economic position of developing countries has served as the main criteria for identifying beneficiaries of differential treatment in international law.[164] This is due to the fact that the level of economic development is, in many cases, correlated with a state's political and military clout in the international community. Further, economic development constitutes one of the factors constraining the capacity of a state to effectively implement international commitments requiring domestic action. More generally, this categorization reflects the historical division between colonized and colonizers as well as the distinction between industrialized and industrializing countries. These categories have now been in use in international law for over three decades and the implied recognition of the existence of a 'Third World' through international instruments represents, in legal terms, an official recognition of the existence of inequalities.

Countries have firstly been generally categorized as developed and developing countries.[165] The limits of a broad categorization which puts all 'non-developed' countries in the same group has led to the creation of various sub-groups. It has thus become common to differentiate developing from least developed countries.[166]

---

[164]   No clear definition of developed and developing countries has emerged in international law. Ad hoc classifications have often been used and the categorization can, thus, be based upon negotiations among states, state practice or self-election. Maurice Flory, *Droit international du développement* (Paris: Presses universitaires de France, 1977) and Wil D. Verwey, 'The Principle of Preferential Treatment for Developing Countries', 23 *Indian J. Int'l L.* 343 (1983). For a case of classification being decided on the basis of negotiations, Decision IX/27, Application of South Africa for Developing Country Status under the Montreal Protocol, Report of the Ninth Meeting of the Parties to the Montreal Protocol on Substances that Deplete the Ozone Layer, Montreal, 15-17 Sept. 1997, Doc. UNEP/OzL.Pro.9/12. In this case, the criteria used to determine South Africa's status include the fact that it is classified as a developing country by the UNDP and the OECD and that it is regarded as a developing country in all other international environmental agreements and protocols to which it is a party and where this distinction is made.

[165]   Concerning the criteria used to distinguish countries, see supra Chapter 1 at p. 11.

[166]   The special situation of least developed countries was first acknowledged in UNCTAD Res. 24 (II), Special Measures to be Taken in Favour of the Least Developed Among Developing Countries Aimed at Expanding their Trade and Improving their Economic and Social Development, 7 Mar. 1968, in Proceedings of the UNCTAD, Second Session, New Delhi, 1 Feb.-29 Mar. 1968, UN Doc. TD/97

Some instruments and institutions further refine the distinction by adding categories such as 'other low-income countries' and 'lower middle-income countries'.[167] Further complications have arisen in the case of the European countries, now known as economies in transition. While these countries used to be donors, they have become substantial recipients of aid from developed countries and are, for instance, entitled to aid under the Montreal Protocol Fund.[168] There are, however, a number of instances where their situation dramatically differs from that of developing countries. Thus, in the case of climate change, since they have substantially contributed to the build-up of greenhouse gases in the long-term, they have been put alongside developed countries in the Climate Change Convention's Annex I. Similarly, there are some countries that may generally be clearly classified as developed or developing but find themselves on the margin in some specific cases. This happened, for instance, in the case of Turkey in the climate change negotiations where significant debates took place over its appropriate categorization. Eventually, it was in principle agreed that Turkey would be deleted from Annex II and would remain in Annex I, as first decided in 1992, but with the recognition of its special circumstances.[169]

Differentiation has also been applied among developed and among developing countries. In the case of the former group, the Kyoto Protocol on climate change is an example of different binding commitments for developed countries.[170] With regard to developing countries, the Global System of Trade Preferences clearly offers special conditions to least developed countries without any expectations of reciprocal concessions.[171]

While categorizations on the basis of economic indicators have been the most frequent, new ones have been progressively introduced. Factors considered include, a specific country's share in the trade of a specific commodity, the share of a particular resource under the sovereignty of a given state, or the geographical situation of certain states, such as landlocked states in the context of the law of the sea. Thus, the Climate Change Convention singles out the needs of countries with

---

(Vol. I). Three special conferences on the situation of least developed countries have been held.

167 Article 7 of the Food Aid Convention, London, 13 Apr. 1999, *Official Journal* L 222, 24/08/1999 p. 40.

168 For further details Decision II/8 Financial Mechanism, Second Meeting of the Parties to the Montreal Protocol on Substances that Deplete the Ozone Layer, London, 27-29 June 1990, Doc. UNEP/OzL.Pro.2/3.

169 Decision 26/CP.7, Amendment to the list in Annex II to the Convention, UNFCCC, *Report of the Conference of the Parties on its Seventh Session*, Marrakesh, 29 Oct.-10 Nov. 2001, UN Doc. FCCC/CP/2001/13/Add.4.

170 Annex B of the Kyoto Protocol to the United Nations Framework Convention on Climate Change, Kyoto, 11 Dec. 1997, Decision 1/CP.3/Annex, UNFCCC, *Report of the Conference of the Parties on its Third Session*, Kyoto, 1-11 Dec. 1997, UN Doc. FCCC/CP/1997/7/Add.1.

171 Article 3 of the Agreement on the Global System of Trade Preferences among Developing Countries, Belgrade, 13 Apr. 1988, reprinted in 27 *ILM* 1204 (1988).

low-lying coastal areas and small island countries, while documents regarding the future implementation of the Kyoto Protocol recognize the need to take into account the situation of developing countries so that they do not have to bear a disproportionate or abnormal burden under the Convention.[172] Similarly, the Law of the Sea Convention specifically addresses the situation of landlocked countries in the context of the setting up of exclusive economic zones.[173]

The reliance on environmental indicators can in some cases lead to categories which do not follow the conventional developed/developing separation. In the context of the Montreal Protocol Fund, contributions are expected from all countries whose annual calculated level of consumption of controlled substances is above a given threshold. The result is that all developed countries have to contribute together with some developing countries.[174]

Generally, the search for new ways to group countries has involved mixing developmental indicators with other elements, such as environmental factors. Categories which blend different factors include the 'food deficit countries' and the widely used 'landlocked' countries.[175] In some commodity agreements, a division between producers and consumers – reflecting mainly a North-South dichotomy – and further divisions based on the relative importance of each country in the producer or consumer group have been adopted. In the International Tropical Timber Agreement, exporters and importers each hold 1000 votes. Among the producers, 40 per cent of the votes are distributed equally among Africa, Asia-Pacific and Latin America, and then redistributed equally among each producing member in the region. Thirty per cent of the votes are distributed in accordance with the respective shares of the total tropical forest resources of all producing members. Finally, the remaining 30 per cent is allocated in proportion to the producing members' respective shares in tropical timber trade.[176] This arrangement is significant for several reasons. It not only gives equal power to producing and

---

[172] Article 4.8 of the Framework Convention on Climate Change, New York, 9 May 1992, reprinted in 31 *ILM* 849 (1992) [hereafter Climate Change Convention] and preamble of the Draft decision -/CMP.1 (Matters relating to Article 3, paragraph 14, of the Kyoto Protocol), in Decision 9/CP.7, Matters relating to Article 3, paragraph 14, of the Kyoto Protocol, UNFCCC, *Report of the Conference of the Parties on its Seventh Session*, Marrakesh, 29 Oct.-10 Nov. 2001, UN Doc. FCCC/CP/2001/13/Add.1.

[173] Article 69 of the Law of the Sea Convention, supra note 100.

[174] Articles 5 and 10 of the Protocol on Substances that Deplete the Ozone Layer, Montreal, 16 Sept. 1987, reprinted in Ozone Secretariat – UNEP, *Handbook for the International Treaties for the Protection of the Ozone Layer* (5th ed. 2000).

[175] Concerning the former, the Food Aid Convention, supra note 167, concerning the latter, the Law of the Sea Convention, supra note 100.

[176] Article 10 of the International Tropical Timber Agreement, Geneva, 26 Jan. 1994, reprinted in 33 *ILM* 1014 (1994).

consuming nations but also specifically allocates part of the voting power in accordance with producing countries' respective shares of forest resources.[177]

Categorizations which take into account several factors are useful in that they try to identify more precisely the states which ought to benefit from differentiation. However, this may not be sufficient. In the case of climate change, for instance, it is not enough to decide that the rights and obligations of states should be apportioned according to their contributions to the problem at stake. It is also necessary to decide whether absolute or per capita measures should be used as the basis for determination since this dramatically influences the outcome. This highlights the difficulties in finding categories valid across the board for a series of instruments and the difficulties in finding categorizations which do not rely heavily on moral, ethical and political valuations.

The search for more precise categories The distinction between developed and developing countries has been used extensively over the past few decades. The limits of these broad categorization has led to the definition of sub-groups, such as that of the least developed countries. The distinction between developing and least developed is extremely useful since the gap between the poorest least developed countries and newly industrialized countries is more significant than the gap between the latter and the average OECD country. However, even these sub-categories do not entirely reflect the reality accurately. Thus, countries of the former Soviet bloc do not fit well in either of these categories. Indeed, while they have had important contributions to some environmental problems such as climate change, their current capacity to alleviate these problems is relatively low and they actually require aid from OECD countries to contribute to improvements in environmental quality. Further, it is noteworthy that even within the group of developing or least developed countries, the indicators used to identify them may still be insufficient to make sure differential treatment measures are accurately targeted. There are significant differences in size and population between countries in the same group and the bigger ones are in a much better position to benefit from differential treatment than a tiny state with the same development ranking according to the indicators in use. This is included to a certain extent in the criteria used to distinguish developing from least developed countries in the UN since even countries with low income per capita, low level of human resource development and high level of economic vulnerability are not eligible if their population is above 75 millions.[178]

The problems which may arise because of these various categorizations have sometimes been resolved by using more fundamental development criteria. Thus,

---

177 A similar arrangement is also provided for in the 1993 Cocoa Agreement. International Cocoa Agreement, Geneva, 16 July 1993, UN Doc. TD/COCOA.8/17/Rev.1 (1995).

178 ECOSOC – Committee for Development Policy, Report on the Second Session, 3-7 April 2000, UN Doc. E/2000/33.

resource allocation in the context of the Multilateral Fund for the Implementation of the Montreal Protocol (Montreal Protocol Fund) has been based on overall levels of development. For this reason, the needs of developing countries have taken precedence over Eastern European countries which are not entitled to any aid under the Fund. However, the special needs of the latter countries have also been taken into account since GEF funding has been open to them.[179]

The limitations of all the various categories have led to the adoption of a more radical stand and to the design of differential treatment on an individual basis. The UN has from the very beginning assessed the contributions of each member state on an individual basis.[180] If this type of differentiation were extended to the granting of aid, aid allocation could be inversely proportional to the countries' per capita income, the poorest receiving a larger share of distributed funds on account of their laggardness.[181] Individualized differentiation does not present major difficulties in relation to the international community of states as their numbers are relatively small. However, in cases where the allocation of the benefits of differential treatment is to be renegotiated, it is obvious that the use of broad categories constitutes a convenient means to avoid lengthy debates over each state's claim to a specific share. This is why, despite the attraction of individualized differentiation in principle, it is unlikely to become the only system in use in practice.

In cases where the benefits of differentiation have to be allocated among individuals or among a greater number of entities, the need to use categories becomes obvious. However, it is remarkable that similar problems arise insofar as it is extremely difficult to define categories in such a way that they cover exactly those groups which have objectively the greatest need for differential measures.

Other Categories

International law remains primarily focused on states.[182] However, the growing importance of other actors in areas covered by international agreements is being acknowledged in various ways. There is a growing recognition that the implementation of international norms at local levels involves a number of non-governmental actors and local state actors, which were previously overlooked at the international level. There have consequently been a number of proposals to accord more space to these important but neglected actors within international law. It has firstly been suggested that in international organizations people should be represented on the basis of population according to the practice of many countries where parliamentary seats are divided among the different constituencies on the

---

[179]   Global Environment Facility, *Operational Strategy* (1996).
[180]   See further, Chapter 3 at p. 72.
[181]   This is, for instance, advocated by Keith Griffin and Terry McKinley, *New Approaches to Development Cooperation* (New York: UNDP, 1996).
[182]   Rosalyn Higgins, *Problems and Process – International Law and How we Use it* 39 (Oxford: Clarendon, 1994).

basis of their population.[183] Secondly, the recognition that international law's ultimate function is to benefit individuals and not states has also been emphasized.[184] Indeed, as long as fairness in international law is only a matter of allocation between states, it is impossible to ensure that the benefits of differentiation reach individuals on the ground. This has been the case in a number of countries where aid is siphoned off by the leaders of the recipient country. Thirdly, even in countries with highly centralized governments, there is a growing recognition of the need to take into account regional and local disparities and inequalities. This is leading to calls for decentralized governance which is slowly being implemented, as in the case of India.[185]

In practice, measures targeting non-state entities have only been adopted in a limited number of cases. These include, for instance, the modest step taken in the Climate Change Convention which demands that specific regions of developing countries should be targeted because of their special environmental features.[186] The European Union's regional policy, however, represents a much more significant attempt to directly target entities other than states. The Community is specifically directed to reduce disparities between the levels of development in the various regions and to alleviate the backwardness of the least favoured regions.[187] This has led to the development of a series of financial mechanisms targeting directly the needy regions. It is remarkable that in the context of the regional policy, Community operations can only be established after close consultations between the Commission, the concerned member state and the competent authorities designated by the latter at national, regional and local levels.[188] This is derived from the broader concept of partnership, which seeks to give local actors a role in the formulation of measures destined to benefit them directly, and also from the principle of subsidiarity.[189] Despite the positive elements highlighted, the principle of partnership is currently limited in scope and does not allow for the active participation of the regions at all levels of decision making.

---

183 Franck, supra note 6 at 482.
184 D.P. O'Connell, *International Law* 106 (London: Stevens, 2nd ed. vol. 1, 1970) and Nico Schrijver, 'The Dynamics of Sovereignty in a Changing World', in Konrad Ginther et al. eds, *Sustainable Development and Good Governance* 80 (Dordrecht: Nijhoff, 1995).
185 Constitution of India (Seventy-third Amendment) Act, 1992 and Constitution of India (Seventy-fourth Amendment) Act, 1992.
186 Article 4.8 of the Climate Change Convention, supra note 172 recognises the needs and concerns of low-lying coastal areas, areas prone to natural disasters or areas prone to desertification of developing countries.
187 Article 130A.2 of the Single European Act, The Hague, 17 Feb. 1986, reprinted in 25 *ILM* 503 (1986).
188 Article 4 of Regulation 2052/88 of 24 June 1988 on the Tasks of the Structural Funds and their Effectiveness, OJ L 185 (15 July 1988).
189 Cf. Opinion of the Committee of the Regions on the role of regional and local authorities in the partnership principle of the Structural Funds, 20 July 1995, OJ C 100 (2 Apr. 1996).

Apart from attempts at the international level to provide differential treatment for actors which are not states, it is noteworthy that a number of countries have provided differential treatment at the domestic level for a number of years. Among the problems faced by these various programmes, the definition of the target groups has been one of central importance. In most cases, domestic differentiation seeks to enhance the position of the weakest groups in society. These often happen to be the most disadvantaged economic groups. While the measures taken by states often seek primarily to improve the economic conditions of the target groups, non-economic criteria are also used. Thus, in both the United States and India, the beneficiary groups are identified as being historically oppressed or excluded endogamous groups at bottom of, or outside, a stratified system in which their status is determined by birth.[190] The Indian Constitution specifies, for instance, that the preferential treatment of socially and educationally backward classes, Schedules Castes and Scheduled Tribes is permissible.[191] It has been widely debated whether membership of a particular group should constitute the main criterion for benefiting of differential measures or whether other factors such as poverty are more relevant.[192] In the case of the United States, it has, for instance, been noted that dealing with the legacy of discrimination through racial preferences may not be the most desirable option. Class-based affirmative action may be more apt to provide equal opportunity than either the current system of affirmative action or the absence of any programme.[193] The problems faced at the domestic level demonstrate the difficulty of finding appropriate criteria for dealing with existing and past inequalities in economic and social terms. Overall, it is apparent that whether differentiation is proposed among a small group of 200 states or for millions of individuals, the definition of the target group is a very intricate matter which cannot receive a single definitive answer.

---

190   Nesiah, supra note 83 at 66.
191   Article 15 of the Constitution of India. See also, M.R. Balaji v. States of Mysore, 28 Sept. 1962, A.I.R. (50) 1963 S.C. 649.
192   Faundez, supra note 65 at 35.
193   Richard D. Kahlenberg, 'Class-Based Affirmative Action', 84 *California L. Rev.* 1037 (1996).

Chapter 3

Differential Treatment in International Law

This chapter focuses on differentiation as an exception to reciprocity. It focuses on the traditional distinction between reciprocal and non-reciprocal obligations and on the specific regimes which seek to bring about substantive equality by enhancing the position of weaker states. This chapter first examines the development of differential treatment at the international level. It distinguishes two main periods, separating the 1960-70s, when differential treatment was mainly based on unilateral claims from developing countries, from the more recent period, when developments in differential treatment – mainly in international environmental law – have generally been based on a commonality of interests among all states. Further, this chapter goes beyond the analysis of differential norms to examine other forms of differential treatment such as differential contributions to international organizations or differential voting procedures in financial institutions. Finally, the third section assesses the impacts of differential treatment on the international legal order. In particular, it analyzes the legal status of differential treatment provisions and explores some of the principles of international law which are most directly linked to differential treatment.

Development of Differential Treatment

As noted earlier, international law has for a long time been based on the principle of legal equality of all entities recognized as states. One of the corollaries of legal equality is that international legal obligations have traditionally been framed as strictly reciprocal commitments binding all signatories in exactly the same way.[1] The most favoured nation clause in the General Agreement on Tariffs and Trade (GATT) is one example of a rule allowing each State to demand the fulfilment of the same obligations from all other member states. Article 1.1 states that 'any advantage, favour, privilege or immunity granted by any contracting party to any product originating in or destined for any other country shall be accorded immediately and unconditionally to the like product originating in or destined for

---

[1]   Emmanuel Decaux, *La réciprocité en droit international* (Paris: Librairie générale de droit et de jurisprudence, 1980) and Antonio Cassese, *International Law in a Divided World* 28 (Oxford: Clarendon, 1986).

the territories of all other contracting parties'.[2] Reciprocity has thus been at the root of the acceptance and fulfilment of international obligations.[3]

Absolute reciprocity was, however, not upheld in all circumstances. The development of 'objective regimes' is a case in point. Despite continuing doctrinal controversy, it is often acknowledged that some treaties, such as treaties providing for the neutralization of a state or territory or treaties creating a regime for international waterways, do create rights and duties for third states.[4] In treaty law, the development of reservations constitutes another interesting example of non-reciprocity.[5] At first, reservations were conceived within a contractual framework and were, thus, only possible if all parties agreed to them.[6] However, by the 1950s, the ICJ rejected this approach. In its advisory opinion on reservations to the Genocide Convention, the Court determined that a state having made a reservation which has been objected to by some but not all state parties can be seen as a member of the convention unless the reservation is incompatible with the object and purpose of the convention.[7] Rules concerning the formulation of reservations were later codified in the Convention on the Law of Treaties which provides that states can make reservations unless they are prohibited by the treaty or are incompatible with the object and purpose of the treaty.[8] The fact that treaty law provides a form of exception to the contractual basis of obligations indicates that differentiation has been a long-standing concern for the international community.[9] In fact, differential treatment is in some ways merely a more recent way to provide the same kind of flexibility as reservations with the similar goal of making the adoption of a given treaty possible for a greater number of states.[10]

Further developments in international law did not occur until the end of the Second World War which was followed by a rapid enlargement of the international

---

[2]   General Agreement on Tariffs and Trade, Geneva, 31 Oct. 1947, 55 *UNTS* 187 (1950) [hereafter GATT Agreement].

[3]   Rosalyn Higgins, *Problems and Process – International Law and how we Use it* 16 (Oxford: Clarendon, 1994).

[4]   Surya P. Subedi, 'The Doctrine of Objective Regimes in International Law and the Competence of the United Nations to Impose Territorial or Peace Settlements on States', 37 *German Yb. Int'l L.* 162 (1994). See also, Article 35 of the Convention on the Law of Treaties, Vienna, 23 May 1969, reprinted in 8 *ILM* 679 (1969).

[5]   The principle of equal sovereignty also implies that states cannot in theory be forced to join any given treaty and that they may withdraw.

[6]   Malcolm N. Shaw, *International Law* 644 (Cambridge: Cambridge University Press, 4th ed. 1997).

[7]   Reservations to the Convention on Genocide, Advisory Opinion, *ICJ Reports 1951*, p. 15, 29.

[8]   Article 19 of the Convention on the Law of Treaties, supra note 4.

[9]   Cf. Felipe Paolillo, 'Final Report', 67/1 *Yb. Institute Int'l L.* 437, 471 (1997).

[10]   Cf. Catherine Redgwell, 'The Law of Reservations in Respect of Multilateral Conventions', in J.P. Gardner ed., *Human Rights as General Norms and a State's Right to Opt Out – Reservations and Objections to Human Rights Conventions* 3 (London: British Institute of International and Comparative Law, 1997).

community. After decolonization, international law became for the first time truly universal in scope and came to encompass a new group of 'developing' states which made the international community much more heterogeneous than ever before.[11] With more entities being recognized as full subjects of international law, the differences in the levels of economic development amongst the members of the international community became much more obvious than they had been in colonial times. These changes came to test the legal foundations of international law. It became, for instance, more and more evident that a strict reliance on the concept of legal equality could not be upheld in all circumstances within a growing community whose members had different economic, political and military capacities. These changes and the ensuing developments reflected to a certain extent the broader forces influencing international law whose function slowly changed from that of ensuring the peaceful coexistence of states to ensuring broad-ranging cooperation on a number of socio-economic issues.[12]

Differential Treatment as Preferential Treatment

Differential treatment measures for the benefit of developing countries were first introduced soon after most colonies achieved independence. Developing countries realized that political independence and the ensuing recognition of sovereignty were not sufficient to guarantee economic independence and control over their own resources, and obtained differential treatment measures in some of the economic agreements they entered into. This eventually led to a broad political movement seeking preferential treatment to foster the economic development of former colonies.

From decolonization to economic sovereignty   Decolonization fundamentally altered the landscape of international relations. In the two decades following the creation of the UN, the number of its member states more than doubled and has continued to increase till today. Given that many new states were born from the demise of colonial empires, a profound destabilization of the international legal order could have been in order. In the event, different factors ensured that developing countries broadly embraced the existing international legal framework.[13] For instance, the new rulers relied upon the *uti possidetis* principle to consolidate their nascent 'nation states' whose existing borders had often been

---

11   On the new universal scope of international law, Shaw, supra note 6 at 34.

12   Georges Abi-Saab, 'Whither the International Community?', 9 *Eur. J. Int'l L.* 248 (1998).

13   R.P. Anand, 'Attitude of the Asian-African States Toward Certain Problems of International Law', 15 *Int'l and Comp. L.Q.* 55 (1966). On the principle of *uti possidetis*, Steven R. Ratner, 'Drawing a Better Line: *Uti Possidetis* and the Borders of New States', 90 *Am. J. Int'l L.* 590 (1996).

drawn under colonial rule. Subsequently, rules concerning the succession of newly independent states to treaties were formalized in a multilateral convention.[14]

Despite the broad acceptance of existing international law, developing countries soon came to voice concerns that political independence could not be equated with economic independence. In particular, claims were made concerning the control of economic resources situated in the territories of newly independent countries. Demands were made for special measures to remedy decades of economic stagnation under colonial rule and an international economic system which appeared to strongly favour vested interests and positions acquired in the course of the colonization process.[15]

A whole body of instruments focusing on economic development from an international perspective developed in the ensuing decades. What came to be known as the international law of development was thus, from the outset, based upon the recognition that real independence requires more than political independence and that special measures should be taken to assist less economically developed countries in realizing economic independence.[16] In other words, the international law of development was based on the principle of equity among nations, which required the adoption of new measures and legal arrangements to allow developing countries to overcome the difficult situation they had inherited from their colonial past.[17] These ranged from the affirmation of redistributive principles such as the recognition of a 'permanent sovereignty over natural resources',[18] to special measures in instruments concerned with economic development.

International trade law constituted one of the most hotly contested areas. This was due to the conditions prevalent as a consequence of colonization. During colonization, colonial and metropolitan economies were integrated in such a way that the former were geared towards meeting the needs of the latter. In many instances, especially for a number of small and least developed countries, this resulted in a high degree of specialization within the economy.[19] Differential

---

[14]   Vienna Convention on Succession of States in Respect of Treaties, 22 Aug. 1978, reprinted in 17 *ILM* 1488 (1978).

[15]   Even though not all developing countries were subjected to colonial rule, a number of the countries that remained independent were in the sphere of influence of one or the other western power. P.J. Cain and A.G. Hopkins, *British Imperialism – Crisis and Deconstruction 1914-1990* (London: Longman, 1993).

[16]   Guy Feuer and Hervé Cassan, *Droit international du développement* 29 (Paris: Dalloz, 2nd ed. 1991).

[17]   Ahmed Mahiou, 'Le droit au développement', in *International Law on the Eve of the 21st Century – Views from the International Law Commission* 217 (New York: United Nations, 1997).

[18]   UNGA Res. 1803 (XVII), Permanent Sovereignty over Natural Resources, 14 Dec. 1962, reprinted in 2 *ILM* 223 (1963).

[19]   This is still reflected today, for instance, in sub-Saharan Africa where the share of manufacturing exports is only 18.4% while primary commodities account in a number

treatment in trade agreements thus constituted the first focal point for newly independent countries.[20] One of the earliest instances can be found in the revision of Article XVIII of the GATT in the mid-1950s, when developing countries with low standards of living were granted permission to derogate from some of the obligations which applied to all other members.[21] A decade later, a new Part granting developing countries more specific exemptions was added to the GATT. Article XXXVI (3) thus states that '[t]here is need for positive efforts designed to ensure that less-developed contracting parties secure a share in the growth in international trade commensurate with the needs of their economic development'. The Article further asserts that '[t]he developed contracting parties do not expect reciprocity for commitments made by them in trade negotiations to reduce or remove tariffs and other barriers to the trade of less-developed contracting parties'.[22]

Around the same time, UNCTAD was established as an organ of the UN General Assembly to promote, *inter alia*, international trade, particularly with a view to accelerating economic development among countries at different stages of development and with different forms of social organization. More generally, it was also to review and facilitate the coordination of activities of the other UN institutions in the field of international trade and economic development.[23] The establishment of UNCTAD demonstrated the international community's recognition of the need for institutions to deal specifically with the concerns and problems of developing countries,[24] albeit as a weaker counterpart of the GATT.[25]

---

of sub-Saharan Africa countries for about 75% of exports. UNCTAD, Economic Development in Africa: Policy, Prospects and Policy Issues, UN Doc. UNCTAD/GDS/AFRICA/1-TD/B/48/12 (2002).

[20] Edwini Kessie, 'Enforceability of the Legal Provisions Relating to Special and Differential Treatment under the WTO Agreements', 3 *J. World Intellectual Property* 955, 959 (2000) mentioning that newly independent countries challenged the basis on which the GATT was built, namely a rules-based, non-discriminatory multilateral trading system.

[21] Article XVIII of the GATT Agreement, supra note 2. On preferential treatment in GATT, see generally Wil D. Verwey, 'The Principles of a New International Economic Order and the Law of the General Agreement on Tariffs and Trade (GATT)', 3 *Leiden J. Int'l L.* 117 (1990).

[22] Article XXXVI.3 and 8 of the GATT Agreement, supra note 2.

[23] UNGA Res. 1995 (XIX), Establishment of the United Nations Conference on Trade and Development as an Organ of the General Assembly, 30 Dec. 1964, in Resolutions Adopted by the General Assembly During its 19th Session, 1 Dec. 1964-1 Sept. 1965, UN Doc. A/5815.

[24] Participants recognized in the first UNCTAD session that developed countries must grant concessions to all developing countries. General Principle 8, Proceedings of the UNCTAD 1, Final Act and Report, UN Doc. E/Conf.46/139-E/Conf.46/141 (Vol. I) at Annex A.I.1.

[25] Ian Brownlie, 'Legal Status of Natural Resources in International Law (Some Aspects)', 162 *RCADI* 245 (1979) noting that UNCTAD is in the institutional sphere

Calls for a new international economic order In the early 1970s, it was often felt in developing countries that despite some significant changes in preceding years traditional international economic law put too much emphasis on the protection of alien property against nationalization.[26] Even though these countries still maintained their willingness to uphold international law on the whole, they now demanded the creation of new rules allowing them to benefit more from the international system.[27] Their arguments centred around the denunciation of injustice in economic relations among developed and developing countries.[28] Their claims focused on the protection of their economic interests, positive discrimination and non-reciprocity. Though the protection and utilization of global commons was one of the controversial areas, the main points at issue were regarding international trade, international monetary matters and the financing of development through aid, loans and foreign direct investment.[29] The new international economic order (NIEO) marked a turning point in North-South relations insofar as developing countries drifted away from full cooperation with the North towards trying to impose on developed countries a new set of principles of international law.[30] The NIEO was thus marked by unilateral calls from developing countries for changes in the international economic and legal system.[31]

A series of factors allowed developing countries to voice these concerns at the level of the UN General Assembly. The global energy crisis of the early 1970s, which highlighted the dependence of developed countries on natural resources, and the fact that developing countries had by then a majority of votes in the General Assembly constituted important elements in the development of these issues in international forums.[32] The most visible result was a series of non-binding instruments seeking to establish an NIEO. These General Assembly resolutions aimed at creating rules of international law meeting the specific needs of

---

what the NIEO is in the normative one. The establishment of UNCTAD is also significant because it paved the way for the establishment of two other major development-oriented bodies, the UNDP in 1965 and UNIDO in 1966.

[26]   Thomas W. Wälde, 'A Requiem for the "New International Economic Order" – The Rise and Fall of Paradigms in International Law', in Najeeb Al-Nauimi and Richard Meese eds, *International Legal Issues Arising under the United Nations Decade of International Law* 1301 (The Hague: Nijhoff, 1995).

[27]   Surya Prakash Sinha, *Legal Polycentricity and International Law* 16 (Durham, North Carolina: Carolina Academic Press, 1996).

[28]   René-Jean Dupuy, *La communauté internationale entre le mythe et l'histoire* 129 (Paris: Economica, 1986) and Mohammed Bedjaoui, *Towards a New International Economic Order* (Paris: UNESCO, 1979).

[29]   A.A. Fatouros, 'The International Law of the New International Economic Order: Emerging Patterns of Norms', XII *Thesaurus Acroasium* 445 (1981).

[30]   Maurice Flory, 'Mondialisation et droit international du développement', 101 *Revue générale de droit international public* 609 (1997).

[31]   R.St.J. McDonald, 'Solidarity in the Practice and Discourse of Public International Law', 8 *Pace Int'l L. Rev.* 259 (1996).

[32]   Feuer and Cassan, supra note 16 at 18.

developing countries on the basis of their different levels of economic development. The Declaration for the establishment of an NIEO specifically provided that the new order should be founded, *inter alia*, on the principle of giving developing countries access to the achievements of modern science and technology, and should consequently promote the transfer of technology and the creation of indigenous technology for their benefit.[33] The Charter on Economic Rights and Duties of States was even more specific in asserting that '[e]very State has the right to benefit from the advances and developments in science and technology for the acceleration of its economic and social development'.[34] At the close of the decade, the Vienna Programme of Action on Science and Technology for Development further stated that as long as there was no restructuring of existing international economic relations on a just and equitable basis, there would be limits to the ability of developing countries to realize their full potential.[35]

The NIEO called, in essence, for a form of distributive justice aimed at meeting the needs of developing countries.[36] It was based on a series of principles emphasizing the need for developing countries to gain effective control over their natural resources and economic development. This explains the central importance of the principle of permanent sovereignty over natural resources. One of the main thrusts of NIEO proposals was thus to strengthen the position of states as economic actors against foreign private investors. This implied a stronger involvement of the state in the management of the economy.[37]

Due to the prevalence of an extremely skewed distribution of technologies across the world, technology transfer was also very prominent among the NIEO demands.[38] It was felt that easier access to modern technologies would promote the realization of economic self-determination for developing countries.[39] Technology

---

[33]   UNGA Res. 3201 (S-VI), Declaration on the Establishment of a New International Economic Order, 1 May 1974, reprinted in 13 *ILM* 715 (1974), at § 4 (p).

[34]   UNGA Res. 3281 (XXIX), 12 Dec. 1974, Charter of Economic Rights and Duties of States, in Resolutions Adopted by the General Assembly during its 29th Session, 17 Sept.-8 Dec. 1974, UN Doc. A/9631, at § 13.

[35]   Vienna Programme of Action on Science and Technology for Development, in Report of the United Nations Conference on Science and Technology for Development, Vienna, 20-31 Aug. 1979, UN Doc. A/CONF.81/16, preamble.

[36]   M. W. Janis, 'The Ambiguity of Equity in International Law', 9 *Brooklyn J. Int'l L.* 7 (1983).

[37]   Susan K. Sell, *Power and Ideas – North-South Politics of Intellectual Property and Antitrust* 72 (Albany: State University of New York Press, 1998).

[38]   I.A. Shearer, *Starke's International Law* 348 (London: Butterworths, 11th ed. 1994) and Gaëtan Verhoosel, 'International Transfer of Environmentally Sound Technology: The New Dimension of an Old Stumbling Block', 27 *Envtl. Pol'y and L.* 470 (1997).

[39]   UNGA Res. 3201 (S-VI), supra note 33. See also, Alan Boyle, 'Comment on the Paper by Diana Ponce-Nava', in Winfried Lang ed., *Sustainable Development and International Law* 137 (London: Graham and Trotman, 1995).

transfer already figured in the Stockholm Declaration.[40] In the mid-1970s negotiations for a Code of Conduct on the Transfer of Technology were initiated. The Draft Code recognized, *inter alia*, that there was a need for developed countries to grant special treatment to developing countries in the field of technology transfer.[41] The Code was however never formally adopted even in a non-binding form.[42] After the publication of a revised draft in 1985, negotiations were stalled for several years. Finally, the secretary-general of UNCTAD proposed that negotiations should be formally suspended in view of the changed circumstances in the international arena.[43] The fate of the proposed technology transfer code is symptomatic of the larger failure of the NIEO movement to bring about any substantive results beyond the series of political declarations in the mid-1970s. By the early 1980s, with the onset of the debt crisis, differential treatment in the NIEO style had been largely abandoned.[44]

Overall, the series of General Assembly resolutions had significant political impacts but the principles put forward were never fully implemented.[45] One of the major projects that the international community embarked upon to realize NIEO principles was the promotion of an Integrated Programme for Commodities. Its central funding mechanism was to be a Common Fund for Commodities whose rationale was to limit fluctuations in the prices of commodities.[46] The negotiations eventually led to the conclusion of a diminutive agreement establishing a common fund for commodities in 1980 that only came into force in 1989.[47] The most

---

[40]   Principle 20 of Declaration of the United Nations Conference on the Human Environment, Stockholm, 16 June 1972, reprinted in 11 *ILM* 1416 (1972) states that 'environmental technologies should be made available to developing countries on terms which would encourage their wide dissemination without constituting an economic burden on the developing countries'.

[41]   Preamble of the Draft International Code of Conduct on the Transfer of Technology, 5 June 1985, reprinted in UNCTAD, International Investment Instruments: A Compendium – Volume I, UN Doc. UNCTAD/DTCI/30(Vol. I) (1996).

[42]   The legal status of the code remained a source of disagreement throughout the negotiations. Sell, supra note 37 at 90.

[43]   UNCTAD, Negotiations on an International Code of Conduct on the Transfer of Technology, UN Doc. TD/CODE TOT/60 (1995).

[44]   Chakravarthi Raghavan, *Recolonization – GATT, the Uruguay Round and the Third World* 53 (London: Zed, 1990) noting that after the call for a new international economic order in the 1970s, the consideration of differential treatment subsided totally for a number of years.

[45]   See generally Jerzy Makarczyk, *Principles of a New International Economic Order* (Dordrecht: Nijhoff, 1988).

[46]   UNCTAD Res. 93 (IV), Integrated Programme for Commodities, 30 May 1976, in Proceedings of the UNCTAD, Fourth Session, Nairobi, 5-31 May 1976, UN Doc. TD/218 (Vol. I). See also Keith Griffin, *International Inequality and National Poverty* 107 (London: Macmillan, 1978).

[47]   Agreement Establishing the Common Fund for Commodities, Geneva, 27 June 1980, reprinted in 19 *ILM* 896 (1980). See also Gamani Corea, *Taming Commodity Markets*

significant sign of the failure of the NIEO movement to bring about significant changes in the field of commodities was the absence of progress on these issues at UNCTAD IV and the following two sessions.[48]

Globalization and the Development of Differential Treatment

The lack of implementation of NIEO demands reflected in some sense the rapid changes in the global economic and political scenario. In other words, the process of economic globalization and the collapse of most communist regimes progressively provided conditions under which it became more difficult for developing countries to put forward claims for preferential treatment. However, while increasing economic integration was leading to a reduction in preferences for developing countries, the emergence of a growing number of international environmental issues and the recognition of close links between development and environmental problems gradually led to the creation of a new wave of differential treatment provisions. These reflected, in part, the growing interdependence of all states in certain fields.

Decline of the new international economic order The NIEO movement was based on solidarity claims by developing countries. These unilateral demands which were to be matched by unilateral obligations of developed countries to compensate for the wrongs of the colonial period were eventually not successful either at the level of principles or in practice.[49] The eventual demise of the NIEO was linked to several factors. The onset of the debt crisis in 1982 constituted a turning point in the NIEO debate. Broader forces were also at play during the 1980s, such as economic globalization. This received a tremendous boost with the collapse of the socialist regimes of Eastern Europe, allowing the world economy to become unified to a much larger extent.

While the NIEO had emphasized the possibility of an alternative economic development path based largely on state intervention, the new economic environment and its accompanying policies were becoming less and less conducive to their realization.[50] By 1990, following what came to be known as the lost development decade for many developing countries, the NIEO rhetoric had faded away and had given way to a new understanding of solidarity which emphasized the mutual responsibility of both developed and developing countries concerning the various international issues necessitating cooperation.[51] This was, for instance,

---

– *The Integrated Programme and the Common Fund in UNCTAD* (Manchester: Manchester University Press, 1992).

48   Feuer and Cassan, supra note 16 at 21.

49   Bruno Simma, 'From Bilateralism to Community Interest in International Law', 250 *RCADI* 217 (1994/VI).

50   Flory, supra note 30 at 621.

51   Simma, supra note 49 at 238.

reflected in the Declaration on International Economic Cooperation adopted in 1990 by the General Assembly which assigns proportionally greater responsibility to the North for the economic problems of the 1980s and for meeting the challenges of the 1990s while providing at the same time that the South will assume the main burden of macroeconomic policy reform at the national level.[52] It was seen as the blueprint for new relations among states because it avoided the NIEO rhetoric but recognized the immense economic problems plaguing the world.[53]

The waning of the NIEO rhetoric has been matched by a greater reluctance to provide differential treatment, in particular in trade agreements. The GATT 1994 agreement has, for instance, maintained the principle of differential treatment, but qualified by several limitations and it provides that such measures are generally temporary in nature.[54] As confirmed by the 1997 decision concerning the regime for the importation, sale and distribution of bananas in the EU, trade preferences such as those provided in the context of the EU-ACP agreements will be considered more and more severely in coming years.[55] In fact, the long-standing practice of providing non-reciprocal trade preferences to African Caribbean and Pacific (ACP) states by the EU is being phased out. The Lomé IV Convention was still premised on the granting of trade preferences to ACP countries, and included, for instance, a stabilization mechanism to remedy the 'harmful effects of the instability of export earnings' for ACP countries.[56] The more recent Cotonou Agreement, however, seeks to progressively remove barriers to trade with a view to achieving WTO compatibility.[57]

---

[52]   UNGA Res. S-18/3, Declaration on International Economic Cooperation, in particular the Revitalization of Economic Growth and Development of the developing Countries, 1 May 1990, General Assembly 18th Special Session, UN Doc. A/S-18/15 (1990). See also, Russel Lawrence Barsh, 'A Special Session of the UN General Assembly Rethinks the Economic Rights and Duties of States', 85 *Am. J. Int'l L.* 192 (1991).

[53]   Statement of the President of the Eighteenth Special Session of the UN General Assembly on UNGA Res. S-18/3: 'First, it does not hark back to the unproductive posturing of the past, yet it recognizes the stark contrasts that scar the international economic landscape', in Provisional Verbatim Record of the Eleventh Meeting, 1 May 1990, UN Doc. A/S-18/PV.11.

[54]   W. Benedek, 'Implications of the Principle of Sustainable Development, Human Rights and Good Governance for the GATT/WTO', in Konrad Ginther et al. eds, *Sustainable Development and Good Governance* 274 (Dordrecht: Nijhoff, 1995).

[55]   European Communities – Regime for the Importation, Sale and Distribution of Bananas, Report of the Appellate Body, 22 Aug. 1997, WTO Doc. WT/DS27/AB/R.

[56]   Article 186 of the Fourth ACP-EEC Convention, Lomé, 15 Dec. 1989, reprinted in 29 *ILM* 783 (1990).

[57]   Article 36 of the Partnership Agreement Between the Members of the African, Caribbean and Pacific Group of States of the one Part, and the European Community and its Member States, of the other Part, Cotonou, 23 June 2000, *Official Journal* L 317, 15/12/2000 p. 3.

Trends in international trade law have become increasingly blurred in recent years. Differential treatment is still, to a large extent, seen unfavourably in the eyes in international trade law. However, in recent years, an increasing number of events point to a possible revival of differentiation in the WTO context. These include specific calls from developing countries for differential treatment, such as in the 1999 declaration of trade ministers of least developed countries, which requested that differential treatment in the multilateral trading system should be binding and should constitute an integral part of the rules in place.[58] Further, the WTO itself has been increasingly concerned with differential treatment measures. The WTO General Council had already decided by 1999 to extend the waiver of the most favoured nation clause with regard to implementation schedules for least developed countries in furtherance of the need to ensure that least-developed countries secure a share in the growth in international trade commensurate with the needs of their economic development.[59] Subsequently, the declaration adopted at the 2001 WTO ministerial conference also stated that consideration should be given in forthcoming negotiations to the ways in which special and differential treatment can be incorporated into WTO rules.[60]

Differential treatment among interdependent states While the emergence of the new economic paradigm heralded the decline of differential treatment in the economic field, other factors have ensured a revival under a different guise. Firstly, the progressive internationalization of environmental concerns and the realization that some problems are global in scope have led to a profound change in international environmental policy making and to the search for new ways to ensure the participation of all countries in relevant agreements.[61] Issues such as the allocation of natural resources, responsibility for conserving and controlling pollution, and the distribution of costs arising from pollution prevention and environmental harms have brought the issue of equity to the fore.[62] Secondly, globalization in the economic and financial sectors and the end of the cold war have led many developing and other countries to be much more integrated in the world economy. This is fostering new relations of interdependence among all countries. Thirdly, globalization has been proceeding simultaneously within the economic, technological and environmental fields and strong linkages between

---

[58]   Declaration of the Meeting of the Ministers of Trade of Least Developed Countries, Seattle, 29 Nov. 1999, § 14.

[59]   WTO, Preferential Tariff Treatment for Least-developed Countries – Decision on Waiver, 15 June 1999, WTO Doc. WT/L/304.

[60]   WTO, Implementation-Related Issues and Concerns, Ministerial Conference – Fourth Session, WTO Doc. WT/MIN(01)/17 (2001).

[61]   South Commission, *The Challenge to the South* 214 (Oxford: Oxford University Press, 1990).

[62]   Edith Brown Weiss, 'Environmental Equity and International Law', in Sun Lin ed., *UNEP's New Way Forward: Environmental Law and Sustainable Development* 7 (Nairobi: UNEP, 1995).

them have become apparent.[63] For instance, the economic impact of measures to stem climate change or the economic potential of biological resources are now evident.

The recognition of the global dimensions of environmental problems, the shift away from state controlled economies and events such as the end of the cold war have contributed to make the NIEO obsolete in international forums.[64] Foreign private investment in developing countries has become comparatively much more important and the existence of unified markets is forcing all countries to compete on par.[65] While granting differential treatment in the economic sphere is thus becoming more and more difficult to justify, other factors bearing on the economy have given rise to a new wave of differential provisions and instruments. The importance accorded to global environmental problems has become such that nearly all recent international environmental agreements include provisions and/or specific mechanisms which take into account the specific characteristics of various groups of countries.

Even though the NIEO rhetoric has subsided, some of the substantive elements which formed the core of the debate in the 1970s are still present. A case in point is the premium placed on the issue of technology transfer which remains central to current differential treatment debates, even though its modalities may be different.[66] What has changed is the rationale for granting differential treatment which now focuses on global environmental needs rather than on development priorities of individual countries. A certain measure of continuity is indeed discernible. In some cases, recent agreements still refer to NIEO era instruments. Thus, Article 34 of the International Timber Trade Agreement states that the Council must consider taking appropriate differential and remedial measures in accordance with the UNCTAD Integrated Programme for Commodities adopted in 1976.[67] More significantly, while some of the NIEO demands were never met in the period when they were formulated as unilateral demands from developing countries, their realization has sometimes been enhanced in recent years. The voting structure adopted in the

---

[63]   R.P. Anand, 'A New International Economic Order for Sustainable Development?', in Najeeb Al-Nauimi and Richard Meese eds, *International Legal Issues Arising Under the United Nations Decade of International Law* 1209 (The Hague: Nijhoff, 1995).

[64]   Wälde, supra note 26 at 3128.

[65]   This impact is much less pronounced for least developed countries. As of 2000, least developed countries received only 5.7% of non-concessional financial flows but 94.7% of all concessional loans and grants provided to developing countries. UNCTAD, *The Least Developed Countries Report 2002* (Geneva: UNCTAD, 2002).

[66]   Cf. Rudolph Dolzer, 'The Global Environment Facility – Towards a New Concept of the Common Heritage of Mankind', in Gudmundur Alfredsson and Peter McAlister-Smith eds, *The Living Law of Nations – Essays on Refugees, Minorities, Indigenous Peoples and the Human Rights of Other Vulnerable Groups* 331 (Kehl: N.P. Engel, 1996).

[67]   International Tropical Timber Agreement, Geneva, 26 Jan. 1994, reprinted in 33 *ILM* 1014 (1994) and UNCTAD Res. 93 (IV), supra note 46.

Montreal Protocol Fund constitutes an example of this trend.[68] Among the factors explaining this resurgence of differential treatment is the fact that it is no more linked to the call for an overhaul of the economic and legal system.[69] Further, in the case of technology transfer, for instance, countries owning environmentally sound technologies have realized that their transfer not only contributes to a better global environment but is also often in their own economic interest.[70] Global environmental problems are thus allowing a second wave of differential treatment, one largely devoid of controversial ideological undertones.[71]

Interdependence in solving environmental problems has been a key factor in the revival of differential measures. Differential measures must, for instance, be seen in the light of the fact that countries relatively less industrialized hold most of the remaining biodiversity. This is partly due to non-industrialization and partly due to the fact that the tropics happen to be more gene-rich than temperate zones. Industrialization in developing countries is likely to wipe out part of this heritage. Another element contributing to the rapid development of differential measures is that certain environmental problems identified as global are currently of major concern for developed countries while they may only be a future concern for developing countries. Thus, the supply of fresh water is presently of much greater concern to numerous developing countries than climate change. These elements and a host of others, such as the fact that the overwhelming majority of environmentally sound technologies are produced in the North, create a situation in which developed countries will agree to differential treatment measures in favour of other countries. As illustrated by the flexibility mechanisms of the climate change regime which are examined in more detail in the next chapter, the rationale may be diverse, ranging from concern for the global environment to the search for the cheapest options to solve a given problem or the creation of new markets for environmentally sound technologies. In any case, the result is that countries which often lack resources to meet the most basic needs of their populations can avoid diverting necessary resources from these essential tasks, while still contributing to solving global environmental problems.[72] In practice, differential treatment has thus become the price to be paid to ensure universal participation in environmental agreements concerned with global problems.[73]

---

68   See also Frank Biermann, 'Financing Environmental Policies in the South – Experiences from the Multilateral Ozone Fund', 9 *Int'l Envtl. Aff.* 179 (1997).
69   Dolzer, supra note 66 at 338.
70   Cf. Verhoosel, supra note 38 at 472.
71   Pierre-François Mercure, 'Le choix du concept de développement durable plutôt que celui du patrimoine commun de l'humanité afin d'assurer la protection de l'atmosphère', 41 *McGill L.J.* 595 (1996).
72   Cf. Mohamed Abdelwahab Bekhechi, 'Une nouvelle étape dans le développement du droit international de l'environnement: La Convention sur la désertification', 101 *Revue générale de droit international public* 5 (1997).
73   Boyle, supra note 39 at 138.

Forms of Differential Treatment

Differentiation has been incorporated into international law in various ways. While it has generally been associated with non-reciprocity in international legal norms, it also encompasses a number of other differential instruments falling within the two broad categories of positive discrimination and resource redistribution.

Positive Discrimination

Differentiation in international environmental agreements In recent environmental agreements, differential treatment has been widely used.[74] This reflects the complexity of the problems addressed as well as the fact that the use of differentiation has the potential to foster cooperation among states with widely different interests and capabilities regarding the problems at stake.

The most common provisions simply acknowledge the existence of different groups of states and provide, for instance, that the special situation of developing countries should be taken into account. Thus, one of the central principles of the Desertification Convention is that '[p]arties should take into full consideration the special needs and circumstances of affected developing country Parties, particularly the least developed among them'.[75]

More specific exclusions to the principle of reciprocity of obligations have been agreed to in several cases. A given instrument may provide that different groups of countries will have different obligations under the convention. The Climate Change Convention distinguishes, for instance, between obligations of all states and the specific obligations of developed countries that include a commitment to provide financial resources for technology transfer needed by developing countries to meet the incremental costs of implementing their own commitments.[76] The Kyoto Protocol to the Climate Change Convention constitutes another interesting example of differential treatment. It not only distinguishes between countries which take on binding commitments and those which do not but also provides for differentiated commitments for each country taking on a quantified emission limitation or reduction commitment.[77] Differential treatment measures are also found in other

---

[74]   Cf. Dominik McGoldrick, 'Sustainable Development and Human Rights: An Integrated Conception', 45 *Int'l and Comp. L.Q.* 796 (1996).

[75]   Article 3.d of the Convention to Combat Desertification in Those Countries Experiencing Serious Drought and/or Desertification, Particularly in Africa, Paris, 17 June 1994, reprinted in 33 *ILM* 1328 (1994) [hereafter Convention to Combat Desertification].

[76]   Article 4.1-3 of the Framework Convention on Climate Change, New York, 9 May 1992, reprinted in 31 *ILM* 849 (1992) [hereafter Climate Change Convention].

[77]   Kyoto Protocol to the United Nations Framework Convention on Climate Change, Kyoto, 11 Dec. 1997, Decision 1/CP.3/Annex, UNFCCC, *Report of the Conference of the Parties on its Third Session*, Kyoto, 1-11 Dec. 1997, UN Doc. FCCC/CP/1997/7/Add.1.

parts of the Kyoto regime. Of special interest is Article 3.14 which requires countries with commitments to make sure they minimize adverse social, environmental and economic impacts on developing countries while implementing their commitments. Among the measures agreed, the Conference of the Parties has emphasized the need for reduction in the diffusion and transfer of advanced fossil-fuel technologies and technologies relating to fossil fuels that emit less greenhouse gases, capture or store them, as well as the need to strengthen developing countries' capacity to improve efficiency activities relating to fossil fuels.[78] Further, differentiation has influenced the design of the institutional mechanisms adopted to foster the implementation of the Protocol. Thus, two different mechanisms are instituted to increase the cost effectiveness of emission limitation or reduction measures. Parties taking on commitments are authorized to participate in emissions trading among themselves.[79] Additionally, a Clean Development Mechanism (CDM), a form of joint implementation, is set up to assist parties with quantified commitments in achieving compliance with their obligations. Under the CDM, these parties can invest in developing countries and apply the certified emission reductions accruing from such project activities towards the fulfilment of their own commitments.[80]

Other conventions retain the principle of reciprocity but grant specific countries longer implementation periods. The Montreal Protocol authorizes, for instance, countries with low per capita emissions of ozone depleting substances to delay by ten years the implementation of their obligations, while other countries must implement their commitments immediately.[81] The GATT 1994 Agreement on Agriculture also entitles developing countries to delay implementation by a decade while least developed countries do not have to abide at all.[82] Another option has been to give developing countries the option to defer implementation until such time as other countries have fulfilled their own commitments. The two conventions which opened for signature at Rio, the Montreal Protocol and the Convention on Persistent Organic Pollutants state that the extent to which developing countries

---

[78]   Decision 9/CP.7, Matters relating to article 3, paragraph 14, of the Kyoto Protocol, UNFCCC, *Report of the Conference of the Parties on its Seventh Session,* Marrakesh, 29 Oct.-10 Nov. 2001, UN Doc. FCCC/CP/2001/13/Add.1.

[79]   Article 17 of the Kyoto Protocol, supra note 77.

[80]   Article 12 of the Kyoto Protocol, supra note 77.

[81]   Article 5.1 of the of the Protocol on Substances that Deplete the Ozone Layer, Montreal, 16 Sept. 1987, reprinted in Ozone Secretariat – UNEP, *Handbook for the International Treaties for the Protection of the Ozone Layer* (5th ed. 2000) [hereafter Montreal Protocol].

[82]   Agreement on Agriculture, Marrakesh, 15 Apr. 1994, in World Trade Organization, *The Legal Texts – The Results of the Uruguay Round of Multilateral Trade Negotiations* (Cambridge: Cambridge University Press, 1999).

will effectively implement their commitments is dependent upon the North fulfilling their pledges on aid and technology transfer.[83]

In keeping with public international law's focus on states, differential treatment provisions usually concern states. Some environmental agreements have, however, taken cognizance of the fact that there is a multitude of relevant actors who should be taken into account in the management and protection of the environment. Thus, the Biodiversity Convention provides for the fair and equitable sharing of benefits arising out of the utilization of genetic resources and the guidelines adopted as guidance for member states in this field clearly recognize the importance of different categories of non-state actors in this area.[84]

Differentiation in international organizations   International organizations are usually organized on the basis of the legal equality of states. There are, however, a number of significant exceptions to this rule. These cover situations where the principle of legal equality is abandoned to favour the weaker states and cases where it is the stronger states which benefit. Exceptions to the rule of formal equality can be found in the assessment of each state's financial contribution to a particular organization, in the voting arrangements or at the level of states' participation in the meetings of international organizations.

The case of the United Nations deserves particular mention. The UN decision making structure is generally based on the principle of the equality of all states which is reflected in the fact that each state has one vote in the General Assembly.[85] However, different kinds of exceptions to this rule are provided. On the one hand, an important example of differential treatment is found in the way member states' contributions are assessed. Indeed, contributions are individually assessed on the basis of members' capacity to pay.[86] This is tempered by the application of other criteria, such as the level of external debt and the level of per capita income to make the assessment acceptable to all. Assessed rates vary from a floor rate of 0.001 per cent, a maximum level of 0.01 per cent for least developed countries to an

[83]   Article 20.4 of the Convention on Biological Diversity, Rio de Janeiro, 5 June 1992, reprinted in 31 *ILM* 818 (1992) [hereafter Biodiversity Convention], Article 4.7 of the Climate Change Convention, supra note 76, Article 5.5 of the Montreal Protocol, supra note 81 and Article 13.4 of the Convention on Persistent Organic Pollutants, Stockholm, 23 May 2001, reprinted in 55 *ILM* 531 (2001).

[84]   Article 1 of the Biodiversity Convention, supra note 83 and Bonn Guidelines on Access to Genetic Resources and Fair and Equitable Sharing of the Benefits Arising out of their Utilization, in Dec. VI/24, 'Access and Benefit-Sharing as Related to Genetic Resources', *Report of the Sixth Meeting of the Conference of the Parties to the Convention on Biological Diversity*, The Hague, 7-19 April 2002, UN Doc. UNEP/CBD/COP/6/20.

[85]   Article 18 of the UN Charter.

[86]   UNGA Res. 14 (I), Budgetary and Financial Arrangements, 13 Feb. 1946, in Resolutions Adopted by the General Assembly During the First Part of its First Session from 10 Jan. to 14 Feb. 1946.

absolute maximum of 22 per cent which caps the contribution of the United States which would be the only country to pay more without a cap.[87] On the other hand, there are other departures from the rule of formal equality which do not constitute differential treatment. These include the voting structure in the Security Council where decisions with the most immediate practical effect can be taken. The decision making pattern is heavily biased in favour of a few politically and militarily important states.[88]

A number of other international organizations apply differentiation principles in the assessment of member states' contributions. Indeed, a majority of them assess their members according to a scale reflecting the size and importance of their economies.[89] In the World Bank, for instance, all states contribute to the capital according to a scale which broadly reflects their economic, financial and political importance on the world stage.[90] In some cases, environmental considerations also come into play. Thus, the level of contributions to the Montreal Protocol Fund depends on the per capita consumption of controlled substances.[91]

The division of contributions among states often cannot be analyzed separately from the decision-making procedures. Indeed, in the World Bank it is the level of capital subscribed that determines a given member's weight in the Board of Governors.[92] This is remarkable because the same mechanism works in favour of different groups of states in different situations. While economically weaker countries are allowed to contribute less, their power within the organization is also commensurately less as a consequence. The GEF has tackled this issue to an extent since recipient countries do not have to contribute to the trust fund but still get a privileged position in the decision making organs.[93]

---

[87]   UNGA Res. 55/5, Scale of Assessments for the Apportionment of the Expenses of the United Nations, 22 Jan. 2001, UN Doc. A/RES/55/5 B-F.

[88]   Article 27.3 UN Charter.

[89]   Henry G. Schermers and Niels M. Blokker, *International Institutional Law – Unity Within Diversity* at § 967 (The Hague: Nijhoff, 1995) note that even in 1961, only 8 out of 122 organizations and none of the principal universal or regional organizations assessed their member states to expenditure in equal shares.

[90]   World Bank, *The World Bank Annual Report 2001 – Volume 2 – Financial Statements and Appendixes* (Washington, DC: World Bank, 2001).

[91]   Articles 5 and 10 of the Montreal Protocol, supra note 81. See also, Dec. V/4, Classification of Certain Developing Countries as not Operating under Article 5 and Reclassification of Certain Developing Countries Earlier Classified as not Operating Under Article 5, *Report of the Fourth Meeting of the Parties to the Montreal Protocol on Substances that Deplete the Ozone Layer*, Copenhagen, 23-25 Nov. 1992, UN Doc. UNEP/OzL.Pro.4/15.

[92]   Article 5.3 of the Articles of Agreement of the International Bank for Reconstruction and Development, 27 Dec. 1945, 2 *UNTS* 134.

[93]   Note however that some of the recipients of GEF funds contributed to the replenishment. Annex C of the Instrument for the Establishment of the Restructured Global Environment Facility, Geneva, 16 Mar. 1994, reprinted in 33 *ILM* 1273 (1994).

Both equality of votes and weighted voting have been proposed and both have shortcomings in different contexts. On the one hand, in bodies like the UN General Assembly formal equality constitutes a form of differential treatment because it reduces the influence of the more powerful states. However, it also gives disproportionate importance to tiny states,[94] and as a result, the General Assembly has never been given any substantive power.[95] Formal equality has also been criticized by authors who fear that this is an incentive for smaller and smaller entities to secede and claim an equal voice on the international scene.[96] On the other hand, an institution like the World Bank works on the basis of weighted voting and votes are attributed in a way which broadly reflects the distribution of economic, military and political power in the world.[97] This arrangement gives very little weight to economically weaker states who are meant to benefit from World Bank aid.[98] However, this has had the advantage of allowing the institution to take potentially controversial decisions that could possibly not have been passed in the context of an international body voting in the one state-one vote manner.[99]

The examples of the World Bank and the UN show that there is no single formula which can be said to constitute differentiation in all cases. However, it is more and more widely accepted that existing differences in population, economic development levels, political and military power between states in many cases necessitate adjustments to decision making structures. Size or population may be relevant factors to determine a state's interest in a global environmental problem, but it is noteworthy that a comparatively small island state may have a relatively bigger stake in the specific fisheries it is most dependent upon than major fishing nations.[100] Inequalities may thus have to be taken into account both to provide more equitable outcomes and to meet, for instance, the expectations of a small nation

---

[94]   Daniel Bodansky, 'The Legitimacy of International Governance: A Coming Challenge for International Environmental Law?', 93 *Am. J. Int'l L.* 614 (1999).

[95]   Calls for giving the General Assembly pre-eminence within the UN system have been made. Dodo Aïchatou Mindaoudou, 'La notion de majorité comme preuve de démocratie à l'Assemblée générale des Nations Unies', 8 *African J. Int'l and Comp. L.* 447 (1996).

[96]   Thomas M. Franck, *Fairness in International Law and Institutions* 480 (Oxford: Clarendon, 1995).

[97]   *Note* that in the World Bank, there are both basic votes allocated equally to all states and weighted voting. The share of basic votes has come down from 14% in 1955 to 3%. Ngaire Woods, 'The Challenge of Good Governance for the IMF and the World Bank Themselves', 28 *World Development* 823 (2000).

[98]   Ngaire Woods, 'Making the IMF and the World Bank more Accountable', 77 *Int'l Aff.* 83 (2001).

[99]   William N. Gianaris, 'Weighted Voting in the International Monetary Fund and the World Bank', 14 *Fordham Int'l L.J.* 910 (1990-91).

[100] Note that this is not limited to developing nations. In the case of the textile machinery industry, Switzerland, a small economic power within the OECD context, holds a strategic position in this industry. Peter Marsh, 'Swiss Build up Their Stake in Textile Machinery Market', *Financial Times,* 26 Feb. 1998, p. 6.

with an important stake in a given industry. In this context, some form of weighted voting is more likely to bring about equitable outcomes even though the complexity of the problems addressed may not allow for solutions favoured by every state.[101]

The need to provide voting systems which do not favour only the bigger and more powerful states has been taken into account in a number of cases. The new environmental trust funds are noteworthy in this context. Both the Montreal Protocol Fund and the GEF give aid recipients a say in the decision making process that is not related to their share of the capital to be distributed. The governance structure in the restructured GEF thus aims to foster decisions with sustainable environmental management goals which are acceptable to both donors and recipients.

Another example is the decision making structure of the regime for the exploitation of deep seabed minerals put in place under the Law of the Sea Convention. The composition of the Council, which is the executive organ of the Authority, reflects partly the share of exploitable minerals consumed by each country, the importance of investments made for the conduct of activities in the Area, the importance of these minerals as export products, the necessity to take into account the situation of developing countries and partly the principle of equitable geographical representation.[102] Within the Council, decisions are in principle taken by consensus. In cases where voting has to take place, the intricate voting procedure tries to take into account all the different interests at stake, including producers, exporters, developed and developing countries, in accordance with the principle of common heritage of humankind and the realization that the consent of the major countries had to be obtained to make the regime viable. Thus, in practice, the introduction of 'chamber voting' gives different interest groups such as the group of deep seabed mining states and other developed countries a blocking vote. Finally, it is noteworthy that there have been attempts to reform the UN Security Council to broaden its representativeness. The enlargement of its membership is being explored by a special working group since 1994 but there have been no concrete results to-date. Besides agreeing that a two-third majority should be found for any change in the composition of the Security Council and reiterating the Millennium Declaration goal of comprehensively reforming the Security

---

101   Cf. Schermers and Blokker, supra note 89 at § 792 who find that equality of voting
       power is a poor basis for decision making.
102   Section 3.15 of the Agreement Relating to the Implementation of Part XI of the
       United Nations Convention on the Law of the Sea of 10 December 1982, New York,
       28 July 1994, reprinted in 33 *ILM* 1309 (1994) [hereafter 1994 Law of the Sea
       Agreement].

Council, the General Assembly has not done more in this regard.[103] The working group has carried on its work but consensus remains elusive.[104]

Finally, differentiation is also noteworthy with regard to the participation of states in meetings, negotiating sessions and conferences. The increasing number of meetings and the decentralization of negotiation sessions often put an unsustainable burden on small developing countries which may not have the capacity to send representatives to all the sessions which would be relevant for them. The international community has reacted to this through the establishment of funding mechanisms to assist developing countries to participate in treaty negotiations. Voluntary funds were, for instance, established for the negotiations of the climate change and desertification conventions.[105] The rationale of the latter was to assist developing countries affected by desertification and drought to participate fully and effectively in the negotiation process.[106] This scheme has been maintained and broadened. There is now a Special Fund to support the participation of developing countries, and in particular least developed countries, in sessions of the Conference of the Parties and a Supplementary Fund to support the participation of representatives of NGOs from affected developing country parties in sessions of the Conference of the Parties.[107]

Resource Redistribution

Resource redistribution has been a lingering concern of the international community which has taken cognizance of a number of existing problems in the

---

[103]   UNGA Res. 53/30, Question of the Equitable Representation on and Increase in the Membership of the Security Council and Related Matters, 1 Dec. 1998, UN Doc. A/RES/53/30 and UNGA Res. 55/2, United Nations Millenium Declaration, 18 Sept. 2000, UN Doc. A/RES/55/2.

[104]   Report of the Open-ended Working Group on the Question of Equitable Representation on and Increase in the Membership of the Security Council and Other Matters related to the Security Council, UN Doc. A/55/47 (2001).

[105]   UNGA Res. 45/212, Protection of Global Climate for Present and Future Generations of Mankind, 21 Dec. 1990, in Resolutions and Decisions Adopted by the General Assembly During its 45th Session, UN Doc. A/45/49.

[106]   UNGA Res. 47/188, Establishment of an Intergovernmental Negotiating Committee for the Elaboration of an International Convention to Combat Desertification in those Countries Experiencing Serious Drought and/or Desertification, Particularly in Africa, 22 Dec. 1992, in Resolutions and Decisions Adopted by the General Assembly During its 47th Session, UN Doc. A/47/49.

[107]   Dec. 7/COP.1, The Supplementary Fund and the Special Fund of the Convention, Convention to Combat Desertification, *Report of the Conference of the Parties on its First Session*, Rome, 29 Sept.-10 Oct. 1997, UN Doc. ICCD/COP(1)/11/Add.1. For recent developments concerning these funds, Dec. 4/COP.5, Programme and Budget for the Biennium 2002-2003, Convention to Combat Desertification, *Report of the Conference of the Parties on its Fifth Session*, Geneva, 1-12 Oct. 2001, UN Doc. ICCD/COP(5)/11/Add.1.

international distribution of resources. Within the context of differential treatment, the single most important example of resource redistribution is 'implementation aid', or aid provided specifically to foster the capacity of states to effectively implement their international obligations. This can take the form of funding mechanisms and technology transfers. Implementation aid will be analyzed in more detail in the next chapter. A number of other examples of resource redistribution schemes can be found in the practice of states. The specific case of debt relief and the allocation of marine resources constitute the focus of this section.

Debt relief As noted above, economics and trade have historically been one of the main focuses of differential treatment. Even though the call for a new international economic order did not materialize as such, a number of specific developments can be noted. Debt relief stands out as a practical application of the principles of differential treatment. In this case, the differential content is linked to the relaxation of the obligation to repay on the basis of broader interests and considerations.

The problem of developing country debt has been on the international agenda for at least two decades and has been a focal point for discussions on the international economic order.[108] The debt burden of least developed countries in particular has often been unsustainable, with outstanding debt exceeding GDP in a number of countries.[109] The realization that the exceedingly high levels of debt are explained in part by the international economic environment and that some of the highly indebted countries are also among the poorest has led the international community to devise different ways to provide debt relief to these countries. Attention has, for instance, focused on the fact that the debt crisis was partly caused by external factors, such as fluctuations in oil prices and the sharp rise in interest rates at the beginning of the 1980s.[110]

The principle of debt relief itself has been and remains controversial. Two opposed claims are made in this regard. Some argue that debts should always be repaid in full and that developing countries cannot claim any special mitigating

---

[108] For an early discussion of the rationale for debt relief, Peter B. Kenen, 'Debt Relief as Development Assistance', in Jagdish N. Bhagwati ed., *The New International Economic Order: The North-South Debate* 50 (Cambridge, Mass: MIT Press, 1977). The Monterrey consensus recently reiterated the importance of external debt relief. Monterrey Consensus of the International Conference on Financing for Development, 22 March 2002, UN Doc. A/CONF.198/11.

[109] Even though the numbers of countries with ratios of total debt to GDP above 100% has been on the decline in recent years, there remained 17 least developed countries (out of 43) in that category in 2000. UNCTAD, supra note 65.

[110] Other external or internal causes of the debt problem include the recycling of petro-dollars and imprudent excessive lending to sovereign borrowers, the uneconomic spending of loan funds by borrower states and the capital flight in heavily indebted countries. August Reinisch, *State Responsibility for Debts – International Law Aspects of External Debts and Debt Restructuring* 8 (Vienna: Böhlau Verlag, 1995).

circumstances.[111] Others contend that extraneous factors should be taken into account:[112] it has, for instance, been suggested that creditor states may be under a duty to grant debt relief as a consequence of an obligation flowing from the general principles of solidarity and cooperation. Further, violations of the duty to enhance the well-being and development of all human beings expressed in the Declaration on the Right to Development may give rise to claim of state responsibility.[113] These claims have however not developed into customary international law.

While no rules of international law require debt relief, a number of initiatives have been taken towards effectuating debt relief with different rationales. Creditors and debtors have, for instance, tried for some time to resolve some of the debt related issues by meeting regularly in the London and Paris clubs. In the Paris club, significant rescheduling of bilateral official debt of the poor and heavily indebted countries has been achieved. However, debt has not been forgiven but rescheduled over long periods of time, ranging from thirty to forty years.[114] The World Bank has on its part put in place a special initiative for heavily indebted poor countries which has resulted in the setting up of a trust fund to finance on a grant basis debt relief for heavily indebted poor countries.[115] Relief is only provided to countries demonstrating though a sustained track record of good performance under IMF-monitored economic programmes, their ability to put to good use the resources that will be released. Further, the debt initiative is designed to preserve the financial integrity of multilateral donors and their preferred creditor status so that they can continue to provide financing on the best possible terms.[116] The main significance of the Initiative is that it constitutes the first comprehensive approach to address the debt problem of the poorest countries and that it also includes multilateral debt.[117]

---

[111]   Dominique Carreau, 'Rapport du directeur d'études de la section de langue française du Centre', in Dominique Carreau and Malcolm N. Shaw eds, *The External Debt* 3 (London: Kluwer Law International, 1995) stating that debt reduction can be envisaged in situations where creditors cannot hope to be fully reimbursed even though this does not affect the binding nature of the obligations of the debtors.

[112]   Cheryl Payer, *Lent and Lost – Foreign Credit and Third World Development* (London: Zed Books, 1991).

[113]   Reinisch, supra note 110 at 132.

[114]   UNCTAD, *The Least Developed Countries 1997 Report* at 29 (Geneva: UNCTAD, 1997).

[115]   *See,* World Bank, Resolution No. 96-9/Resolution No. IDA 96-5, Establishment of the Heavily Indebted Poor Countries (HIPC) Debt Initiative Trust Fund, reprinted in 36 *ILM* 997 (1997). This initiative is part of a larger agenda and is linked to the broader question of policy performance.

[116]   *Id.*

[117]   Bernhard G. Gunter, 'What's Wrong with the HIPC Initiative and What's Next?', *20 Development Pol'y Rev.* 5 (2002). The HIPC remains controversial even among international organizations and has, for instance, been severely criticized by UNCTAD for not providing 'a durable exit from the debt problem' for heavily indebted least developed countries. UNCTAD, supra note 65 at 210.

Overall, efforts at reducing developing country debt have only met with partial results. This has been acknowledged by the UN General Assembly which has expressed its concern

> that despite the debt-relief measures taken so far, those measures have not yet fully provided effective, equitable, development-oriented and durable solutions to the outstanding debt and debt-servicing problems of a large number of developing countries, in particular the poorest and heavily indebted countries, which continue to face serious debt problems.[118]

Other proposals to reduce debt include, for instance, the reimbursement in local currency or default.[119] The rationale for such suggestions is that debtors should not be responsible for the often significant depreciation of their currencies and that they should not be liable to pay more than what they borrowed in nominal terms. While not taking direct action itself, the UN Human Rights Commission has taken a strong stance on the need for debt reduction. It has argued that debt payments should not take precedence over the basic rights of the people of debtor countries to food, shelter, clothing, employment, health services and a healthy environment.[120] The Commission has further stressed the need for a political dialogue between creditor and debtor countries based on the principle of shared responsibility.[121]

Attempts have also been made to link debt relief and environmental protection. These have led to the creation of debt-for-nature swaps. The rationale is that in countries with high ratios of debt to GNP and high ratios of interest payments to export revenues, debt becomes a factor in environmental degradation and contributes to increased pressure on natural resources.[122] Debt-for-nature swaps have been used by environmental non-governmental organizations and by governments in creditor countries to simultaneously foster developmental and environmental objectives.[123] A number of swaps have focused on the prevention of deforestation, and more specifically on conservation of the rainforests whose

---

[118]   UNGA Res. 52/185, Enhancing International Cooperation Towards a Durable Solution to the External Debt Problem of Developing Countries, 18 Dec. 1997, UN Doc. A/RES/52/185.

[119]   Barry Wilkins, 'Debt and Underdevelopment: The Case for Cancelling Third World Debts', in Robin Attfield and Barry Wilkins eds, *International Justice and the Third World – Studies in the Philosophy of Development* 169 (London: Routledge, 1992).

[120]   Res. 1995/13, 'Effects on the full enjoyment of human rights of the economic adjustment policies arising from foreign debt and, in particular, of the implementation of the Declaration on the Right to Development', Report of the Commission on Human Rights on its fifty-first Session, 1995, UN Doc. E/1995/23.

[121]   Commission on Human Rights, Ways and Means to Carry out a Political Dialogue Between Creditor and Debtor Countries in the United Nations System, based on the Principle of Shared Responsibility, 52nd Session, UN Doc. E/CN.4/1996/22.

[122]   Catherine A. O'Neill and Cass R. Sunstein, 'Economics and the Environment: Trading Debt and Technology for Nature', 17 *Columbia J. Envtl. L.* 93 (1992).

[123]   Amanda Lewis, 'The Evolving Process of Swapping Debt for Nature', 10 *Colorado J. Int'l Envtl. L. and Pol'y* 431 (1999).

preservation is seen as an area of major concern in developed countries.[124] Other transactions have focused, for instance, on the purchase of waste treatment equipment.[125] Debt-for-nature swaps offer strong incentives for debtor states to undertake conservation measures and contribute to environmental protection at the local and global levels.[126]

In a context where obligations entered into are meant to be valid for all times, save for some special circumstances such as force majeure, debt relief constitutes a significant concession to the reciprocity of obligations. This explains why it has been extremely controversial even though it is being considered and used in various contexts. On the whole, debt relief is both a reflection of relations of solidarity at the international level and a reflection of pragmatic considerations on the part of creditors.

Allocation of natural resources   The allocation of natural resources has been the subject of numerous international legal instruments. This is due to the fact that they constitute the primary material of all industrial activity, that they are unequally distributed around the world and that they do not all fall under the sovereignty of a state. Natural resources are necessary but marginal in the economies of industrialized countries. However, their exploitation often constitutes one of the mainstays of developing country economies. The combination of these two elements has led to the development of a number of legal regimes taking into account the unequal capacity of states to access and benefit from certain resources. Deep seabed resources are particularly noteworthy. Different trends can be observed in the development of differentiation concerning access to and the management of these resources. Depending on the context, one observes either a tendency towards the setting up of common regimes for exploitation or towards the strengthening of sovereign claims over the resources. It is noteworthy that some developments in this field have been influenced by the recognition that current international mechanisms for the appropriation of resources have either not given all countries a reasonable level of command over their resources or have contributed to the depletion of natural resources.[127]

The concept of common heritage of humankind has been applied to the access and exploitation of some resources. In the case of the law of the sea, for instance, deep seabed resources in the high have been declared a common heritage of humankind.[128] Before the adoption of the Law of the Sea Convention of 1982,

---

[124]   United States, Tropical Forest Conservation Act of 1998, 22 *US Code* 2431.

[125]   Italy Becomes Fifth Western Nation to Sign 'Debt-for-Nature' Swap with Poland, *BNA Int'l Envtl. Daily,* 23 Apr. 1998, d5.

[126]   Carlos A. Quesada Mateo ed., *Debt-For-Nature Swaps to Promote Natural Resource Conservation* (Rome: FAO, 1993).

[127]   Ian Brownlie, *Principles of Public International Law* 258 (Oxford: Clarendon, 5th ed. 1998).

[128]   UNGA Res. 2749 (XXV), Declaration of Principles Governing the Sea-Bed and the Ocean floor, and the Subsoil Thereof, Beyond the Limits of National Jurisdiction, 17

resources found in and under the high seas had the status of *res communis* and could be freely appropriated by all states. Deep seabed resources had not been the object of any regulation because they were of no immediate use to any state. With the discovery of vast deposits of minerals in the deep seabed whose commercial exploitation appeared possible, a regime for access and exploitation became necessary.[129] Since these resources had never been under the sovereignty of any state, it was agreed that a special status be granted to resources found in the Area.[130]

The concept of common heritage as applied to the Area implies first that no state can claim sovereignty over deep seabed resources.[131] Second, the exploitation of the resources is to be internationally managed. Thus, a central regulatory and administrative agency supervises the exploitation of these resources, collects and redistributes the fees that users must pay to access the Area.[132] Third, benefits arising from the exploitation of these resources are to be shared equitably among all states. In effect, even the states which do not exploit the resources themselves are entitled to a share of the benefits.[133] The Authority is thus mandated to establish an economic assistance fund to compensate developing countries that suffer adversely from a price reduction of the minerals exploited in the Area.[134] Fourth, the resources should be used exclusively for pacifist purposes, should be accessible to all for scientific research and their utilization must take into account the renewability of the resources.[135]

Dec. 1970, in Resolutions Adopted by the General Assembly During its 25th Session, UN Doc. A/8028 and article 136 of the United Nations Convention on the Law of the Sea, Montego Bay, 10 Dec. 1982, reprinted in 21 *ILM* 1261 (1982) [hereafter Law of the Sea Convention].

129   Richard Young, 'The Legal Regime of the Deep-Sea Floor', 62 *Am. J. Int'l L.* 641 (1968).

130   Martti Koskenniemi and Marja Lehto, 'The Privilege of Universality – International Law, Economic Ideology and Seabed Resources', 65 *Nordic J. Int'l L.* 533 (1996). The Area is defined in article 1 of the Law of the Sea Convention, supra note 128 as 'the sea-bed and ocean floor and subsoil thereof, beyond the limits of national jurisdiction'.

131   Kemal Baslar, *The Concept of the Common Heritage of Mankind in International Law* 82 (The Hague: Kluwer Law International, 1998).

132   Part XI Section 4 of the Law of the Sea Convention, supra note 128.

133   Nico Schrijver, *Sovereignty over Natural Resources – Balancing Rights and Duties* 220 (Cambridge: Cambridge University Press, 1997) and Alexandre Kiss, 'Conserving the Common Heritage of Mankind', 59 *Revista Juridica de la Universidad de Puerto Rico* 773 (1990).

134   Article 151.10 of the Law of the Sea Convention, supra note 128 and Section VII of the 1994 Law of the Sea Agreement, supra note 102.

135   R.St.J. MacDonald, 'The Common Heritage of Mankind', in Ulrich Beyerlin et al. eds, *Recht zwischen Umbruch und Bewahrung* 153 (Berlin: Springer, 1995) and Mercure, supra note 71 at 605.

The Convention could not come into force because of disagreements over the regime regulating the exploitation of deep seabed resources as adopted in 1982.[136] This led to a compromise agreement which restricted the application of the principle of common heritage and altered the compensatory package to make exploitation more attractive to contractors.[137] In particular, the 1994 agreement reinforces the power of the Council, reduces the preferential position of the Enterprise as compared to the contractors, and abolishes compulsory technology transfers.[138]

Overall, despite the restrictions placed by the 1994 agreement on the application of the principle of common heritage, the regime very clearly articulates differential concerns and provides a basis for exploitation of the resources which is significantly different from that governing resources under national sovereignty. It is noteworthy that the 1994 adjustments do not seek to modify the principles governing the management of the resources but only adapt a selected number of elements to make the regime acceptable to all states. In this sense, it constitutes another example of the more pragmatic approach taken in recent years which leaves out some of the ideological debates of the NIEO but manages to at least get limited practical results.

While the trend towards internationalizing the management of deep seabed resources constitutes a clear case of a regime seeking to provide weaker and less economically advanced states a say and a share in the management of resources beyond national sovereignty, it is noteworthy that the development of exclusive economic zones (EEZs) fundamentally stems from similar concerns. The difference between the regime for the Area and EEZs is that the latter constitutes an extension of the concept of state sovereignty to areas previously part of the high seas. The claims for EEZs, first made by some Latin American countries and then by most coastal states were premised on the desire to regulate access to resources for the benefit of the coastal states.[139] While the concept of EEZ was first put forward by developing countries, it was very quickly accepted by all coastal states because most of them, including major powers like the US, stood to gain significantly.[140] This thus constitutes another case of differentiation gaining wide acceptance

---

136   Günther Jaenicke, 'The United Nations Convention on the Law of the Sea and the Agreement Relating to the Implementation of Part XI of the Convention', in Ulrich Beyerlin et al. eds, *Recht zwischen Umbruch und Bewahrung* 121 (Berlin: Springer, 1995).

137   Bernard H. Oxman, 'The 1994 Agreement and the Convention', 88 *Am. J. Int'l L.* 687 (1994).

138   Jaenicke, supra note 136 at 123.

139   Schrijver, supra note 133 at 229. Cf. Simma, supra note 49 at 241 stating that the extension of jurisdiction and sovereign rights in the EEZ shows a tension between the traditional instinct of 'first come first served' and the acceptance of community interests.

140   Oscar Schachter, *Sharing the World's Resources* 43 (New York: Columbia University Press, 1977).

because a majority of developed and developing countries had an interest in promoting these claims. The case of the EEZ is also illustrative of the difficulties in finding solutions which benefit all states. Indeed, developing landlocked states were the most significant group of states not benefiting from the establishment of EEZ. In Africa, the problem is particularly acute because of the number of landlocked countries which are also among the poorest countries. Admittedly, the Law of the Sea Convention does attempt to remedy the potential loss that the enclosure of common resources represents to these countries by enjoining coastal states to share their surplus with regional landlocked countries. However, the relevant provisions seem to show that the entitlements of landlocked countries are rather weak and that coastal states in effect have unregulated discretion in deciding what the extent of their surplus resources is.[141]

The Influence of Differential Treatment on the Development of International Law

Examples analyzed in this chapter show that differentiation has been widely used in different contexts. It is noteworthy that the form through which differentiation is carried out is not in itself a mark of differentiation. Indeed, both reciprocal and non-reciprocal arrangements can amount to differential treatment depending on the aim and intent of the provision or regime. This is illustrated by the case of the World Bank voting mechanism which is non-reciprocal but is not differential or the case of the former Multifibre Agreement which constituted an exception to free trade rules but was also not differential in intent.[142] Differential treatment examined here is thus not linked to particular forms or procedures but to the intent to remedy existing or potential inequalities.

The various forms taken by differential treatment reflect the complexity of the problems at stake and the numerous factors which must be taken into account to have rules which effectively promote substantive equality. The furtherance of substantive equality sometimes comes at the cost of complicating the legal system. However, the fact that the international community is constantly looking for ways to adapt the standard formula of legal equality so that adopted regimes foster substantive equality demonstrates that on the whole the disadvantages of

---

[141] S.C. Vasciannie, *Land-Locked and Geographically Disadvantaged States in the International Law of the Sea* 57 (Oxford: Clarendon, 1990) and David Joseph Attard, *The Exclusive Economic Zone in International Law* (Oxford: Clarendon, 1987).

[142] For the new regime, Agreement on Textiles and Clothing, Marrakesh, 15 Apr. 1994, in World Trade Organization, *The Legal Texts – The Results of the Uruguay Round of Multilateral Trade Negotiations* (Cambridge: Cambridge University Press, 1999). See also Ann Weston, 'The Uruguay Round: Unravelling the Implications for the Least Developed and Low-Income Countries', in UNCTAD, *International Monetary and Financial Issues for the 1990s – Volume VI* at 61 (New York: UNCTAD, 1995).

complexity do not outweigh the benefits that can be gained through differential measures.

Overall, the rather frequent use of differential measures seems to indicate a recognition of the limits of the principle of formal equality in an international community encompassing states of varying sizes and population, with widely different economic and political clout and unequal stocks of natural resources and biodiversity. Differential treatment is not limited to cases where the situation of one state or a group of states is taken into account in formulating treaty norms. It can also constitute the very basis of a given legal regime, such as in the case of the regime for the management of deep seabed resources which is based on the principle of common heritage of humankind. In these cases, differential treatment fundamentally builds on the concept of judicial equity by proactively giving effect to concerns over substantive equality.

In practice, a number of motives can be found for granting differential treatment but two main justifications seem to prevail. Firstly, 'weaker' states have been able to propose differential regimes where their bargaining power is stronger than usual, such as in a number of environmental agreements where their participation is necessary for the overall success of the regime. Secondly, and much more consistently, differential treatment has developed where it has been in the 'stronger' states' interests to do so. Global environmental problems provide an interesting test case since these are problems usually identified by developed countries which require the cooperation of, often unwilling, developing countries.

Legal Status of Differential Norms

The widespread utilization of differential instruments in international law does not provide any indication with regard to their legal status in international law. Indeed, judicial equity developed over several centuries but its 'validity' was questioned until relatively recently. While judicial equity is now widely accepted even at the international level, the legal status of differential treatment is still the object of significant debate. It has, for instance, been questioned whether differential non-reciprocal provisions constitute hard law. This is linked to the broader debate concerning the existence of soft law provisions in binding international agreements.[143] Unlike General Assembly resolutions whose status as soft law is easily established through a formal legal analysis, the soft law content of a binding provision is more difficult to ascertain. In some cases, a provision will be seen as reflecting a 'soft obligation' if the language of the treaty does not clearly specify states' obligations and is couched in any language other than 'shall'. In other cases, the nature of the obligation itself is 'soft'. The commitments clause in the Climate

---

[143]   Pierre-Marie Dupuy, 'Soft Law and the International Law of the Environment', 12 *Michigan J. Int'l L.* 420 (1991). See generally Dinah Shelton ed., *Commitment and Compliance – The Role of Non-binding Norms in the International Legal System* (Oxford: Oxford University Press, 2000).

Change Convention thus reads as follows: 'All Parties, taking into account their common but differentiated responsibilities and their specific national and regional development priorities, objectives and circumstances, shall . . .' This introductory paragraph is then followed by specific commitments, one of which reads: The parties shall

> [t]ake climate change considerations into account, to the extent feasible, in their relevant social, economic and environmental policies and actions . . . with a view to minimizing adverse effects on the economy, on public health and on the quality of the environment, of projects or measures undertaken by them to mitigate or adapt to climate change.[144]

Here, the actual content of the obligation undertaken by state parties is so weak that it may eventually be compared to a non-binding commitment made in the context of a resolution or declaration.[145]

These soft binding obligations constitute a defining trait of some recent international environmental conventions but do not define differential treatment.[146] This 'contextualization' may affect both absolute norms and differential treatment.[147] Differential treatment is neither limited to contextual clauses nor primarily concerned with them. Entirely different 'hard' obligations are a much more significant example of differential treatment. An important example of such differential treatment is given by the Montreal Protocol which grants countries with low per capita emissions of ozone depleting substances a ten-year window to implement commitments which apply similarly to all countries. In the field of human rights, article 2.1 of the Covenant on Economic Social and Cultural Rights, which grants member states the possibility to implement the rights progressively in accordance with their respective capabilities, illustrates that differentiation does not diminish the binding nature of a given obligation.[148] In this case, differentiation does not make obligations to respect economic and social human rights less binding for all states but constitutes at most a temporary derogation.[149]

---

144   Article 4.1 and 4.1 (f) of the Climate Change Convention, supra note 76.

145   Cf. Christine Chinkin, 'Normative Development in the International Legal System', in Dinah Shelton ed., *Commitment and Compliance – The Role of Non-binding Norms in the International Legal System* 21 (Oxford: Oxford University Press, 2000).

146   On soft international environmental law, Maria Gavouneli, 'Compliance With International Environmental Treaties: The Empirical Evidence', 91 *Am. Society Int'l L. Proceedings* 234 (1997).

147   Daniel Barstow Magraw, 'Legal Treatment of Developing Countries: Differential, Contextual and Absolute Norms', 1 *Colorado J. Int'l Envtl. L. and Pol'y* 69 (1990).

148   Article 2.1 of the International Covenant on Economic, Social and Cultural Rights, New York, 16 Dec. 1966, reprinted in 6 *ILM* 360 (1967).

149   Cf. Michael R. Anderson, 'Human Rights Approaches to Environmental Protection', in Alan E. Boyle and Michael R. Anderson eds, *Human Rights Approaches to Environmental Protection* 1 (Oxford: Clarendon, 1996).

Differentiation as a Principle of International Law?

Differential treatment has become a common feature of international law but it is still disputed whether granting differential treatment has become compulsory and if so, in which situations. Differentiation has been used extensively in agreements pertaining to international trade and economic development, and environmental conservation and management agreements. By the early 1980s, one comprehensive study of differential treatment exposed the extent of its application. Verwey, however, carefully avoided any suggestion that there may be a customary duty to grant differential treatment in the economic field and stated that it should be 'left to the United Nations Member Governments to decide what legal significance they would attach to the evidence presented in the present report'.[150]

A cursory analysis of developments over the past twenty years in the various fields where differentiation has developed constitute a guide to assess the present status of differential treatment in international law. Firstly, it is apparent that differentiation to enhance the economic situation of poorer countries has been upheld till date. It is striking that the international law of sustainable development encompasses several principles put forward in the context of the NIEO or the international law of development.[151] Thus, despite the fact that both the international law of development and the NIEO have been largely discarded some of their underlying principles have survived in a different form.[152]

Secondly, as highlighted above, even though economic differentiation is less frequently granted than before, differential treatment has developed rapidly in international environmental law in recent years. This can be explained in part by the fact that there has been a much greater convergence of interests among countries in environmental law than in the field of economic development. This is linked to historical, geographical and economic reasons which make developing, tropical and populous countries necessary participants in the fight against a number of global problems which are currently of concern mostly in developed countries. It is remarkable that there has been a consistent practice of granting differential treatment in global environmental agreements since the adoption of the Montreal Protocol in 1987. Further, there has been a marked diversification of differentiation techniques and a definite strengthening of their 'differential' content. This is, for instance, the case with provisions making the implementation of developing

---

[150]   Wil D. Verwey, 'The Principle of Preferential Treatment for Developing Countries', 23 *Indian J. Int'l L.* 343, 359 (1983). See also, Ndiva Kofele-Kale, 'The Principle of Preferential Treatment in the Law of GATT: Toward Achieving the Objective of an Equitable World Trading System', 18 *California Western Int'l L.J.* 291 (1987/88).

[151]   Cf. Andrew Jordan and Jacob Werksman, 'Incrementality and Additionality: A New Dimension to North-South Resource Transfers?', 6 *World Resource Rev.* 178 (1994).

[152]   Kamal Hossain, 'Sustainable Development: A Normative Framework for Evolving a More Just and Humane International Economic Order', in Subrata Roy Chowdhury et al. eds, *The Right to Development in International Law* 259 (Dordrecht: Nijhoff, 1992). See also, Cassese, supra note 1 at 368.

countries' obligations dependent upon developed countries first fulfilling their own pledges.[153]

The principle which captures most closely the essence of differential treatment in international environmental law is the principle of common but differentiated responsibility (CBDR). In substance, it posits that states should be held accountable in different measure according to their respective historical and current contributions to the creation of global environmental problems and their respective capacities to address these problems.[154] In practice, this implies that developing countries must have, at least in some situations, different or fewer obligations than developed countries.[155] The principle of CBDR has been applied both to the question of the responsibility of states for the creation of specific global environmental problems and to the responsibility for solving international environmental problems on the basis of differing capacity to provide resources to address these problems.[156] While CBDR focuses on the allocation of responsibilities, it also seeks to bring all states together to cooperate in solving international environmental problems.[157] The essence of the principle of CBDR is thus its twin emphasis on partnership and differential treatment.[158]

The principle of CBDR received recognition in the Rio Declaration which provides that

States shall cooperate in a spirit of global partnership to conserve, protect and restore the health and integrity of the Earth's ecosystem. In view of the different contributions to global environmental degradation, States have common but differentiated responsibilities. The developed countries acknowledge the responsibility that they bear in the international pursuit of sustainable development in view of the pressures their societies place on the

---

[153] *See above* at note 83.

[154] *Note* that the principle of CBDR does not entail a punishment for faults committed either by previous or current generations in developed countries. It only constitutes an acknowledgment of the responsibility that individuals and states in developed countries have by virtue of their specific development patterns. On this point, Henry Shue, 'Global Environment and International Inequality', 75 *Int'l Aff.* 531 (1999).

[155] Cf. Duncan French, 'Developing States and International Environmental Law: The Importance of Differentiated Responsibilities', 49 *Int'l and Comp. L.Q.* 35 (2000).

[156] Oran R. Young, 'Environmental Ethics in International Society', in Jean-Marc Coicaud and Daniel Warner eds, *Ethics and International Affairs – Extent and Limits* 161 (Tokyo: UNU Press, 2001).

[157] Cf. Paul G. Harris, 'Common but Differentiated Responsibility: The Kyoto Protocol and United States Policy', 7 *New York University Envtl. L.J.* 27 (1999).

[158] On the notion that the concept of common but differentiated responsibility is promoting a sense of partnership, International Committee on Legal Aspects of Sustainable Development, 'Second Report', in International Law Association, *Report of the Sixty-Seventh Conference* (1996).

global environment and of the technologies and financial resources they command.[159]

It has also found recognition in international treaties such as the Climate Change Convention of which it constitutes one of the basic principles.[160]

The principle of CBDR is in large part an economic principle, as illustrated by the emphasis on the temporal dimension of each nation's responsibility in the creation of international environmental problems. As noted, there is a clear relationship between industrialization and climate change. Since industrialization has not proceeded at a similar pace in all parts of the world, some countries have contributed a higher overall share of greenhouse gases while others may increasingly contribute in the future. In the Climate Change Convention the principle of CBDR is applied through developed countries' pledges of financing the full incremental costs of measures to be taken by developing countries to alleviate the greenhouse effect on the basis of their higher past and present contributions to the problem.[161] The economic dimension of the principle of CBDR is extremely important since it highlights continuity with differential treatment in economic instruments. This implies that differential treatment in environmental agreements has roots in development-based differential treatment and that the two strands are not totally unconnected even though circumstances surrounding their respective development are notably different.[162]

Recent state practice with regard to CBDR indicates that there is no clear consensus on the issue of differentiated responsibilities and the principle of CBDR is clearly not yet part of customary law.[163] However, the increasing recognition of differentiated responsibilities in different contexts read together with the development of differential treatment generally may at some point in the future lead to the recognition of CBDR as a general principle of international environmental law.[164] Despite a rather disjointed history, the practice of granting differential treatment may be slowly finding stronger roots in the specific context of

---

[159]   Principe 7 of the Rio Declaration on Environment and Development, 14 June 1992, Rio de Janeiro, reprinted in 31 *ILM* 874 (1992).

[160]   Article 3.1 of the Climate Change Convention, supra note 76 and Article 10 of the Kyoto Protocol, supra note 77.

[161]   Jyoti K. Parikh, 'North-South Cooperation for Joint Implementation', in J.K. Parikh et al. eds, *Climate Change and North-South Cooperation – Indo-Canadian Cooperation in Joint Implementation* 192 (New Delhi: Tata McGraw-Hill, 1997).

[162]   Jason M. Patlis, 'The Multilateral Fund of the Montreal Protocol: A Prototype for Financial Mechanisms in Protecting the Global Environment', 25 *Cornell Int'l L.J.* 181 (1992).

[163]   Bettina Kellersmann, *Die gemeinsame, aber differenzierte Verantwortlichkeit von Industriestaaten und Entwicklungsländern für den Schutz der globalen Umwelt* (Berlin: Springer, 2000).

[164]   Pierre-Marie Dupuy, 'Où en est le droit international de l'environnement à la fin du siècle?', 101 *Revue générale de droit international public* 873 (1997).

international environmental law.[165] It is moreover noteworthy that while the founding instruments of the NIEO were in most cases cast in the form of non binding instruments, such as UN General Assembly resolutions, 'new' differential treatment provisions are usually contained in treaties and that a fairly consistent state practice in this regard can be observed over the last few years.[166] The new importance of differential treatment in international environmental law has been reflected in a resolution of the Institute of International Law which states that multilateral environmental treaties shall 'on the basis of the differences in the financial and technological capabilities of States and their different contribution to the environmental problem, provide for economic incentives, technical assistance, transfer of technologies and differentiated treatment where appropriate'.[167]

Developments in environmental law seem to show that granting differential treatment is becoming more and more firmly established in international law.[168] However, even if a principle of differentiation is emerging, it is probably rather limited. Thus, in the case of economic development instruments, despite some advances, it is doubtful whether state practice is more conclusive than it was at the time of Verwey's study.[169] Rather, the 'old' style differential provisions have become almost obsolete in the current international framework and the development of customary norms in this sphere has been significantly restricted as exemplified by the GATT 1994 agreements and associated agreements such as the Cotonou Agreement.[170] In environmental law, even if a generic principle of differentiation is emerging, it may be difficult to ascertain the existence of specific customary norms. Thus, if developed countries have agreed in several environmental treaties to make the provision of aid a condition for the implementation of obligations by developing countries, this is unlikely to constitute

---

165   Interestingly, the World Summit on Sustainable Development Plan of Action singles out CBDR among the principles required for the successful realization of the goals of Agenda 21. Paragraph 2 of the Plan of Action, Johannesburg, 4 Sept. 2002.

166   Frank Biermann, '"Common Concern of Humankind": The Emergence of a New Concept of International Environmental Law', 34 *Archiv des Völkerrechts* 426 (1996).

167   Article 4 of the Procedures for the Adoption and Implementation of Rules in the Field of Environment, 67/2 *Yb. Institute Int'l L.* 515 (1997).

168   Frank Biermann, 'Justice in the Greenhouse: Perspectives from International Law', in F.L. Tóth ed., *Fair Weather? Equity Concerns in Climate Change* 160 (London: Earthscan, 1999).

169   Verwey, supra note 150. See also, H. Beck, *Die Differenzierung von Rechtspflichten in den Beziehungen zwischen Industrie- und Entwicklungsländern – Eine völkerrechtliche Untersuchung für die Bereiche des internationalen Wirtschafts-, Arbeits- und Umweltrechts* (Frankfurt: Peter Lang, 1994). Cf. Magraw, supra note 147 at 79 stating that there may be 'a "soft law" principle or an emerging customary norm that international conventional regimes – environmental and other – should, as a general matter, take the interests of developing countries in achieving sustainable development into account'.

170   See above text at note 54.

a rule of customary law at present.[171] In fact, the actual scope of differentiation can be difficult to ascertain as in the case of the Biodiversity Convention. While the technology transfer commitments in article 16 are not strongly differential because their implementation depends on mutual agreement between the provider and the recipient of technology, the same treaty also provides at article 20 that the implementation of technology transfer commitments is a pre-condition for developing countries' implementation of their own obligations.

Differentiation and Sovereignty: Fostering Partnerships

As noted, sovereignty constitutes a cornerstone of international law. It defines the boundaries between the domestic and international spheres and implies that states have a duty to refrain from intervening in matters which are essentially within the domestic jurisdiction of another state.[172] Sovereignty further entails independence.[173] The scope of sovereignty is however not fixed since states can of their own accord choose to restrict it.[174] Further, developments in international law can lead to changes in the ambit of the principle. Thus, the development of human rights in the UN has resulted in the consequence that sovereignty is today no bar to international consideration of internal human rights situations.[175]

In environmental law, sovereignty has been subjected to contradictory trends. As noted above, the principle of permanent sovereignty over natural resources which emerged after decolonization was chiefly asserted as a way to promote a redistribution of global wealth so that developing countries would be in a better position to realize their development plans and included, for instance, a right to nationalize foreign-owned resources.[176] It has since been repeatedly reaffirmed in international treaties. Traditional international environmental law was thus based primarily on a simple balancing of competing sovereign interests which fostered confrontation between independent and competing entities rather than cooperation.[177]

Despite this emphasis on sovereignty, exceptions qualifying the principle have progressively developed in both treaty and customary rules.[178] Thus, one of the

---

171 Biermann, supra note 166 and Beck, supra note 169. Cf. Schrijver, supra note 133.
172 Article 2.7 of the UN Charter.
173 Island of Palmas Case (Netherlands v. USA), the Hague, April 1928, 2 *Rep. Int'l Arbitral Awards* 829 (1949).
174 Steven Lee, 'A Puzzle of Sovereignty', 27 *California Western Int'l L.J.* 241 (1997).
175 Shaw, supra note 6 at 202.
176 Schrijver, supra note 133 at 229.
177 Jutta Brunnée and André Nollkaemper, 'Between the Forests and the Trees – An Emerging International Forest Law', 23 *Envtl. Conservation* 307 (1996).
178 Patricia W. Birnie and Alan E. Boyle, *International Law and the Environment* 138 (Oxford: Oxford University Press, 2002) and Günther Handl, 'Environmental Security and Global Change: The Challenge to International Law', 1 *Yb. Int'l Envtl. L.* 3 (1990).

central customary principles in modern international environmental law is that states have the responsibility to ensure that activities within their jurisdiction do not cause damage to the environment of other states.[179] The internationalization of environmental problems has further led the international community to acknowledge that some global environmental problems are a common concern of humankind.[180] The principle of common concern expresses the common interest and responsibility of states in solving international environmental problems. Different issues illustrate this point. The recognition of the global significance of climate change is, for instance, meant to foster further cooperation to alleviate its consequences. In other words, states agree that a limited loss of authority with regard to specific problems can be offset by a strengthened collective environmental control over such issues.[181]

Another example is the internationalization of some environmental resources situated under national sovereignty which is having a profound impact on traditional notions of sovereignty. A number of conservation treaties have already introduced the notion that the international community has an interest in the sustainable management of wildlife.[182] This implies that states may have a responsibility towards other states or the international community to preserve or sustainably manage wildlife stocks.[183] While conservation has been relatively uncontentious, attempts to have some natural resources under state jurisdiction, such as forests, recognized as common concern of humankind have met with stiff opposition.[184] In fact, the latest consensus position reiterates that states have a sovereign and inalienable right to manage their forests in accordance with their own national policies. The only concession made to international concerns is that such

---

179   Principle 2 of the Rio Declaration, supra note 159.
180   Cf. Claudio Grossman and Daniel Bradlow, 'Are we Being Propelled Towards a People-Centered Transnational Legal Order?', 9 *Am. University J. Int'l L. and Pol'y* 1 (1993) who argue that one of the factors accounting for the steady diminution of sovereignty since the end of the Second World War is the increasing occurrence of activities whose effects spill over national boundaries. See also, William R. Moomaw, 'International Environmental Policy and the Softening of Sovereignty', 21 *Fletcher F. World Aff.* 7 (1997).
181   Marian A.L. Miller, 'Sovereignty Reconfigured – Environmental Regimes and Third World States', in Karen T. Litfin ed., *The Greening of Sovereignty in World Politics* 173 (Cambridge, Mass: MIT Press, 1998).
182   Convention on the Conservation of European Wildlife and Natural Habitats, Berne, 19 Sept. 1979, *European Treaty Series* N° 104 and Convention for the Protection of the World Cultural and Natural Heritage, Paris, 23 Nov. 1972, reprinted in 11 *ILM* 1358 (1972).
183   The international function that states may have in this situation has been referred to as 'role splitting'. Georges Scelle, *Précis de droit des gens – Principes et systématique* (1932/1934). Concerning role splitting in international environmental law, Michel Virally, 'Panorama du droit international contemporain', 183 *RCADI* 9 (1983/V).
184   Progress on the negotiation of an international forest convention has, for instance, been extremely slow. Chapter 1 above at p. 5.

policies must be consistent with sustainable development.[185] The cautious attitude adopted by some states is partly linked to the significant impact of setting aside forested land on behalf of the international community on the economic development of developing countries. However, even though the exploitation of forests by developing countries cannot be dissociated from economic development in these countries, forest management like the rest of biodiversity management has important international implications which increase the pressure to 'internationalize' the problem of deforestation.[186] Despite this strong opposition on the issue of forest management, the Desertification Convention illustrates the fact that at least limited international supervision in the field of natural resources is not any more completely inconceivable.[187]

Apart from various qualifications to the traditional concept of sovereignty, other elements show that international environmental law has been moving towards new forms of cooperation which may signal a gradual move away from the 'confrontational' conception of international law.[188] In areas beyond sovereignty, such as the high seas which used to be devoid of international management, states have found ways to set up a regime for the exploitation of deep seabed which is slowly taking shape.[189] The fact that there have been moves towards both the strengthening and weakening of sovereignty shows that a broader dynamic is at play. This broader trend is linked to globalization which has been occurring at different levels and is bringing new relations of interdependence between all states.[190] While economic globalization does not necessarily favour economically less developed states, the peculiarity of international environmental problems has in a number of cases resulted in the favouring of states which are among the economically less developed.[191] This is fostering the development of new relations based on cooperation and partnership. Differential treatment in international environmental law may thus constitute one of the external representations of the

[185]   UN Forum on Forests Res. 2/1, Ministerial Declaration and Message from the United Nations Forum on Forests to the World Summit on Sustainable Development, UN Doc. E/2002/42-E/CN.18/2002/14 (2002).
[186]   Brunnée and Nollkaemper, supra note 177 at 309.
[187]   Alistair Iles, 'The Desertification Convention: A Deeper Focus on Social Aspects of Environmental Degradation', 36 *Harvard Int'l L.J.* 207 (1995).
[188]   Cf. French, supra note 155 at 56 noting that differentiation based on a global partnership between North and South may prove, in the future, to be an important justification for differentiated responsibilities.
[189]   Regulations on Prospecting and Exploration for Polymetallic Nodules in the Area, in International Seabed Authority, Decision of the Assembly Relating to the Regulations on Prospecting and Exploration for Polymetallic Nodules in the Area, 13 July 2000, Doc. ISBA/6/A/18.
[190]   Cf. Wolfgang H. Reinicke and Jan Martin Witte, 'Interdependence, Globalization, and Sovereignty: The Role of Non-binding International Legal Accords', in Dinah Shelton ed., *Commitment and Compliance – The Role of Non-binding Norms in the International Legal System* 75 (Oxford: Oxford University Press, 2000).
[191]   Cf. Miller, supra note 181 at 188.

concept of partnership. Indeed, it may provide a framework where all states can work on a common platform which has not been brought about by the reliance on sovereign equality. New developments in the notion of sovereignty may thus partly lead to the establishment of more substantively equal relations. The UN Watercourse Convention accepts, for instance, that cooperation cannot be based only on the principle of sovereign equality. Article 8 thus states that watercourse states must not only cooperate on the basis of sovereign equality but also on the basis of 'mutual benefit and good faith in order to attain optimal utilization and adequate protection of an international watercourse'.[192] Overall, the apparent interdependence of states in their efforts to preserve the global environment seems, in fact, to have already positively impacted relations between developed and developing countries. For the first time, nations may genuinely have found a common platform on which effective cooperation can be based.[193]

Overall, differentiation is promoting the development of legal relations which focus less rigidly on the principle of sovereign equality while retaining it as the fundamental principle against which departures are to be measured. In other words, globalization seems to have the twin impact of upholding reliance on sovereignty while fostering relations of partnership or solidarity in some areas, in particular where common interests can be identified.[194] This closely corresponds with the message of the 2001 Least Developed Countries Conference which emphasized on the one hand that these countries have the primary responsibility for their own development, and on the other hand recognized that this same process of development implies the recognition of shared responsibility which must come about through the establishment of genuine partnerships.[195]

---

[192] Convention on the Law of the Non-navigational Uses of International Watercourses, 12 May 1997, reprinted in 36 *ILM* 700 (1997).

[193] Dolzer, supra note 66.

[194] Cf. the definition of solidarity by McDonald, supra note 31 at 290.

[195] Brussels Declaration, Third United Nations Conference on the Least Developed Countries, 20 May 2001, UN Doc. A/CONF.191/12, at § 3.

Chapter 4

Differential Treatment at the Implementation Level: Technology Transfer and Implementation Aid

This chapter focuses on the use of differentiation at the level of the implementation of international instruments.[1] This may concern the application of rules which are themselves differential such as in the case of the different commitments in the climate change regime. It can also relate to reciprocal rules like the commitments to develop strategies for the conservation and sustainable use of biodiversity that all parties undertake under Article 6 of the Biodiversity Convention but whose implementation is backed by implementation aid only in the case of developing countries. In many ways, differential implementation constitutes the most vibrant and promising side of differential treatment. Further, innovations like the setting up of the Global Environment Facility (GEF) are important because they are at the interface between positive discrimination and resource redistribution.

The basic thrust of differentiation at the implementation level is to foster the prompt and effective implementation of measures agreed upon by all parties. Providing funding or technology transfer to countries lacking either thus fundamentally constitutes an instrument to further the implementation of international conventions globally. At the same time, implementation-related differential treatment also constitutes an instrument to foster the participation of developing countries in cases like the Montreal Protocol where the problem addressed may not feature in the list of national environmental law and policy priorities. Further, in the course of the provision of technology transfer or implementation aid the specific needs and situations of individual countries can be taken into account. In this sense, differential treatment presents an avenue for making the implementation of international environmental treaties more sensitive to local conditions and needs.

---

[1]   On general issues related to the implementation of international environmental treaties David G. Victor et al. eds, *The Implementation and Effectiveness of International Environmental Commitments – Theory and Practice* (Cambridge, Mass: MIT Press, 1998) and Edith Brown Weiss and Harold K. Jacobson eds, *Engaging Countries – Strengthening Compliance with International Accords* (Cambridge, Mass: MIT Press, 1998).

This chapter focuses on technology transfer and aid, two of the most important instruments of differential treatment at the implementation level which play a key role in fostering the effective implementation of global environmental instruments. The first section examines technology transfer which constitutes one of the most practical instruments of differential treatment. Its importance in the context of this study is heightened by the fact that the transfer of technology as an agent of development has been an important focus of international policy making for several decades. The second section considers financial mechanisms in the context of the implementation of international environmental treaties. Together with technology transfer, environmental financial mechanisms constitute an easily identifiable indicator of commitments towards the effective realization of differential treatment measures. In this respect, the GEF constitutes the single most important contribution towards the implementation of differential treatment measures in the environmental field. The third section focuses on joint implementation in the climate change regime, a novel implementation instrument in international environmental law. Joint implementation is significant in the context of differential treatment because one of the mechanisms instituted under the Kyoto Protocol, the Clean Development Mechanism, is a direct consequence of the existence of differential commitments under the Protocol. Further, the involvement of the private sector is significant because it potentially provides new avenues for the financing of measures to implement international environmental treaties and the transfer of environmentally sound technologies. The last section critically assesses the benefits delivered by the three instruments examined and concludes that a lot remains to be done to bring about effective differential treatment at the implementation level.

Technology Transfer

Technology transfer in the environmental field constitutes one of the most interesting differential mechanisms currently used as it directly contributes to developing countries' capacity to implement their international obligations while serving environmental goals. By its very nature technology transfer is usually a process which involves mainly the private sector. This is due to the fact that technology transfer involves the dissemination of commercial technology which is usually protected by intellectual property rights.[2] There has historically been relatively little direct international regulation of technology transfers whereas there exists a significant corpus of international legal rules concerning the protection of intellectual property rights. However, the development of international environmental law highlights the continuing significance of international law concerning technology transfer. Accordingly, this section examines general issues

---

[2]   Peter Muchlinski, *Multinational Enterprises and the Law* 426-7 (Oxford: Blackwell, 1995).

concerning technology transfer and the use of technology transfer provisions in international environmental treaties.

Technology, Development and Environment

Global environmental problems cover a wide range of issues, from desertification to the depletion of the ozone layer. Responses to these global challenges rely on a mix of policy, legal and institutional measures but also require, in many cases, new technological solutions. Relevant technologies range from CFC-free propellants to stem the destruction of the ozone layer to stoves with improved energy efficiency to lower the rates of deforestation which contribute to desertification and to lower greenhouse gas emissions which contribute to climate change. While incentives for technological innovations can be created at the local level in some cases, there are cases where developing countries are not directly concerned with a specific environmental problem and its technological solutions. In the case of the ozone layer, for instance, concern over its global environmental impacts firstly arose in countries which were the major producers of CFCs. The search for CFC-free replacement substances was logically undertaken in developed countries. The implementation of a global regime to ban CFCs thus implies transfers of technologies already developed in the North.

One of the by-products of industrialization and associated new technologies is increased pressure on the environment.[3] This can take the form of intensified natural resource extraction or increased air, water or other pollution released as a by-product of new activities.[4] However, the relationship between technology and the environment does not stop there since technological improvements also constitute the source of solutions to some environmental problems. In international debates, two opposed views of the technology environment nexus are apparent. On the one hand, technological development is today perceived as a crucial factor for environmental conservation and management. This is reflected in Agenda 21 which states that biotechnology promises to enable the development of better health care,

---

[3]   Article 1.2 of the Draft International Code of Conduct on the Transfer of Technology, 5 June 1985, reprinted in UNCTAD, International Investment Instruments: A Compendium – Volume I, UN Doc. UNCTAD/DTCI/30(Vol. I) (1996) [hereafter Draft Code of Conduct] defines technology as 'systematic knowledge for the manufacture of a product, for the application of a process or for the rendering of a service'.

[4]   W.W. Rostow, *The Stages of Economic Growth: A Non-Communist Manifesto* (Cambridge: Cambridge University Press, 3rd ed. 1990) acknowledging that for countries attaining technological maturity in the 21st century, one may expect concomitant strains on the physical environment brought about by the global industrialization and urbanization.

enhanced food security and improved supplies of potable water.[5] On the other hand, the success story of the green revolution hides significant environmental problems. In fact, while crop output has dramatically increased in the short-run, the green revolution has had significant environmental costs. These include falling water tables due to the overuse of tube-wells, waterlogged and saline soils from many large irrigation schemes, declining soil fertility with excessive chemical fertilizer use and water pollution with pesticides.[6]

Technologies known as environmentally sound technologies have an important role to play in solving global environmental problems.[7] Their importance in the context of differential treatment in environmental agreements stems firstly from the fact that existing environmentally sound technologies and R&D capacity in this field are heavily concentrated in OECD countries. The trend seems to be towards increasing inequalities in technological capacity. Thus, while in Japan and the United States expenditure on R&D accounted for 2.8 per cent and 2.63 per cent of gross national income respectively between 1987 and 1997, the average for middle income and low income countries was 0.90 per cent and 0.47 per cent during the same period. Even large countries like India and China do not spend more than 0.73 per cent and 0.66 per cent respectively.[8] Recent trends towards the greater direct involvement of private firms in technology transfer transactions does not seem to have improved the situation of developing countries apart from a few countries.[9] Such inequalities in holdings and development capacity, when dealing with global environmental problems, call for some measure of technology transfer.

The capacity of technology transfer to foster both development and environmental quality is another important element. Technology ownership, for instance, increases the likelihood that benefits to recipients are sustained over time, even after completion of the project and also avoids some of the pitfalls associated

---

5   Agenda 21, *Report of the United Nations Conference on Environment and Development*, Rio de Janeiro, 3-14 June 1992, UN Doc. A/CONF.151/26/Rev.1 (Vol. 1), Annex II, at § 16.1.

6   Bina Agarwal, *Gender, Environment and Poverty Interlinks in Rural India* 7 (Geneva: UNRISD, 1995).

7   Environmentally sound technologies are defined as technologies which 'protect the environment, are less polluting, use all resources in a more sustainable manner, recycle more of their wastes and products, and handle residual wastes in a more acceptable manner than the technologies for which they were substitutes'. Agenda 21, supra note 5 at § 34.1. They include technologies that focus on cleaning processes such as end-of-pipe technologies like filters or remedial technologies like waste disposal or water treatment systems and technologies focusing on the design of clean technologies such as new process technologies and new products. On this point, UNCTAD, Promoting the Transfer and Use of Environmentally Sound Technologies: A Review of Policies, UN Doc. UNCTAD/DST/12 (1997).

8   World Bank, *World Development Indicators* (Washington, DC: World Bank, 2001).

9   UNCTAD, Partnerships and Networking in Science and Technology for Development, UN Doc. UNCTAD/ITE/TEB/11 (2002).

with traditional aid, such as the diversion of funds.[10] Similar arguments have been put forward where the process of liberalization and privatization leads to important increases in portfolio equity flows that are not matched by a similar rise in foreign direct investment flows. Such portfolio investments may give local economies more flexibility but overall tend not to contribute to long-term sustainable development since investors' priorities focus on the liquidity of their investments so as to facilitate rapid divestment should better opportunities arise elsewhere.[11]

Technological development contributes mostly to the process of industrialization but also has the potential to help meet people's basic needs.[12] In fact, there is an intrinsic link between technological advancement to foster the development process and the generation of technologies that meet local people's needs and provide employment.[13] The link between technology, the environment and development has generally been endorsed at the international level. Thus, Agenda 21 recognizes that access to and transfer of environmentally sound technology are essential requirements for the realization of sustainable development.[14] More specifically in the context of global environmental instruments, technology transfers are seen as essential to help developing countries meet their differentiated responsibilities in abating environmental problems.[15]

The Evolution of Technology Transfer Policies at the International Level

Technology transfer was conceived for a long time as an instrument through which modernization could be brought about in developing countries. The rationale was to allow them to start their industrialization with the best technologies currently available instead of developing for themselves technologies previously developed

---

10   Christopher D. Stone, *The Gnat is Older than Man – Global Environment and Human Agenda* (Princeton, NJ: Princeton University Press, 1993).

11   Jayati Ghosh et al., 'Privatising Natural Resources', XXX/38 *EPW* 2351 (1995) concerning India.

12   An example of emphasis on local technological development is the Society for Research and Initiatives for Sustainable Technologies and Institutions in Gujarat, India. For further information, visit www.sristi.org.

13   R.C. Mascarenhas, *Technology Transfer and Development – India's Hindustan Machine Tool Company* 9 (Boulder, CO: Westview Press, 1982).

14   Agenda 21, supra note 5 at § 34.7.

15   Programme for the Further Implementation of Agenda 21, UNGA Res. S-19/2 (Annex), reprinted in 36 *ILM* 1639 (1997) at § 88, recognizing that '[t]here is an urgent need for developing countries to acquire greater access to environmentally sound technologies if they are to meet the obligations agreed at the United Nations Conference on Environment and Development and in the relevant international conventions'. See also, Amrita Achanta and Prodipto Ghosh, 'Technology Transfer and Environment', in Vicente Sanchez and Calestous Juma eds, *Biodiplomacy – Genetic Resources and International Relations* 157 (Nairobi: African Centre for Technology Studies, 1994).

in the North during its process of industrialization.[16] It was also hoped that this would foster the development of comparative advantage. Generally, it was assumed that technologies were available only from developed countries and that technology transfer would help domestic production replace imports in a protected market.[17] Developing countries were viewed more as recipients of technology than potential innovators.[18] Developed countries were to support and facilitate the internal efforts of developing countries to achieve development through the establishment of endogenous scientific and technological capacities.[19] It was further posited that technology transfer would improve developing countries' material circumstances by facilitating a more productive use of resources and providing a technological base from which the development of indigenous technologies could proceed.[20] The idea that international technology transfer would promote economic growth in developing countries was, for instance, reflected in the Draft Code of Conduct on the Transfer of Technology which provided that '[s]tates should co-operate in the international transfer of technology in order to promote economic growth throughout the world, especially that of the developing countries'.[21]

One corollary of this traditional conception of technology transfer was the emphasis on the concept of appropriate technologies which focused on perceived problems associated with the transposition of technologies in socio-economic and ecological environments for which they were not specifically created and the problems that adaptation to the particular situation could pose. Schumacher argued, for instance, that an appropriate technology should be 'conducive to decentralization, compatible with the laws of ecology, gentle in its use of scarce resources and designed to serve the human person'.[22] At the international level, it was hotly disputed whether technologies could be transferred from one country to the next without adaptation. Some authors argued that what was appropriate in one country would be appropriate everywhere. State-of-the-art technologies were thus to be transferred without modification because technologies made to measure for poor countries would be poor technologies and a technology appropriate for

[16] Michael Blakeney, *Legal Aspects of the Transfer of Technology to Developing Countries* 63 (Oxford: ESC Publishing, 1989).

[17] John H. Barton, 'The Economic and Legal Context of Contemporary Technology Transfer', in Edgardo Buscaglia et al. eds, *The Law and Economics of Development* 83 (Greenwich, Conn: JAI Press, 1997).

[18] John Mugabe and Norman Clark, *Technology Transfer and the Convention on Biological Diversity – Emerging Policy and Institutional Issues* 3 (Nairobi: African Centre for Technology Studies, 1996).

[19] Vienna Programme of Action on Science and Technology for Development, in Report of the United Nations Conference on Science and Technology for Development, Vienna, 20-31 Aug. 1979, UN Doc. A/CONF.81/16.

[20] Blakeney, supra note 16 at 60.

[21] Section 2.2(iv) of the Draft Code of Conduct, supra note 3.

[22] E.F. Schumacher, *Small is Beautiful: A Study of Economics as if People Mattered* 143 (London: Blond and Briggs, 1973).

'underdeveloped' countries would be an underdeveloped technology.[23] Others opined on the contrary that the development of technologies in the North by definition begged the question whether, if at all, such technologies could also be used in totally different socio-economic environments.[24]

Today, the policy environment into which technology transfer takes place is fundamentally different.[25] Firstly, while in the 1970s states were very much at the centre of debates on technology transfer, by the early 1990s, a dramatic shift had occurred in favour of the private sector.[26] Concurrently, it has become more and more common to assume that technology transfers must take place on a commercial basis and that they cannot be based on preferential measures.[27] This, in turn, is linked to the expanding scope of intellectual property rights.[28] In recent years, inter-firm cooperation has become an important mechanism for accessing technology in different parts of the world, especially in the high and medium technology industries where joint ventures, joint R&D and co-production are increasingly used.[29] Secondly, the bipolar world of the cold war has given way to a global economy in which all economic actors compete under increasingly similar trade rules in all parts of the world. In a situation where most nations are moving toward export-oriented strategies, the mainstream view is now that all countries need to gain access to world-class technologies if they are to produce goods which can be sold competitively on the market. Competitiveness at the global level can only be achieved by acquiring at the outset world-class technologies.[30] Thirdly, new global environmental concerns have introduced a new set of levers which have fostered a revival of technology transfer from developed to developing countries.[31] This seems to be leading to a new approach where the various actors recognize that technology transfer is a complex process which by definition involves the public

[23]   Arghiri Emmanuel, *Technologie appropriée ou technologie sous-développée* (Paris: Presses universitaires de France, 2nd ed. 1982).
[24]   Frances Stewart, *Technology and Underdevelopment* 96 (London: Macmillan, 2nd ed. 1978).
[25]   As noted by Muchlinski, supra note 2 at 446, developing countries attempted to challenge the established international technology transfer system for a number of years but by the early 1990s, their opposition was fast receding.
[26]   UNCTAD/Andrew Barnett, Do Environmental Imperatives Present Novel Problems and Opportunities for the International Transfer of Technology?, UN Doc. UNCTAD/DST/4 (1995). See also Michael J. Trebilcock, 'What Makes Poor Countries Poor? – The Role of Institutional Capital in Economic Development', in Edgardo Buscaglia et al. eds, *The Law and Economics of Development* 15 (Greenwich, Conn: JAI Press, 1997).
[27]   Gaëtan Verhoosel, 'Beyond the Unsustainable Rhetoric of Sustainable Development: Transferring Environmentally Sound Technologies', 11 *Georgetown Int'l Envtl. L. Rev.* 49 (1998).
[28]   For further developments on intellectual property rights, see infra at chapter 5.
[29]   UN Doc. UNCTAD/ITE/TEB/11, supra note 9 at vii.
[30]   Barton, supra note 17 at 86.
[31]   Barnett, supra note 26 at 5.

and private sectors in partnership.[32] Finally, while obtaining technologies from abroad remains important to most developing countries, it is now seen primarily as a means of accumulating internal technological capacity. The emphasis is thus less on the problem of choosing the most appropriate technology but on what firms do with technologies after securing them.[33]

As noted, the emergence of global environmental problems has given renewed importance to technology issues. Thus, Agenda 21 devotes a whole chapter to the transfer of environmentally sound technologies.[34] Generally, a number of recent instruments have recognized the importance of technological solutions to some global environmental problems. Both the Climate Change Convention and the Kyoto Protocol emphasize the importance of technology transfer. The Protocol provides that all parties must

> [c]ooperate in the promotion of effective modalities for the development, application and diffusion of, and take all practicable steps to promote, facilitate and finance, as appropriate, the transfer of, or access to, environmentally sound technologies, know-how, practices and processes pertinent to climate change, in particular to developing countries, including the formulation of policies and programmes for the effective transfer of environmentally sound technologies that are publicly owned or in the public domain.[35]

The Convention to Combat Desertification also strives to define the kinds of technologies that are to be transferred, acquired, adapted or developed in the context of the implementation of the convention. It implies that these technologies should not only be environmentally sound but also economically viable, socially

---

32   Verhoosel, supra note 27 at 50.

33   UNCTAD, Fostering Technological Dynamism: Evolution of Thought on Technological Development Processes and Competitiveness, UN Doc. UNCTAD/DST/9 (1996).

34   Chapter 34 of Agenda 21, supra note 5.

35   Article 10.c of the Kyoto Protocol to the United Nations Framework Convention on Climate Change, Kyoto, 11 Dec. 1997, in Decision 1/CP.3/Annex, UNFCCC, *Report of the Conference of the Parties on its Third Session*, Kyoto, 1-11 Dec. 1997, UN Doc. FCCC/CP/1997/7/Add.1. *Note* that the Kyoto Protocol chooses a different approach from the Climate Change Convention. While in the latter, only developed countries have technology transfer obligations, under the former, all countries must cooperate in this regard, possibly implying the necessity for developing countries to strengthen their intellectual property rights regimes. On this point, Verhoosel, supra note 27. *Note also* that the COP decided in 2001 to establish an expert group to enhancing the implementation of the provision on technology transfer. Decision 4/CP.7, Development and Transfer of Technologies, UNFCCC, *Report of the Conference of the Parties on its Seventh Session*, Marrakesh, 29 Oct.-10 Nov. 2001, UN Doc. FCCC/CP/2001/13/Add.1.

acceptable and that they should generally be relevant to combating desertification while contributing to the realization of sustainable development.[36]

Differentiation through Technology Transfers

In a context where not all countries have the same capacity to take measures to solve global environmental problems and where some legal instruments have recognized the principle of common but differentiated responsibilities, the transfer of environmentally sound technologies constitutes one of the instruments through which developed and developing countries can fulfil their differentiated responsibilities, the former by transferring the technologies, the latter by applying them so as not to increase their contribution to, say, greenhouse gas emissions. Technology transfer also has the capacity to contribute to the development process which is an underlying aim of differential treatment. A number of instruments have recognized the link between technology transfer and the implementation of their provisions either directly or indirectly. For example, the Biodiversity Convention explicitly provides that the extent to which developing countries implement their commitments depends on the effective implementation by developed countries of their own commitments related to transfer of technology.[37]

The case of the ozone depletion regime warrants special mention in this context since the adoption of the Montreal Protocol constituted a turning point in the development of differentiation in international environmental law.[38] The importance of the Montreal Protocol stems firstly from the nature of the problem at stake. Ozone depletion is caused mostly by gases produced by human industrial activity and in practice, the production and consumption of ozone depleting substances (ODS) is mainly attributable to OECD countries. At first, negotiations for an international treaty involved mainly OECD countries which were the main producers of ODS. These were characterized for a while by the lead of the United States and the reluctance of the European Community.[39] The ozone negotiations were marked by the importance of two factors which had not previously held such sway in international environmental diplomacy. Firstly, evolving scientific knowledge concerning the extent of the ozone layer depletion had an important, if not decisive, impact on the results of the negotiations leading to the Vienna Convention, the Montreal Protocol and its subsequent amendments. Secondly,

[36] Article 18.1 of the Convention to Combat Desertification in Those Countries Experiencing Serious Drought and/or Desertification, Particularly in Africa, Paris, 17 June 1994, reprinted in 33 *ILM* 1328 (1994) [hereafter Convention to Combat Desertification].

[37] Article 20.4 of the Convention on Biological Diversity, Rio de Janeiro, 5 June 1992, reprinted in 31 *ILM* 818 (1992) [hereafter Biodiversity Convention].

[38] Cf. Gaëtan Verhoosel, 'International Transfer of Environmentally Sound Technology: The new Dimension of an old Stumbling Block', 27 *Envtl. Pol'y and L.* 470 (1997).

[39] Anne Gallagher, 'The "New" Montreal Protocol and the Future of International Law for the Protection of the Global Environment', 14 *Houston J. Int'l L.* 267 (1992).

technological developments concerning the production of replacement substances played an important role in making the adoption of an international agreement widely acceptable.[40] Different actors in the negotiations used scientific knowledge and technological improvements as bargaining tools. Thus, in the United States while industry repeatedly questioned the underlying science and claimed that no replacements were available, substitutes quickly came on the market once regulations were in place. It appears that the availability of substitutes was more contingent on the dominant policy discourse, translated into market signals, than on any scientific or technical factors.[41] At the international level too, the availability of scientific knowledge to the negotiators was a necessary but far from sufficient condition for the success of the negotiations.

By the time the negotiations for the Montreal Protocol got under way, it had become clear to negotiators that the problem could not be solved by unilateral action on the part of developed countries. This led to the development of a new dimension in the negotiations. While developing countries consumed about 12 per cent of total CFCs and their per capita consumption was only a fraction of that of developed countries,[42] it was recognized that rapid industrialization, escalating populations, increasing demand for controlled substances and products containing or produced with ODS and, in several countries, the development of substantial CFC production capacity to satisfy these new markets would probably lead to a significant increase in developing countries consumption of ODS.[43]

The specificities of the ozone layer problem led to important innovations. This was partly due to the strong bargaining position of developing countries in the negotiations. The widespread availability of CFC technology would have allowed many developing countries to enter into large-scale production of refrigeration and air cooling systems in the near future.[44] It is partly due to this leverage that differential treatment to foster better implementation, and in particular technology transfer, has received significant attention. The evolution of differential treatment provisions in the Montreal Protocol reflects in part the evolution of the whole regime. In 1987, the main preoccupation of developing countries was to maintain maximum usage of CFCs for the longest possible grace period. This was reflected in the adoption of Article 5 granting developing countries a ten-year window to

---

40   James K. Sebenius, 'Designing Negotiations Towards a New Regime – The Case of Global Warming', 15 *Int'l Security* 110 (1991) notes that Dupont's advance in the development of substitutes to CFCs constituted one significant factor in its acceptance of the proposed ozone regime.

41   Karen T. Litfin, *Ozone Discourses – Science and Politics in Global Environmental Cooperation* (New York: Columbia University Press, 1994).

42   Richard Elliot Benedick, *Ozone Diplomacy – New Directions in Safeguarding the Planet* 148 (Cambridge, Mass: Harvard University Press, enlarged ed. 1998).

43   Gallagher, supra note 39 at 311.

44   Frank Biermann, *Saving the Atmosphere – International Law, Developing Countries and Air Pollution* (Frankfurt am Main: Peter Lang, 1995).

implement the provisions of the Protocol.[45] When it became clear that developed countries would soon phase out their production and consumption of CFCs, the grace period became much less important than the ability to move rapidly to the new technologies.[46] The negotiations thus focused on the creation of a financial mechanism and the modalities for technology transfer. These proved to be the most difficult issues in the revision process. The negotiations were marred by entrenched positions on both sides but the result,[47] considering the specificities of the issue at stake, was surprisingly progressive in legal and institutional terms. This was brought about by a common willingness of all states supported by scientific assessments.[48] It is also noteworthy that when the revision got under way, many key developing country players, in particular China and India, had not ratified the Protocol. Their refusal to ratify unless aid and technology transfer provisions were strengthened added another dimension to the problem.[49] The revision process was thus aimed both at strengthening the regime from within and at attracting universal membership.[50] The revisions resulted in the setting up of a financial mechanism to offset the cost of compliance with the Protocol for developing countries. Further, the 1990 meeting agreed to add an article on technology transfer which provides that all parties must take every practicable step to ensure that the best available environmentally safe substitutes and related technologies are expeditiously transferred to developing countries and that the transfers occur under fair and most favourable conditions.[51]

The example of the Montreal Protocol indicates that technology transfer can be an important vehicle for the realization of differential treatment in practice. The importance of technology transfer in this context has been acknowledged in other contexts such as Forest Principles which enunciate that technology transfer should be promoted and financed to enable developing countries to enhance their capacity

---

45   Article 5 of the Protocol on Substances that Deplete the Ozone Layer, Montreal, 16 Sept. 1987, reprinted in Ozone Secretariat – UNEP, *Handbook for the International Treaties for the Protection of the Ozone Layer* (5th ed. 2000) [hereafter Montreal Protocol].

46   Benedick, supra note 42 at 149. One of the reasons was that the phase-out could lead to CFCs becoming more expensive for countries dependent on CFC imports.

47   Palitha T.B. Kohona, 'The Environment: An Opportunity for North/South Cooperation', *Third World Legal Studies* 71 (1993).

48   David Hurlbut, 'Beyond the Montreal Protocol: Impact on Nonparty States and Lessons for Future Environmental Protection Regimes', 4 *Colorado J. Int'l Envtl. L. and Pol'y* 344 (1993).

49   In the event, China ratified the Protocol in 1991 and India in 1992.

50   Cf. Stella Papasavva and William R. Moomaw, 'Adverse Implications of the Montreal Protocol Grace Period for Developing Countries', 9 *Int'l Envtl. Aff.* 219, 223 (1997) who criticize the current regime, in particular the grace period which may 'produce serious environmental harm, raise the cost of compliance, and do nothing to ensure that these countries will be in compliance at the end of that period'.

51   Article 10 A of the Montreal Protocol, supra note 45.

to better manage, conserve and develop their forests.[52] Generally, the emphasis on technology transfer as an instrument of differential treatment reflects changes at the policy level which increasingly seek to promote 'technology cooperation' rather than 'technology transfer' in a bid to ensure that transfers are accompanied by long-term cooperation and partnership.[53]

Overall, developments under the Montreal Protocol indicate that there is significant scope for technology transfer to give substance to differential treatment commitments. Two points must, however, be noted in this regard. Firstly, the specific conditions under which the ozone regime arose are unlikely to be replicated in other areas. Secondly, the goals of the technology transfer provisions in environmental agreements such as the Montreal Protocol or the Biodiversity Convention are generally much more modest than what was sought in the NIEO era. The difference is that within this more restricted framework, implementation is more effective than before.

Implementation Aid

In the past, development aid was one of the main instruments through which developed countries discharged their duties to foster economic development in the South. It was promoted for a long time as the most effective mechanism to foster socio-economic change in developing countries. The rationale for giving aid ranges from humanitarian, ethical or moral imperatives to ties arising, for instance, from a history of colonialism to more pragmatic considerations such as furthering the strategic, political and economic interests of the donor.[54]

Traditional development aid suffers from shortcomings in the context of differential treatment, as it is generally not based on equal relations of partnership. It tends to reflect an inequality between the donor and the recipient, and depends upon the former's willingness to commit funds and the conditions posed. The practice of granting aid in effect tends to institutionalize the substantive inequality between donors and recipients.[55] Despite this unpromising background, the creation of aid mechanisms to solve specific environmental problems has coincided with a rethinking of their functions and potential. Recent international environmental law

---

[52]   Principle 11 of the Non-Legally Binding Authoritative Statement of Principles for a Global Consensus on the Management, Conservation and Sustainable Development of all Types of Forests, Rio de Janeiro, 14 June 1992, reprinted in 31 *ILM* 881 (1992) [hereafter Forest Principles].

[53]   Elizabeth J Bush and L.D. Danny Harvey, 'Joint Implementation and the Ultimate Objective of the United Nations Framework Convention on Climate Change', 7 *Global Envtl. Change* 265 (1997).

[54]   Roger Riddell, *Aid in the 21st Century* (New York: UNDP, 1996).

[55]   Edward Kwakwa, 'Emerging International Development Law and Traditional International Law – Congruence or Cleavage?', in Anthony Carty ed., *Law and Development* 407 (Aldershot: Dartmouth, 1992).

treaties have thus tried to place aid within the context of the implementation of differential or reciprocal commitments and have in some cases changed the basic rules for allocating funds. In any case, environmental financial mechanisms constitute today one of the most important incentives for the effective implementation of international agreements in the field of sustainable development.[56]

Environmental Financial Mechanisms

The implementation of environmental obligations often necessitates the allocation of substantial financial resources. The inability or unwillingness of a majority of developing countries to divert substantial funds to tackle problems like climate change or the ozone layer depletion which do not necessarily have any immediate relevance to the realization of sustainable development at local levels has led to calls for the development of financial mechanisms to provide the necessary resources to these countries. In this context, the creation of financial mechanisms whose function is specifically to help countries effectively implement their international obligations is significant. Indeed, these mechanisms directly reflect a will to provide differentiated rights and obligations among member states as well as directly provide resources through which these commitments can be implemented. The setting up of specific financial mechanisms in an environmental context is not new in itself but their use and prominence has significantly increased in the 1990s.[57]

One of the first mechanisms to have been set up is the World Heritage Fund (WHF) instituted in 1972.[58] It constituted one of the first attempts at solving global environmental problems cooperatively and giving financial incentives to achieve the goals of the World Heritage Convention. The Fund is designed to make payments to assist in the protection of properties forming part of the world cultural and natural heritage.[59] It compensates states for certain protection or conservation activities undertaken in the global interest. Thus, countries which make special preservation efforts that benefit the world at large can claim some compensation for the global benefits generated by their local actions.[60] Financial compensation can be obtained by any country that is a Party to the World Heritage Convention and

---

56   Peter H. Sand, 'International Economic Instruments for Sustainable Development: Sticks, Carrots and Games', 36 *Indian J. Int'l L.* 1 (1996).

57   Edith Brown Weiss, 'The Five International Treaties: A Living History', in Edith Brown Weiss and Harold K. Jacobson eds, *Engaging Countries: Strengthening Compliance with International Accords* 89 (Cambridge, Mass: MIT Press, 1998).

58   Convention for the Protection of the World Cultural and Natural Heritage, Paris, 23 Nov. 1972, reprinted in 11 *ILM* 1358 (1972).

59   Financial Regulations for the World Heritage Fund, Convention Concerning the Protection of the World Cultural and Natural Heritage, Doc. WHC/7.

60   Peter H. Sand, 'Trusts for the Earth: New International Financial Mechanisms for Sustainable Development', in Winfried Lang ed., *Sustainable Development and International Law* 167 (London: Graham and Trotman, 1995).

eligibility is not limited to developing countries. The different forms of assistance it offers include preparatory assistance, for instance, to prepare lists of cultural and natural properties, emergency assistance, training, technical cooperation and assistance for promotional activities.[61] The WHF is designed for small-scale assistance and its budget has been around 3.5 million dollars for several years. Assessments of its effectiveness have however been positive since it is often difficult for countries to acquire quickly and easily small-scale funds for specific conservation activities.[62]

Another significant small-scale mechanism is the Ramsar Fund.[63] The original wetlands convention signed in 1971 did not provide for the establishment of a financial mechanism,[64] but the Conference of Contracting Parties decided in 1990 to establish a fund supported by voluntary contributions to provide assistance to developing countries for activities undertaken in furtherance of the purposes of the convention.[65] Funding can be allocated for activities that improve the management of listed sites, the initial process of designation of sites and generally for the wise use of wetlands, such as providing seed money for the preparation of proposals to be submitted to development assistance agencies and multilateral development banks.[66] Subsequent meetings of the parties have modified the target group for financial assistance. While the focus remains on developing countries, the parties stated that countries with economies in transition should also be assisted.[67] This illustrates the fact that differential treatment is more and more concerned with groups of countries which do not necessarily include only developing countries or all developing countries. The Ramsar Fund remains a small facility but its existence is significant.[68] It must be understood as an effort by developed countries to foster the implementation of the goals of the convention in other regions of the world where resources may not be forthcoming to ensure proper preservation of listed wetlands. In this case, the establishment of the fund much later than the adoption of

[61]   Intergovernmental Committee for the Protection of the World Cultural and Natural Heritage, Operational Guidelines for the Implementation of the World Heritage Convention, Doc. WHC-97/2 (1997).
[62]   Daniel Navid, 'Compliance Assistance in International Environmental Law: Capacity-Building, Transfer of Finance and Technology', 56 *Zeitschrift für ausländisches öffentliches Recht und Völkerrecht* 810 (1996).
[63]   In full: Ramsar Small Grants Fund for Wetland Conservation and Wise Use.
[64]   Convention on Wetlands of International Importance Especially as Waterfowl Habitat, Ramsar, 2 Feb. 1971, reprinted in 11 *ILM* 963 (1972).
[65]   See generally M.J. Bowman, 'The Ramsar Convention Comes of Age', 42 *Netherlands Int'l L. Rev.* 1 (1995).
[66]   Res. C.4.3. on a Wetland Conservation Fund, 4th Meeting of the Conference of the Contracting Parties, Montreux, 1990.
[67]   Res. C.5.8. on the Wetland Conservation Fund, 5th Meeting of the Conference of the Contracting Parties, Kushiro, 1993.
[68]   Concerning the level of funding, Resolution VII.5 on the Small Grants Fund, 7th Meeting of the Conference of the Contracting Parties to the Convention on Wetlands, 1999.

the convention reflects the realization of state parties that implementation in developing countries was lagging partly due to insufficient financial resources.

Most recent agreements dealing with global environmental problems include some form of funding mechanism. The aim is generally both to attract widespread membership by subsidizing compliance for some countries as well as to foster implementation in countries which lack the technical, financial or institutional capacity to effectively fulfil their commitments. In several cases, the establishment of financial mechanisms is linked to the fact that developing countries will only be able to contribute to solving environmental problems if they are given access to cleaner technologies, usually developed in the North. Since private parties usually own these technologies, their diffusion in developing countries is often hampered by difficulties in access to finance.[69] Overall, recent environmental financial mechanisms fund developing countries' activities to tackle global environment problems on the basis of common but differentiated responsibilities.

The importance given by the international community to specific problems has been reflected in the kind of implementation mechanisms set up. On the one hand, the Desertification Convention has not until now benefited from access to any specific financial mechanism.[70] Instead, a Global Mechanism housed at the International Fund for Agricultural Development has been set up to increase the effectiveness and efficiency of existing financial mechanisms.[71] The Global Mechanism is specifically meant to promote actions leading to the mobilization and channelling of financial resources by, for instance, collecting and disseminating information concerning potential sources of funding without in itself being a financial mechanism.[72] On the other hand, the Montreal Protocol, the Biodiversity Convention and the Climate Change Convention have benefited from access to funding specifically earmarked to foster their implementation.[73] Further, in the case of climate change, the Conference of the Parties has progressively recognized the

---

[69] Stephan Schmidheiny et al., *Financing Change: The Financial Community, Eco-Efficiency, and Sustainable Development* (Cambridge, Mass: MIT Press, 1996).

[70] Philippe Cullet, 'Desertification', in UNESCO, *Knowledge for Sustainable Development* (Oxford: EOLSS Publishers, 2002). See however, below at p. 111 concerning recent developments in the GEF.

[71] On the institutional arrangement between the International Fund for Agricultural Development and the Convention to Combat Desertification, Dec. 10/COP.3, Memorandum of Understanding between the Conference of the Parties to the United Nations Convention to Combat Desertification and the International Fund for Agricultural Development Regarding the Modalities and Administrative Operations of the Global Mechanism, *Report of the Conference of the Parties on its Third Session*, Recife, 15-26 Nov. 1999, UN Doc. ICCD/COP(3)/20/Add.1.

[72] Dec. 24/COP.1, Organization to House the Global Mechanism and Agreement on its Modalities, Convention to Combat Desertification, *Report of the Conference of the Parties on its First Session*, Rome, 29 Sept.-10 Oct. 1997, UN Doc. ICCD/COP(1)/11/Add.1.

[73] These financial mechanisms are the Multilateral Fund for the Implementation of the Montreal Protocol and the Global Environment Facility.

need for funding targeted at specific areas in addition to funding available through the Global Environment Facility. It has therefore decided to establish a special climate change fund to finance complementary activities in specific fields such as technology transfer. It has also been decided to establish a least developed countries fund which will support a specific work programme for these countries to help them in particular with adaptation measures in the face of adverse effects expected even after the implementation of the climate change mitigation activities proposed under the Kyoto Protocol.[74] A third fund, the adaptation fund, is meant to finance concrete adaptation projects and programmes in developing countries that are parties to the Kyoto Protocol.[75] The most noteworthy aspect of this fund is that it will partly be financed from a share of the proceeds of the clean development mechanism, a differential implementation mechanism analyzed further in the next section of this chapter.

The Global Environment Facility

The Global Environment Facility (GEF) is by far the biggest financial mechanism specifically devoted to global environmental problems. It derives its significance not so much because of the resources at its disposal, which remain tiny compared to overall development aid, but mostly because of its innovative governance structure and guiding principles. The GEF was first set up in 1991 by the World Bank to specifically address some of the existing global environmental problems and was restructured in 1994.[76] Its mission is to provide new and 'additional grant and concessional funding to meet the agreed incremental costs of measures to achieve agreed global environmental benefits'.[77] The notion of new and additional resources has remained contentious since it has not been defined in treaties and can therefore not be easily operationalized.[78]

One of the main characteristics of the GEF is its focus on the distinction between local and global environmental benefits. The concept of incremental costs

74 Decision 7/CP.7, Funding under the Convention, UNFCCC, *Report of the Conference of the Parties on its Seventh Session,* Marrakesh, 29 Oct.-10 Nov. 2001, UN Doc. FCCC/CP/2001/13/Add.1.
75 Decision 10/CP.7, Funding under the Kyoto Protocol, UNFCCC, *Report of the Conference of the Parties on its Seventh Session,* Marrakesh, 29 Oct.-10 Nov. 2001, UN Doc. FCCC/CP/2001/13/Add.1.
76 World Bank, Res. N° 91-5, Global Environment Facility, reprinted in 30 *ILM* 1735 (1991) and Instrument for the Establishment of the Restructured Global Environment Facility, Geneva, 16 Mar. 1994, reprinted in 33 *ILM* 1273 (1994) [hereafter 1994 Instrument]. On the development of the GEF, GEF/Helen Sjoeberg, From Idea to Reality – The Creation of the Global Environment Facility (Washington, DC: GEF, 1994) and Shoshana K. Mertens, 'Towards Accountability in the Restructured Global Environment Facility', 3 *Rev. Eur. Community and Int'l Envtl. L.* 105 (1994).
77 1994 Instrument, supra note 76 at § 2.
78 GEF/Gareth Porter et al., Study of GEF's Overall Performance (Washington, DC: GEF, 1998).

has been developed to assess global and local benefits and determine the specific cost related to the protection of the global environment.[79] The GEF only covers the difference between the cost of a project undertaken with global environmental objectives in mind and the cost of an alternative that the recipient country would have implemented in the absence of global environmental concerns. It is thus only when global benefits 'cost' more than the base scenario that GEF funding can be obtained.[80] A number of other principles guide GEF activities. GEF resources must be additional to current aid budgets. GEF activities must be based on national priorities designed to support sustainable development and be cost-effective. Finally, eligibility for GEF funding is limited to countries which are eligible to borrow from the World Bank or are eligible recipients of UNDP technical assistance through their Indicative Planning Figure.[81] The GEF has focused until now on four global problems. These are climate change, biological diversity, international waters and the depletion of the ozone layer. Land degradation issues have been taken into account insofar as they relate to one of the four focal areas enumerated above.[82] Other global environmental problems are not included in the GEF mandate. Following criticism that the GEF fails to address some important global environmental issues, a proposal has been put forward to amend the GEF 1994 Instrument and to include among the focal areas land degradation and persistent organic pollutants.[83]

The GEF is particularly noteworthy in the context of differential treatment for two reasons. Firstly, its governance structure warrants attention since it is novel in the context of aid mechanisms. The Council, the main decision making organ, has 16 members from developing countries, 14 from developed countries and 2 from the former communist countries.[84] In principle, decisions are taken by consensus. However, if a vote is called for, decisions must be adopted by a 60 per cent majority of both the total number of participants and total contributions.[85] Though some recipient countries contribute to the trust fund, most of the funds come from developed countries. The decision mechanism thus ensures that decisions are

---

[79]   GEF/Ken King, The Incremental Costs of Global Environmental Benefits (Washington, DC: GEF, 1993).

[80]   *Note* that the 10-year review of the GEF found that there is still confusion among stakeholders over the definitions of the concepts of global environmental benefits and incremental costs and recommended that better operational guidance should be given with regard to these two concepts. GEF, Focusing on the Global Environment – The First Decade of the GEF – Second Overall Performance Study 66 (2002).

[81]   1994 Instrument, supra note 76, at § 4 and 9.

[82]   Global Environment Facility, Clarifying Linkages Between Land Degradation and the GEF Focal Areas: An Action Plan for Enhancing GEF Support, GEF Council, Dec. 1999, Doc. GEF/C.14/4.

[83]   GEF Council, Proposed Amendments to the GEF Instrument, Doc. GEF/C.19/14 (2002).

[84]   1994 Instrument, supra note 76, at § 16.

[85]   1994 Instrument, supra note 76, at § 25.

adopted by a majority of donors and a majority of recipients. This is meant to ensure that the interests of both donors and recipients are taken into account, thus ensuring decisions more easily acceptable to all member states as compared to the case of classical aid institutions such as the World Bank.

Secondly, the significance of the GEF in the context of differentiation stems from the fact that it is partly meant to constitute a source of funding to help countries take measures allowing them to be in compliance with their obligations under environmental treaties in the four focal areas of concentration. In this capacity, the GEF is a mechanism through which developed countries discharge their financial responsibilities under the biodiversity and climate change conventions. Until now, the GEF has been retained as the financial mechanism of both the Biodiversity and Climate Change conventions, according to their respective provisions and the guidance of the conferences of the parties.[86] The institutional link between the GEF and the two conventions is relatively strong since the GEF functions under the guidance of the conferences of the parties which decide on policies, programme priorities and eligibility criteria in their particular field. This is an innovative arrangement in a financial mechanism since this implies that its overall policy is determined by different bodies where the decision making power does not reflect the same balancing of interests.

As an implementation aid mechanism, the GEF fulfils several functions. Firstly, it subsidizes the costs of compliance with the conventions for developing countries and thereby allows both developed and developing countries to fulfil their respective differentiated responsibilities in the creation and solution of international environmental problems. Secondly, by fostering more effective implementation of international conventions, it impacts positively on the global environment. Thirdly, the provision of funding constitutes one of the levers used to attract universal membership in global environmental regimes. Finally, the GEF also contributes to the development of the concept of partnership. While it is in some respects a 'normal' development aid mechanism, the novel governance structure constitutes a significant departure from the premise of inequality usually associated with aid.

The GEF is a clear example of the way in which differentiation has evolved between the 1970s and the present. While GEF resources come overwhelmingly from developed countries, it manages to have a decision-making structure which reflects the interests of the different interest groups within the organization much

---

[86]   The conventions themselves had called for specific changes in the 1991 GEF. Articles 11 and 21 of the Framework Convention on Climate Change, New York, 9 May 1992, reprinted in 31 *ILM* 849 (1992) and Article 21 and 39 of the Biodiversity Convention, supra note 37. Various decisions of each COP have given further guidance to the GEF. Decision 6/CP.7, Additional Guidance to an Operating Entity of the Financial Mechanism, UNFCCC, *Report of the Conference of the Parties on its Seventh Session,* Marrakesh, 29 Oct.-10 Nov. 2001, UN Doc. FCCC/CP/2001/13/Add.1 and Decision VI/17, Financial Mechanism under the Convention, CBD, *Report of the Sixth Meeting of the Conference of the Parties,* The Hague, 7-19 April 2002, UN Doc. UNEP/CBD/COP/6/20.

better than in the World Bank. This seems to be partly due to the fact that the GEF's objectives are to focus on the solution of global environmental problems and this does not pose any challenge to the international economic and legal order. This is in contradistinction with discourses on technology transfer in the 1970s which constituted a direct extension of the call for an NIEO. Overall, the GEF is more driven by global environmental needs rather than the quest for economic or political global reform.[87] More specifically, the GEF is a direct reflection of a new interdependence of all states in their efforts to preserve the local and global environment and may lead to a novel state of international cooperation in which the common interest of humankind is not only defined but also actively pursued.

If the GEF is innovative in a number of ways, its effectiveness in practice remains a matter of debate. The recently concluded review of the GEF's performance in its first decade generally commends the GEF for supporting projects that have been able to 'produce significant results aimed at improving global environmental problems'.[88] However, there remain a number of uncertainties with regard to the effectiveness of the GEF as a mechanism for implementing differential commitments in the context of global environmental problems which include, for instance, its capacity to play a catalytic role given the very limited resources at its disposal.[89]

The Kyoto Mechanisms in the Climate Change Regime

The climate change regime has been quite innovative with regard to the development of new instruments to foster the implementation of the commitments that some state parties have taken up. The so-called flexibility mechanisms, and in particular the Clean Development Mechanism, are particularly noteworthy in the context of differential treatment in international environmental law.

Flexibility in the Climate Change Regime

The introduction of the concept of flexibility represents a conscious attempt to liberate international law from some of its structural constraints, to reflect the reality of the current world order and to facilitate the implementation of inter-state agreements. In international environmental agreements, flexibility mechanisms have been specifically introduced to enhance the cost-effectiveness of measures to address international environmental problems and to attract new sources of

---

[87] See generally, Rudolph Dolzer, 'The Global Environment Facility – Towards a New Concept of the Common Heritage of Mankind', in Gudmundur Alfredsson and Peter McAlister-Smith eds, *The Living Law of Nations – Essays on Refugees, Minorities, Indigenous Peoples and the Human Rights of Other Vulnerable Groups* 331 (Kehl: N.P. Engel, 1996).

[88] GEF, supra note 80 at x.

[89] GEF, supra note 80 at 50.

funding.[90] Nations with high costs for meeting environmental obligations can thus invest funds in other nations that avail low cost opportunities to fulfil the same objectives.[91] This 'spatial flexibility' has the advantage of bringing about global environmental benefits at the lowest possible cost by exploiting comparative advantage opportunities.[92] Flexibility has usually been premised on the idea that it should benefit both parties in addition to fostering international environmental protection.

More specifically, flexibility relates to the fact that the private sector is directly involved in the implementation of an inter-state agreement. International law is thus opening itself to non-state actors in a much more active way than previously. The involvement of the private sector must further be seen in a context of declining official development assistance and the need to find alternative sources of funding for the realization of sustainable development in general.

Flexibility mechanisms have been introduced in different legal regimes but have been the subject of significant attention in the context of the climate change convention. Different types of mechanisms have evolved in this context. Activities Implemented Jointly (AIJ) constitutes historically the first kind of flexibility instrument developed on the basis of Article 4.2(a) of the Convention.[93] AIJ brings together countries with commitments and countries without commitments under the Convention, allowing the former to implement projects in the latter to take advantage of cost differentials. Under the Kyoto Protocol, different types of flexibility mechanisms have been defined. Joint Implementation (JI) refers specifically to cooperative projects between two Parties with commitments through which credits accrue. Participation is voluntary, emission reduction or sink enhancement must be additional to any that would otherwise occur and JI projects must be supplemental to domestic actions for the purpose of meeting commitments.[94] Another type of flexibility is embodied in the option given to a group of countries to aggregate individual commitments and decide amongst

---

90   Cf. Jutta Brunnee, 'A Fine Balance: Facilitation and Enforcement in the Design of a Compliance Regime for the Kyoto Protocol', 13 *Tulane Envtl. L.J.* 223 (2000).

91   Thomas Heller, Joint Implementation and the Path to a Climate Change Regime (Jean Monnet Chair Paper, The Robert Schuman Centre at the European University Institute, 1995).

92   David Pearce, 'Joint Implementation – A General Overview', in Catrinus J. Jepma ed., *The Feasibility of Joint Implementation* 15 (Dordrecht: Kluwer, 1995).

93   Decision 5/CP.1, Activities Implemented Jointly Under the Pilot Phase, UNFCCC, *Report of the Conference of the Parties on its First Session*, Berlin 28 Mar.-7 Apr. 1995, UN Doc. FCCC/CP/1995/7/Add.1. The pilot phase for AIJ was again extended in 2001. Decision 8/CP.7, Activities Implemented Jointly under the Pilot Phase, UNFCCC, *Report of the Conference of the Parties on its Seventh Session*, Marrakesh, 29 Oct.-10 Nov. 2001, UN Doc. FCCC/CP/2001/13/Add.1.

94   Art. 6.1 of the Kyoto Protocol, supra note 35.

themselves on the allocation of the burden.[95] The Clean Development Mechanism (CDM) defined by Article 12 of the Protocol is different from both AIJ and JI but shares characteristics with both. It generally seeks to facilitate joint emission reduction projects between Annex I Parties and developing countries.[96] It specifically provides that projects must assist developing countries in realizing sustainable development and at the same time allows crediting of certified emission reductions to Annex I Parties. Emissions trading constitutes the last type of flexibility mechanism whereby a fully-fledged market mechanism is established. It is modelled on existing tradable emission permits, credits and offsets schemes that have, for instance, been put in place in the United States to facilitate compliance with the Clean Air Act.[97] Under the Kyoto Protocol, emissions trading can only take place among countries with commitments and must be supplemental to domestic actions.[98] Some countries like the UK have already put in place domestic emissions trading schemes while an agreement over an international scheme is still in the making.[99]

Flexibility Mechanisms and Differential Treatment

Flexibility mechanisms are in part driven by differential considerations.[100] They apply into practice the idea that international environmental problems must be solved through partnerships among all countries and all actors. In the case of the climate change regime, flexibility mechanisms fall directly within the general differential framework of the Convention. Thus, even if the rationale for their development is cost-effectiveness, their implementation cannot be dissociated from the guiding principles of the Convention. Further, even if they are implemented through private actors, they must comply with general principles of international law.

Flexibility mechanisms have close links with the question of differential commitments. Firstly, in the case of the CDM, the mechanism is fundamentally

---

95 The EU has, for instance, made use of the possibility to re-allocate the generic EU commitment among member states to allow some less economically advanced countries to increase their emissions. Articles 3 and 4 of the Kyoto Protocol, supra note 35. See also, Fanny Missfeldt, 'Flexibility Mechanisms: Which Path to Take after Kyoto?', 7 *Rev. Eur. Community and Int'l Envtl. L.* 128 (1998).

96 Annex I Parties are member states to the Climate Change Convention listed in Annex I to the Convention. These are, for instance, the countries that are required to take on emission limitation and reduction commitments under the Kyoto Protocol.

97 Clean Air Act, 42 U.S.C. §§ 7401 et seq. (1988). See also Michael Grubb et al., *Greenhouse Gas Emissions Trading* (Geneva: UNCTAD, 1998).

98 Art. 17 of the Kyoto Protocol, supra note 35.

99 UK Greenhouse Gas Emissions Trading Scheme 2002, Doc. ETS(01)06.rev1 (2002) and Richard Rosenzweig et al., *The Emerging International Greenhouse Gas Market* (Arlington, VA: Pew Center on Global Climate Change, 2002).

100 Cf. Albert Mumma, 'The Poverty of Africa's Position at the Climate Change Convention Negotiations', 19 *UCLA J. Envtl. L. and Pol'y* 181 (2000/2001).

premised on the asymmetric position of countries with commitments and those without commitments. It is on this basis that states engage in a new type of collaboration to foster the most effective results possible from a global environmental point of view. The asymmetry of commitments in the Protocol has been one of the most contentious elements of the regime. This is due in particular to the fact that even before the US decided not to ratify the Kyoto regime, the US Senate had already threatened not to ratify the Protocol if developing countries did not take on commitments at Kyoto.[101]

In practice, even though non-Annex I countries do not have commitments under the Protocol, they in effect contribute significantly to the implementation of the Convention and Protocol through their involvement in the implementation of flexibility mechanisms as well as through their reporting obligations. They, thus, indirectly fulfil 'commitments' to mitigate climate change even though, on paper, they do not have any obligations to do so. Their contribution is in some way a reflection of a new worldwide partnership to solve global problems which is also noticeable in other areas. Indeed, by putting to the service of the international community the cheapest climate change mitigation options, host countries make a significant contribution to the realization of the goals of the Convention which would not be possible otherwise. Even though they receive a form of financial compensation for this service, this reward is paltry when one considers that flexibility mechanisms may end up using most of the cheapest mitigation opportunities. In other words, by participating in the CDM, host countries can be said to take on voluntarily climate change mitigation commitments.

The recognition of the contribution of host countries to climate change mitigation makes it possible to address the issue of the exhaustion of cheap mitigation opportunities. Indeed, while using these options is sensible from a global environmental policy point of view, credits should be given to countries which allow the international community to benefit from them. If credits are given to host countries, the problem raised by the exhaustion of cheap mitigation opportunities disappears.[102] In practice, it is significant that the implementation period of some flexibility projects is much longer than the commitments period for Annex I countries. In the case of forestry projects, it is, for instance, noteworthy that host countries may be asked to keep the land under forest cover for periods ranging from 20 to 99 years. Their contribution to climate change mitigation is thus extremely significant. The issue with regard to host countries' contribution is not

---

[101]   Byrd-Hagel Resolution (S. Res. 98), Expressing Sense of Senate Regarding U.N. Framework Convention on Climate Change, 143 *Congressional Record* S8113-05, S8139 (25 July 1997). See also, Lakshman Guruswamy, 'Climate Change: The Next Dimension', 15 *J. Land Use and Envtl. L.* 341 (2000).

[102]   *Contra* Proposal for a Directive of the European Parliament and of the Council Establishing a Scheme for Greenhouse Gas Emission Allowance Trading within the Community and Amending Council Directive 96/61/EC, Doc. COM(2001) 581 final, 23 Oct. 2001 at 17 wherein the Commission argues that in the long term, the inclusion of credits from JI and CDM projects for investor countries is desirable.

necessarily whether credits should be given to them for future use but rather to recognize today their contribution and effort.

Several other elements of the flexibility mechanisms can be mentioned in a general discussion about their differential content. Firstly, an important aspect of the agreed regime for flexibility is that the use of the mechanisms must be supplemental to domestic action.[103] This constitutes an important differential component insofar as the supplemental condition implies a recognition that while host countries participate in flexibility mechanisms for the benefit of the global environment, the principle of differentiated responsibilities requires countries with commitments to take the lead in reducing greenhouse gas emissions.

Secondly, in the specific case of emissions trading, important differential considerations arise at the level of the first allocation of emissions allowances.[104] The premise for emissions trading is that the initial allocation method has no material bearing on the efficiency of the system to achieve a given environmental target at a minimum cost if trading in the market is competitive and transaction costs are low. The initial allocation can thus be used to address differential concerns without affecting the cost-effectiveness of the system. Different allocation methods can be adopted. Each method is based on a different notion of equity. Emissions can firstly be allocated on the basis of current emission levels. The consequences of this allocation – grand fathering – would be the promotion of stability in the international economic order by allowing current polluters to carry on and by limiting low polluters' rights to expand their polluting industries. This allocation has the perceived advantage of limiting the disruption caused to the global economy. Secondly, allotment systems can focus on the environment as a global good and the need to take action to mitigate climate change. A global burden which has to be shared according to specific criteria is thus recognized. The various proposals are based on different rationales. Some focus on egalitarian principles and propose an equal per-capita entitlement; some focus on economic development factors and propose that the allocation should be done according to each nation's ability to pay while other favour an allocation based on the emission intensity of each unit of GDP.[105] They all seek to establish a basis which recognizes the different contributions to the creation of the problem, the different capacities to respond to the problem and the link between economic development and environmental degradation in the form of carbon emissions. Given that none of these proposals attracts widespread support, some attempts have been made to put

---

103   Draft Decision -/CMP.1 (Mechanisms), in Decision 15/CP.7, Principles, Nature and Scope of the Mechanisms Pursuant to Articles 6, 12 and 17 of the Kyoto Protocol, UNFCCC, *Report of the Conference of the Parties on its Seventh Session,* Marrakesh, 29 Oct.-10 Nov. 2001, UN Doc. FCCC/CP/2001/13/Add.2, at § 1.

104   Cf. Russell B. Korobkin and Thomas S. Ulen, 'Efficiency and Equity: What can be Gained by Combining Coase and Rawls?', 73 *Washington L. Rev.* 329 (1998).

105   See generally Prodipto Ghosh and Jyotsna Puri eds, *Joint Implementation of Climate Change Commitments – Opportunities and Apprehensions* (New Delhi: Tata Energy Research Institute, 1994).

forward allocation systems based on a combination of criteria. Thus, to stem the tide of criticism against per capita entitlements, which is widely seen as creating an incentive for increased population levels,[106] emissions could be allocated according to both population and gross national product.[107]

Thirdly, flexibility mechanisms clearly illustrate that the implementation of international treaties such as the climate change will not be fair overall unless its impacts on all actors are taken into account. It is imperative to ensure that climate change mitigation activities benefit all constituencies, especially the weakest. This has implications at several levels. Firstly, to ensure a just distribution of emissions rights around the world, it is, for instance, not sufficient to grant countries allocations according to their populations. Indeed, if the rights are vested at the state level, it is probable that in many countries the benefits will not be equitably distributed.[108] Secondly, all implementation activities should aim at directly benefiting local people and communities. This is because international law is intrinsically meant to eventually benefit individuals, not states.[109] More specifically, local people and groups should, for instance, be integrated in the design and implementation of flexibility projects. These requirements are exactly similar to those of other development projects but need to be clearly integrated in the climate change context where development discourses and practices are not necessarily known by all concerned actors.

The Clean Development Mechanism and Differential Treatment

The Clean Development Mechanism (CDM) is certainly the most important of the three mechanisms from the point of view of differential treatment. As noted, the CDM is closely linked to the principle of common but differentiated responsibility. It constitutes a form of partnership among developed and developing countries to solve a global problem on the basis of the different commitments that countries assume under the Kyoto Protocol. A number of other elements are also relevant from the point of view of differentiation.

The CDM is specifically premised on the need to simultaneously foster sustainable development in host countries and cheap climate change mitigation activities for the investors. In effect, the existence of the CDM – like other flexibility mechanisms – is justified on the lower marginal costs of climate change

106   Cf. Olav Benestad, 'Energy Needs and CO_2 Emissions – Constructing a Formula for Just Distributions', 22 *Energy Pol'y* 725 (1994).
107   Kirk R. Smith et al., 'Who Pays (to Solve the Problem and How Much)?', in Peter Hayes and Kirk Smith eds, *The Global Greenhouse Regime – Who Pays? – Science, Economics and North-South Politics in the Climate Change Convention* 70 (London: Earthscan, 1993).
108   Michael Thompson and Steve Rayner, 'Cultural Discourses', in Steve Rayner and Elizabeth L. Malone eds, *Human Choice and Climate Change – Volume One – The Societal Framework* 265 (Columbus, Ohio: Battelle Press, 1998).
109   D.P. O'Connell, *International Law* (London: Stevens, vol. 1, 2nd ed. 1970).

mitigation in developing countries. It must, however, also be seen in a longer-term perspective which acknowledges the need for developing countries to substantially raise their standards of living. Even if this is achieved with the most energy efficient technologies currently available,[110] both aggregate and per capita greenhouse gas emissions of developing countries are likely to grow. If by hypothesis developing countries need to raise their emissions, fairness requires that the cost-effective options for emission limitation or reduction should be used by developing countries themselves or at least credited to them. One of the ways in which CDM can achieve both aims is by focusing on development activities which ensure that future economic growth in developing countries not in opposition to climate change concerns. In this sense, CDM should focus more on avoiding future emissions than on the cheapest mitigation opportunities.[111] This has now been partly recognized insofar as host countries have been given the right to decide themselves whether a CDM project contributes to achieving sustainable development.[112]

The regime envisioned for the implementation of the CDM provides other differential elements, for instance with regard to financial issues. Given the increasing apprehension in host countries concerning declining levels of official development assistance, it has now specifically been agreed that public funding should not result in the diversion of aid and should be separate from Annex I countries' financial obligations.[113] Further, a part of the proceeds from CDM projects must be used to assist developing countries which are particularly vulnerable to the adverse effects of climate change in carrying out climate change adaptation activities.[114] A commitment to the implementation of this provision is now evident in the setting up of a dedicated adaptation fund which will be financed in part from a share of the proceeds of CDM projects.[115]

The CDM raises significant questions concerning the impact of flexibility mechanism projects on the sovereignty of host countries. Firstly, at a general level, the question of sovereign rights arises because countries undertake activities in other countries which help them fulfil their own obligations. More specifically, concerns exist that CDM projects may exhaust low-cost mitigation opportunities which will not be available to host countries in case they take on commitments in

---

[110] The transfer of environmentally safe and sound technology and know-how is expressly recognised as one of the aims of the CDM. Decision 17/CP.7, Modalities and Procedures for a Clean Development Mechanism as Defined in Article 12 of the Kyoto Protocol, UNFCCC, *Report of the Conference of the Parties on its Seventh Session,* Marrakesh, 29 Oct.-10 Nov. 2001, UN Doc. FCCC/CP/2001/13/Add.2.

[111] Cf. Mumma, supra note 100 at 206 arguing that African countries are not in a position to benefit significantly from CDM unless the additionality criterion is interpreted so as to include the avoidance of future emissions through CDM.

[112] Preamble of Decision 17/CP.7, supra note 110.

[113] Decision 10/CP.7, supra note 75.

[114] Art. 12.8 of the Kyoto Protocol, supra note 35.

[115] Decision 10/CP.7, supra note 75. The adaptation levy will be 2%.

the future.[116] Secondly, in the case of land intensive activities such as forestry, there are trade-offs between maintaining the land under forest cover and food security or more generally development needs in many countries where arable land is in short supply.[117] Thirdly, the CDM raises the issue of credit storing for host countries. If emission reduction or sink enhancement achieved in host countries are credited to the investors, it may be conceived that subsequent emissions which arise as a result of the activities should also be allocated to the investor.[118]

Further differential issues arise in the context of the distribution of projects across the South. The AIJ experience has shown that it is difficult to expect all countries to have the same capacity to attract projects.[119] As a result the need to promote equitable geographic distribution of CDM projects has been specifically recognized.[120] The geographic distribution of projects is nevertheless likely to remain a contentious issue. In fact, the level of support among investor countries for aid-financed CDM projects is not very high. In case the private sector constitutes the main source of finance in CDM, it is likely that a majority of developing countries will attract little or no CDM investment which may be concentrated in a few big countries.[121]

The geographical spread of projects is closely related to the question of 'hot air' or surplus permits that some countries like Russia are likely to have at the end of the commitment period. These surplus permits are a direct consequence of the negative economic trends at the beginning of the 1990s in Russia which implied that it achieved greenhouse gas emission reductions far in excess of its obligations. This significant reduction is attributable to historical circumstances but from the point of view of the global environment, Russia benefits from a huge subsidy for complying with its obligations under the Protocol.[122] From a differential point of view, it would seem logical to offer similar conditions to all developing countries.

---

[116]   The proposed draft decision on mechanisms addresses this issue by mentioning in its preamble that the Kyoto Protocol has not created or bestowed any right, title or entitlement to emissions of any kind on Parties included in Annex I. Draft Decision - /CMP.1 (Mechanisms), supra note 103.

[117]   Philippe Cullet and Patricia Kameri-Mbote, 'Joint Implementation and Forestry Projects – Conceptual and Operational Fallacies', 74 *Int'l Aff.* 393 (1998).

[118]   This is an issue which will take on significance as some projects provide benefits which go beyond 2012. Anonymous, 'Avoiding Emissions by Fuel Wood Plantations in Brazil', 8/2 *Joint Implementation Quarterly* 10 (2002).

[119]   In fact, as of 2001, only 44% of AIJ projects were in developing countries (56% in countries undergoing economic transition). On the other hand, nearly all forestry projects were in non-Annex I Parties. UNFCCC, Fifth Synthesis Report on Activities Implemented Jointly under the Pilot Phase, UN Doc. FCCC/SBSTA/2001/7 (2001).

[120]   Decision 17/CP.7, supra note 110.

[121]   Nancy Kete et al., Should Development Aid be Used to Finance the Clean Development Mechanism? 5 (Washington, DC: World Resources Institute, 2001).

[122]   Benito Müller, Ratifying the Kyoto Protocol: The Case for Japanese-Russian Joint Implementation (London: Royal Institute of International Affairs – Energy and Environment Programme, Briefing Paper – New Series N° 21, 2001).

However, from an environmental point of view, extending hot air to all developing countries would probably be catastrophic. The solution to this problem is probably to be found in seeking increasing transfers of environmentally sound technologies to developing countries as provided for in the Convention. This constitutes one of the only alternatives to increased emissions which under current scenarios are a prerequisite to raising existing people's standards of living and addressing the needs of increasing populations.

Lastly, the question of institutional arrangements for the allocation of CDM projects is of interest. Over time, there have been proposals for a bilateral or multilateral solution to the allocation issue. In the case of a bilateral solution, investor states negotiate directly with host parties on a specific project. This is generally similar to the AIJ system. Despite the apparent simplicity and fairness of a bilateral scheme, there are good grounds for preferring a multilateral arrangement in the case of the CDM. In fact, the method of allocation of projects is of such significance that it will affect the degree to which the CDM can contribute to the implementation of the principle of common but differentiated responsibilities. As noted, the AIJ experience indicates that a bilateral option offers no guarantee that projects will be either equitably shared among countries or that countries whose environmental or development needs are greatest will be prioritized.[123] The advantages of a multilateral solution include the following: Firstly, a multilateral clearing-house can distribute projects around the world according to the fundamental principles of the Convention and make sure that the benefits of the CDM will be accorded in priority to countries which have greater needs for development or technological assistance. Secondly, a multilateral CDM can put all host countries on a more equal footing. It can, in particular, give smaller and poorer countries a better chance of hosting projects and thereby avoid direct trading between countries which may put pressure on the host country. Thirdly, a multilateral institution is in a better position to foster a sectoral distribution of desirable projects, for instance, by striking a balance between adaptation and mitigation activities. In practice, the bilateral option has been chosen for the time being and the CDM Executive Board will only register project activities but will not take on the task of allocating projects.

Involvement of the Private Sector and Differential Treatment

One of the main innovations and challenges of the Kyoto mechanisms is the important role given to the private sector in an inter-state agreement. Traditionally, the private sector has not been directly involved in the design or implementation of international instruments. This subdued role has been due both to the resistance of private sector actors to formal involvement in intergovernmental forums and to

---

[123] Cf. Saleemul Huq, *Applying Sustainable Development Criteria to CDM Projects: The PCF Experience* (World Bank: Prototype Carbon Fund, 2002).

states' fear of loss of power.[124] This has not always been positive from the point of view of the development of international law, as illustrated in the case of codes of conduct developed in the 1980s to regulate multinational companies' international activities, which were largely drafted without the direct formal involvement of private companies.[125]

International law is certainly capable of accommodating actors such as multinational companies. In fact, the ICJ was asked long ago to determine whether the UN was a subject of international law capable of possessing international rights and duties, and having the capacity to maintain its rights by bringing international claims.[126] The Court made it clear that the legal personality of the UN and its rights and duties did not have to be the same as those of a state. The rationale for broadening the number of subjects of international law was that 'the progressive increase in the collective activities of States has already given rise to instances of action upon the international plane by certain entities which are not States'.[127] The rapid internationalization of a number of fields of activity since 1949 makes this conclusion even more relevant today. The significant role of multinational companies in the international economic system calls for their more direct participation in intergovernmental forums.

In the climate change context, the formal involvement of private companies intersects at the level of implementation mechanisms. The participation of the private sector is linked to the search for market mechanisms to foster a more economically efficient implementation of the treaty from a global point of view. The participation of the private sector can also be explained by the move away from aid-financed development and the increased reliance on private finance to foster economic development. Further, the fact that a majority of activities causing climate change are carried out by private entities implies that the involvement of the private sector is of crucial importance to foster the effective implementation of the climate change treaties.[128]

From a legal point of view, the participation of the private sector in the implementation of an international treaty does not pose any significant problem. However, the lack of framework for private sector participation in inter-state agreements is also a challenge. Thus, in the climate change context, the efficiency brought by the private sector should not come at the expense of equity or sustainability. For instance, the CDM is first considered a developmental

---

[124] Jonathan I. Charney, 'Transnational Corporations and Developing Public International Law', 1983 *Duke L.J.* 748 (1983).

[125] *Id.*

[126] Reparation for Injuries Suffered in the Service of the United Nations, 11 Apr. 1949, *ICJ Reports 1949*, p. 174.

[127] *Id.* at 178.

[128] Laura B. Campbell, 'The Role of the Private Sector and other Non-state Actors in Implementation of the Kyoto Protocol', in W. Bradnee Chambers ed., *Inter-linkages – The Kyoto Protocol and the International Trade and Investment Regimes* 17, 20 (Tokyo: UN University, 2001).

instrument which also fosters local and national benefits not directly related to climate change mitigation. In this regard, the Protocol seems to backtrack on previous developments. Article 12.2 of the Protocol states, for instance, that the CDM should assist host parties in achieving sustainable development, a much less precise formulation than the AIJ Decision which seeks projects 'compatible with and supportive of national environment and development priorities and strategies'.[129] Further, while the AIJ Decision called for AIJ to foster 'long-term environmental benefits', Article 12 speaks only of 'benefits' and Articles 6 and 17 omit any mention of this.[130]

At the domestic level, the private sector has often had a role to play in the implementation of international agreements but this has usually not been directly related to the international treaty. In the Kyoto mechanisms, private enterprises are taking on a much more prominent role and benefiting much more directly from the international regime in place. This necessitates the development of a framework to ensure accountability and liability of these actors since international law is not well equipped at the moment for direct enforcement against private actors. This is all the more important in the case of flexibility mechanisms where the involvement of the private sector is driven mainly by considerations of cost-effectiveness while the other objectives outlined in the treaty, such as the promotion of sustainable development in the case of the CDM, may not be taken into account.

In the context of flexibility mechanisms, it is difficult to completely separate private liability from state responsibility. In general international law, the principle is that every international wrongful act of a state entails its international responsibility,[131] but in environmental law, liability rules are still developing.[132] In the climate change context, the question of state liability has surfaced in debates concerning the responsibility of states for past, present and future emissions of greenhouse gases.[133]

Some more specific issues arise in the context of flexibility mechanisms, for instance, in the case of forestry projects whose eligibility under the CDM has now been confirmed.[134] In this case, the issue of the responsibility for emissions arising as a result or following the completion of projects has not been solved and the

---

[129]   Art. 12.2 of the Kyoto Protocol, supra note 35 and Decision 5/CP.1, supra note 93, at § 1.b.

[130]   Decision 5/CP.1, supra note 93 at § 1.d.

[131]   Article 1, Responsibility of States for Internationally Wrongful Acts, in UNGA Res. 56/83, Responsibility of States for Internationally Wrongful Acts, 12 Dec. 2001, UN Doc. A/RES/56/83.

[132]   Institute of International Law, Responsibility and Liability under International Law for Environmental Damage, Resolution of 4 Sept. 1997, reprinted in 7 *Rev. Eur. Community and Int'l Envtl. L.* 99 (1998).

[133]   Frank Biermann, '"Common Concern of Humankind": The Emergence of a New Concept of International Environmental Law', 34 *Archiv des Völkerrechts* 426 (1996).

[134]   Decision 17/CP.7, supra note 110.

accounting of these factors may negate the contribution of these projects to climate change mitigation. Neither of the two possible scenarios constitutes sustainable options from the point of view of climate change and sustainable development. Firstly, where trees are planted for timber exports to the investor nation, all the carbon sequestered in the host country and credited to the investor is eventually released by the investor state, thus negating all gains. Secondly, in cases where trees are used or left to decay in the host country, while current practice which allocates emissions to the final user would make the host responsible for these emissions, the idea of crediting the investor and penalizing the host goes against the very essence of the Convention.

The sharing of responsibility between host and investor states is important in a longer-term perspective. If host countries end up being responsible for emissions linked to the implementation of a flexibility mechanism project, this may involve an indirect transfer of responsibility for emissions from investor to host countries. Further, in the case of non-completion of a project, it is fundamental that responsibility be allocated not only according to normal contract principles but also according to the principles of the Convention. Among the two (private) entities signing the contract for the implementation of a project, contract rules should apply if the host, for instance, fails to deliver the carbon benefits specified in the contract. However, the host entity implementing the project cannot be held responsible if the investor country is in breach of its own international commitment under the Protocol. Similar principles should apply in case of non-completion of a project due, for instance, to force majeure. If, say, a forest under flexibility management is destroyed by a natural cause, such as a volcanic eruption, contractual principles should apply between the two private entities at stake but the investor country should remain responsible for meeting its commitments.[135] In other words, flexibility mechanisms should not become a vehicle for the transfer of responsibility for fulfilling international obligations from a country to a private entity in another country.

Lessons Learnt at the Implementation Level for the Development of Differential Treatment

Differential treatment has been applied in international environmental agreements with a certain amount of consistency in recent years. It has generally involved differentiation in treaty norms as well as differentiation at the implementation level. While 'traditional' differentiation examined in chapter 3 has led to a number of changes in the structure of international law, the very notion of differential treatment is still the object of significant debate, as illustrated by the evolution of international trade law. At the implementation level, differentiation has been less

---

[135]   Cf. Art. 4.6 of the Kyoto Protocol, supra note 35 in the case of 'bubbles'.

associated with ideological battles and has thus had the opportunity to develop in recent years in a slow but regular manner.

Recent developments in differentiation at the implementation level have focused on environmental issues. This is due to the conjunction of a number of factors which have led most states to find a common platform to address global issues such as the depletion of the ozone layer. Differentiation at this level is thus clearly linked more to practical considerations than to the reliance on international customary law or general principles of international law. It is, for instance, significant that technology transfer in the context of inter-state agreements has effectively been revived in this new context now largely devoid of ideological undertones of the NIEO which was based on antagonistic principles dividing the donors and recipients of technology.

Differentiation at the implementation level is generally oriented towards fostering better implementation of international treaties and specifically achieving practical results, such as effective technology transfers. However, it also goes beyond that function to contribute to the development of legal principles fostering more substantive equality in inter-state relations. Further, differential treatment at the implementation level has been associated with new developments, for instance, concerning the governance structure of financial mechanisms or the involvement of new actors in public international law agreements in the case of the flexibility mechanisms.

On the whole, differentiation at the implementation level has neither radically changed the way international agreements are implemented nor led to the rapid acceptance of new principles of international law which would put into question the dominance of the principle of sovereignty as the basic organizing principle of inter-state relations. However, it has led to the realization that changes may be necessary in the current organization of international legal relations to improve the effectiveness of the rules adopted.

The specific case of aid is noteworthy since it has historically been one of the main instruments through which differentiation has been put in practice. In this case, donors have usually refused to make indefinite aid commitments.[136] However, aid still remains a common feature of many international treaties and it has been contended that a right to aid, and thus by extension to differential treatment, would be slowly emerging.[137] It is noteworthy that in the last ten years, allocation structures in aid mechanisms have been strengthened in favour of recipient countries. This represents a significant departure from previous practice and seems to give aid improved international standing even though this is happening in a

---

[136]   Biermann, supra note 44 at 116.
[137]   Maurice Flory, *Droit international du développement* 55 (Paris: Presses universitaires de France, 1977) stating that the international community is progressively recognising a right to aid and Sam Johnston, 'Financial Aid, Biodiversity and International Law', in Michael Bowman and Catherine Redgwell eds, *International Law and the Conservation of Biological Diversity* 271 (London: Kluwer Law International, 1996).

context where public sector funds are becoming relatively less significant with the growing importance of private investment generally and where the percentage of official development assistance has been declining.[138] Developments in environmental trust funds seem to indicate a strengthening of the differential component.[139] In the Montreal Protocol Fund, the North agreed to an innovative decision making structure which gives recipients a say in the main decision making body. This was supposed to be a one-off occurrence which was not supposed to have any counterpart elsewhere.[140] As it turned out, within a couple of years a similar decision making structure was adopted in the GEF.

On the whole, the existence of differentiation seems to be a rather positive factor in the development of international environmental law. However, the current approach is still relatively piecemeal and lacking in many respects. These shortcomings include the difficulties in fully involving the private sector in the context of the implementation of an international law agreement and the still limited scope of the GEF mandate. Broader issues also need to be tackled in this context. While differential implementation brings about more effective implementation of international norms, the current emphasis on cost-effectiveness is not devoid of problems since it does not seem to be necessarily compatible with the broader goals of environmental sustainability, both at the global and local levels. Another concern with cost-effectiveness is that it tends to lead to a preference for large-scale projects which are not necessarily the only desirable alternatives if all factors concerning the protection of the global environment are taken into account.[141] Further, in the context of the climate change convention the focus on flexibility mechanisms has led to sidelining other mechanisms such as state responsibility, liability and compensation. It is therefore useful to determine the direction differential treatment should take to be more effective in realizing the twin objective of effective implementation and substantive equality.

---

[138] Net official development assistance as a percentage of GNP declined from 0.33% to 0.22% between 1990 and 2000. UNDP, *Human Development Report 2002* (New York: Oxford University Press, 2002).

[139] Cf. Rüdiger Wolfrum, 'Means of Ensuring Compliance with and Enforcement of International Environmental Law', 272 RCADI 9 (1998).

[140] This is reflected in the Decision of the Second Meeting of the Parties establishing the Interim Financial Mechanism which states that '[t]he Financial Mechanism set out in this decision is without prejudice to any future arrangements that may be developed with respect to other environmental issues'. Dec. II/8, Report of the Second Meeting of the Parties to the Montreal Protocol on Substances that Deplete the Ozone Layer, UNEP, London 27-29 June 1990, UN Doc. UNEP/OzL.Pro.2/3.

[141] Joyeeta Gupta, *The Climate Change Convention and Developing Countries: From Conflict to Consensus?* 104 (Dordrecht: Kluwer, 1997).

Towards a Broader Conception of International Environmental Problems

Differential treatment for the implementation of international environmental agreements has focused on some specific problems. It is necessary to look into the question of the choice of issues which are covered under differential schemes. Generally, the international community currently only addresses a small sample of all the environmental problems affecting the biosphere. In fact, the problems that are deemed 'global' only represent a small subset of environmental issues of international relevance. These currently comprise climate change, biodiversity, international waters, stratospheric ozone and desertification and constitute, for instance, the focus of the action of the GEF. While these are serious environmental problems, other issues of great concern, such as fresh water management, sanitation, soil erosion, waterborne diseases, environmental health, poverty alleviation and the terms of trade between natural resource products and manufactures are not part of recognized global problems.[142] This seems to imply that the international nature of an environmental problem is not sufficient to earn it appropriate recognition.[143]

Among the problems tackled at the international level, the problems of the depletion of the ozone layer and climate change stand out. In both cases, contributions to the creation of the problems have been 'different' for each country and approximately mirror current levels of per capita income. Both are partly caused by industrial development. Their impacts are either not significant enough as yet such as in the case of climate change or geographically limited such as in the case of ozone depletion.[144] These elements have ensured that while there is worldwide concern for these issues national interests have not been eliminated. Indeed, different countries are likely to suffer or benefit differently from climate change and from the adoption of a binding regime, whether in environmental or economic terms. Similarly, biodiversity conservation and management is also controversial for different reasons. It has long been the subject of environmentalists' concerns but developing countries have tried to reject the notion

---

[142]   Michael Redclift and Colin Sage, 'Introduction', in Michael Redclift and Colin Sage eds, *Strategies for Sustainable Development – Local Agendas for the Southern Hemisphere* 1 (Chichester: Wiley, 1994).

[143]   The 1994 report of the independent evaluation of the GEF on its first phase pointedly stated that the rationale for the selection of the four focal areas was rather obscure in origin 'and can be traced to the World Bank and to a few developed countries interested in 'internationalizing' certain environmental problems'. UNDP, UNEP and World Bank, *Global Environment Facility – Independent Evaluation of the Pilot Phase* 35 (Washington, DC: World Bank, 1994).

[144]   The major current threat seems to be an increase in skin cancers, mostly though not exclusively in areas of the globe occupied by OECD countries. Stone, supra note 10. See also, Brett M. Coldiron, 'Thinning of the Ozone Layer: Facts and Consequences', 27 *J. Am. Academy Dermatology* 653 (1992).

that resources lying inside their boundaries should be viewed as global.[145] These examples show that the prioritization of environmental problems cannot be understood in a political, economic and social vacuum. This is probably partly due to the fact that a number of environmental problems are intrinsically linked to industrial activity and addressing them has significant economic repercussions.

While non-environmental considerations seem to influence the prioritization of problems, this is not usually discussed. Environmental concerns which are currently addressed at the international level seem to focus mostly on an environmental ethic associated with urban lifestyles. The call for setting up nature reserves with limited human intervention constitutes one of the clearest examples of this trend.[146] Similar considerations underlie the issue of climate change which is not one of the most pressing environmental problems the world population as a whole is facing today since it does not as yet have direct impacts.[147] On the other hand, pressing problems like the eradication of malaria have met with little interest from the international community for many years.[148]

If differentiation is to effectively contribute to the realization of sustainable development, it is imperative that it targets the problems which matter most to fulfilling the twin objectives of environmental quality and meeting all human beings' basic needs. To this end, a framework should be adopted to openly determine the relative importance of the various environmental issues of concern at the international level. This framework should focus not only on scientific considerations but also on the importance of environmental problems to the majority of the world population. Given current conditions where hundreds of millions of people lack access to fresh water and are affected by life-threatening waterborne diseases, it is desirable that the nexus between environment and development should be made more explicit. The different kinds of environmental diseases constitute a case in point. The increase in skin cancers caused by the depletion of the ozone layer and the number of deaths caused by water-borne diseases indicates that both should be tackled. However, if one was to be given more prominence, it might be the latter because it affects more people who are generally in more precarious socio-economic situations.

Current global environmental priorities, apart from land degradation, do not necessarily reflect the aims outlined. It is therefore not altogether surprising that they may conflict with the needs of the majority of rural people in developing countries. This is illustrated by the case of biodiversity. As noted, biodiversity conservation is sometimes equated with the setting up of reserves wherefrom local people are excluded. This both obfuscates the often long-standing relationships

---

145   UNDP, UNEP and World Bank, supra note 143.
146   Cf. Patricia Kameri-Mbote, *Property Rights and Biodiversity Management in Kenya – The Case of Land Tenure and Wildlife* (Nairobi: ACTS Press, 2002).
147   Gupta, supra note 141 at 52.
148   Mohamed Larbi Bouguerra, 'Le paludisme, ce fléau si peu combattu', 531 *Monde diplomatique* 23 (1998).

between people and their environment as well as overlooks the fact that some of their activities are part of the ecosystem.[149] If biodiversity conservation constitutes an important environmental goal in itself, it cannot be undertaken in a vacuum since conservation directly impacts on many people's lives.[150] Concerns regarding the existence or recreational value of species should thus give way to more balanced assessments focusing more on people, especially people who are directly affected by biodiversity conservation measures.[151]

Overall, the effectiveness of differentiation at the implementation level could be significantly strengthened if the priorities addressed reflected more accurately the range of problems facing humankind. This would imply not only taking into account problems not currently recognized as 'global' but also devising more comprehensive strategies linking the different problems and related international instruments.[152]

Towards more Effective Technology Transfer Mechanisms

Differential treatment has been associated with a renewed interest in technology transfer provisions. This is significant given the importance of technological solutions to solve a number of environmental problems. However, it is clear that recent technology transfer mechanisms have not had any large-scale impacts even though they contribute to technological capacity building in developing countries. The Commission on Sustainable Development has, for instance, noted that 'there is overall recognition that the level of technology and technology-related investments from public and private sources in developed countries directed towards

---

149   A study by the Bombay Natural History Society in the Bharatpur Sanctuary showed, for instance that buffalo grazing helps to counter the tendency of the wetland to turn into grassland, *cited in* Ashish Kothari et al., 'People and Protected Areas – Rethinking Conservation in India', 25 *Ecologist* 188 (1995).

150   See generally Kameri-Mbote, supra note 146.

151   On the issue of recreational/existence value, Lujan v. Defender of Wildlife, 112 S. Ct. 2130 (1992) determining that American conservationists eager to see some species in foreign tropical countries saved from extinction potentially have standing in American courts.

152   Some limited steps have been taken in this direction. Article 1 of Protocol 10 to the Fourth ACP-EC Convention of Lomé as Revised by the Agreement Signed in Mauritius, 4 Nov. 1995, 155 *The Courier ACP-EU* (1996) recognizing the importance and necessity of the rational and integrated management of forest resources so as to ensure sustainable development in the long term as propounded in the Rio Forest Principles, the Rio Declaration, the Climate Change Convention, the Biodiversity Convention and the Desertification Convention. See also, Article 4.2.a of the Convention to Combat Desertification, supra note 36 which states specifically that in pursuing the objectives of the convention, state parties must adopt an integrated approach addressing the physical, biological and socio-economic aspects of the processes of desertification and drought.

developing countries has not, in general, been realized as envisaged at UNCED'.[153] This has led to calls for commitments concerning concrete measures for the transfer of environmentally sound technologies to developing countries.[154]

More specific concerns relate to the framework into which technology transfer have to be conceived and implemented. It has, for instance, been pointed out that the current emphasis on global problems identified in the North may lead to the transfer of technologies which are more relevant to global concerns than to the more pressing needs of developing countries.[155] Further, while increased private flows have led to investments in industry and technology in some developing countries and economies in transition, there has been a bias against the poorest countries which has slowed the process of technological change in these countries.[156] Technology transfer has generally been very modest and barriers to developmentally sound transfers have remained formidable. This is attributed to the lack of access to relevant technologies, inadequate demand for technology linked to poverty and lack of finance and the lack of necessary infrastructure to support acquisition and utilization of relevant technologies. The divergence between trajectories of technological development which meet the needs of industrial countries and the types and forms of technologies relevant to the needs of the most people in developing countries have resulted in the lack of relevant technologies.[157]

Overall, technology transfer in the context of differential treatment has not led to the endowment of developing countries with the technological tools necessary to compete on a par in international markets. Further, technologies which may be of use in developing countries to foster sustainable development are sometimes not transferred because the investors are not keen on delving into areas they do not know well.[158] Generally, it is thus apparent that while technology transfer as envisaged under the NIEO was not successfully implemented and eventually discarded, the new framework has not fostered much more successful transfers. In fact, the history of the development of industrial technology does not seem to indicate that it can or has contributed to the alleviation of poverty in developing countries.[159]

Other factors which may contribute to this record include the fact that technology transfer is mainly, if not exclusively, conceived as a North-South affair.

---

[153]   UN Commission on Sustainable Development, Overall Progress Achieved Since the United Nations Conference on Environment and Development, Fifth Session, 7-25 April 1997, UN Doc. E/CN.17/1997/2.

[154]   Programme for the Further Implementation of Agenda 21, supra note 15.

[155]   Barnett, supra note 26 at 7.

[156]   UN Doc. E/CN.17/1997/2, supra note 153 at 29.

[157]   Barnett, supra note 26 at 4.

[158]   Swiss Federal Office of Environment, Forests and Landscape/Hari Sharan et al., Activities Implemented Jointly (AIJ): A Review of International Activities and a Study of Policies and Strategies for a Swiss Pilot Phase Programme (Discussion Paper, on file with the author, March 1997).

[159]   Schumacher, supra note 22 at 137.

This tends to overlook, for instance, the extremely wide disparities in levels of economic development among developing countries. The enhancement of South-South technological cooperation has been the subject of many debates but has never been considered as a priority by the international community.[160] Overall, it is clear that differentiation cannot be limited to redressing imbalances between two broad groups of countries when the levels of technological development among developing countries is also extremely unequal.

Finally, while this discussion of technology transfer has not focused on questions of ownership and debates concerning the intellectual property rights legal regime at the international level, a complete assessment of the effectiveness of technology transfers must take into account the impacts of intellectual property rights. As noted, the rationale for technology transfers is the fact that technologies are protected by intellectual property rights, in particular patents. The intellectual property rights system was challenged to an extent from the point of view of differentiation in the context of the NIEO. Not only were these challenges abandoned but the overwhelming trend in the past 15 years has been towards a strengthening of intellectual property rights protection at the international level, as illustrated by the adoption of the Agreement on Trade-Related Aspects of Intellectual Property Rights (TRIPS Agreement).[161] This explains to a large extent why even international environmental agreements which focus on technology transfer as a way to bring substance to the differential treatment debate have not been as successful as could have been hoped. In fact, the strengthening of intellectual property right protection has tended to thwart the growth of technology transfer towards developing countries. However, as chapter 5 explores in further detail, interesting elements arise from the remaining differential provisions found in the TRIPS Agreement.

Differential Treatment and Non-state Actors

Differential treatment at the implementation level has been intrinsically linked to the recognition that the effective implementation of international norms is dependent on the involvement of all concerned actors.[162] This is especially true in the field of environmental management where states are often not in a position to

---

160 See however, initiatives such as the Technical Cooperation among Developing Countries programme which seeks to promote the deliberate and voluntary sharing of experience between developing countries. FAO Handbook on TCDC (Rome: FAO, 1992). See also the TDCD web site at http://tcdc.undp.org.

161 Agreement on Trade-Related Aspects of Intellectual Property Rights, Marrakesh, 15 Apr. 1994, reprinted in 33 *ILM* 1125 (1994).

162 The link between differential treatment and a partnership between all concerned actors is clearly made in section 3 of the Declaration of Principles of International Law Relating to Sustainable Development, International Law Association, New Delhi, 6 April 2002.

effectuate changes on their own. The participation of the private sector in the climate change regime is a reflection of this recognition.

There have also been calls for giving a more important role to non-state actors in international law. The general move towards privatization and liberalization has ensured that the importance of states is diminishing both at the domestic and international levels.[163] Globalization also tends to blur the distinction between national and international, and private and public concerns. In this context, international law cannot focus exclusively on states.[164] Further, states often seem to have great difficulties in fulfilling their international obligations because they lack the necessary resources and because part of the funds allocated do not reach their intended beneficiaries.[165]

For the time being, efforts towards involving non-state actors have been hampered in two different ways. Firstly, the attempt to bring in the private sector is constrained by the lack of an appropriate legal framework to carry this out. Thus, in the case of the flexibility mechanisms, the involvement of the private sector will only strengthen the implementation of the convention if its involvement is driven not only by profit motivation but also by other factors leading to the realization of the environmental and developmental goals of the convention.

Secondly, the drive towards involving the private sector has not been extended to other actors. Thus, the different actors of the civil society have not received as much attention and recognition as business and industry.[166] The necessity to take a broader view is acknowledged, for instance, in Agenda 21 which recognizes that all social groups should be integrated in the process of realizing sustainable development.[167] This includes diverse entities such as business and industry,

---

[163]   While official development assistance received by all developing countries diminished from 1.4% of GDP in 1990 to 0.5% in 2000, net foreign direct investment flows increased from 0.9% to 2.5%. UNDP 2002, supra note 138.

[164]   Edith Brown Weiss, 'Environmental Equity and International Law', in Sun Lin ed., *UNEP's New Way Forward: Environmental Law and Sustainable Development* 7 (Nairobi: UNEP, 1995).

[165]   The Fund for the Development of Indigenous Peoples which was set up to support the process of self-development of indigenous peoples, communities and organizations of Latin America and the Caribbean takes some steps towards involving non-state recipients of aid. Agreement Establishing the Fund for the Development of the Indigenous Peoples of Latin America and the Caribbean, Madrid, 24 July 1992, reprinted in Wolfgang E. Burhenne ed., *International Environmental Law – Multilateral Treaties* 992:55 (1995).

[166]   NGOs are now often granted observer status in intergovernmental proceedings but their 'informal' participation remains subject to state consent. Christine Chinkin, 'Normative Development in the International Legal System', in Dinah Shelton ed., *Commitment and Compliance – The Role of Non-binding Norms in the International Legal System* 21 (Oxford: Oxford University Press, 2000).

[167]   Agenda 21, supra note 5 at §23.1. See also, Brussels Declaration, Third United Nations Conference on the Least Developed Countries, 20 May 2001, UN Doc.

women, farmers or non-governmental organizations. While business, industry and non-governmental organizations have gained varying degrees of recognition as international actors, other groups are still generally outside the purview of international law.[168] In a number of cases, the effective implementation of international norms may require the establishment of new avenues to bypass states when they are incapable of delivering effective measures. At the international level, the establishment of a special facility within the GEF for non-governmental organizations constitutes a step towards 'mainstreaming' non-state actors, even though these initiatives remain relatively limited in scope.

Overall, differential treatment does not necessarily provide direct answers to the question of the participation of non-state actors at different levels of the international legal process. However, it highlights the need for a number of changes to make international environmental law – and other fields of international law – both more substantively equitable and more efficient in terms of implementation. At the international level, the distinction between state and non-state actors remains a serious impediment to the broader participation of the latter as fully-fledged actors. In the case of the private sector, a certain reluctance to take on a more formal role can be discerned. A deeper involvement is necessary in fields like technology transfer where members of the private sector are the main actors in most situations. Some of the implications include, for instance, the need for international law to allocate rights and responsibilities not only to states but also to other important actors. The Kyoto mechanisms constitute a first attempt to integrate the private sector in a more balanced way. As noted, a number of issues, in particular with regard to responsibility, have not been resolved in the Kyoto Protocol context. Few other international environmental law treaties provide a framework with regard to private actors' liability, apart from the treaties concerning civil liability in the field of nuclear energy.[169]

The involvement of the civil society also presents significant, though completely different, challenges. Differential treatment clearly indicates that there are benefits to taking into account the special needs and situations of different countries. It is much more difficult to apply the same principles when dealing with millions of individuals but forms of decentralization within states can provide answers to some of the existing problems. In other words, the effectiveness of differential treatment in international law is constrained by the very framework within which it operates. The distinction between the national and international spheres together with low levels of participation of civil society at the international

---

A/CONF.191/12 at § 3, calling for partnerships also with both the civil society and the private sector.

[168] The case of transnational corporations is subject to an evolving debate. Though their role remains mostly informal, they have received a measure of functional international personality. Nico Schrijver, *Sovereignty over Natural Resources – Balancing Rights and Duties* (Cambridge: Cambridge University Press, 1997).

[169] Protocol to Amend the 1963 Vienna Convention on Civil Liability for Nuclear Damage, Vienna, 12 Sept. 1997, reprinted in 36 *ILM* 1462 (1997).

level ensure that it remains difficult to find international law solutions to make sure the benefits of differential treatment reach their intended beneficiaries.[170] The problem differs widely depending on states but can be significant in cases where states are not genuinely committed to implementing social and environmental justice domestically.[171] Chapter 5 builds on these elements. It examines the specific question of the introduction of intellectual property rights in agriculture in developing countries by way of the TRIPS Agreement. This provides an opportunity to analyze one of the few differential provisions of this treaty in the context of its implementation at the national level in a field which directly concerns a majority of the population in most developing countries.

---

[170]   Cf. Wolfgang H. Reinicke and Jan Martin Witte, 'Interdependence, Globalization, and Sovereignty: The Role of Non-binding International Legal Accords', in Dinah Shelton ed., *Commitment and Compliance – The Role of Non-binding Norms in the International Legal System* 75, 90 (Oxford: Oxford University Press, 2000) mentioning that the international law of cooperation has gained in importance under conditions of globalization but can only succeed if international law moves beyond its narrow focus on states.

[171]   Cf. Andrew Linklater, *Beyond Realism and Marxism – Critical Theory and International Relations* (Basingstoke: Macmillan, 1990).

Chapter 5

Differential Treatment in Practice: The Case of Plant Variety Protection

The preceding chapters have shown that differential treatment has a lot to offer in conceptual and practical terms in bringing about more substantively equal relations among states and in fostering effective solutions to some international environmental problems. They have also shown that both at the conceptual level and at practical levels, there remain a number of uncertainties concerning the legal status of differential treatment in international environmental law and concerning its capacity to be an engine of positive change in practice.

This chapter builds on the findings of the previous chapters and through the study of one particular issue, the protection of plant varieties through intellectual property rights, brings out a number of additional elements which confirm the need for differentiation in practice and highlight the difficulties its further development may face. This chapter includes discussions on the following: Firstly, the case study from India provides an example of the intricacies of translating differential provisions into domestic legal frameworks. Secondly, the clause concerning plant variety protection in the Agreement on Trade-Related Aspects of Intellectual Property Rights (TRIPS Agreement) which incorporates elements of differential treatment constitutes an important example of the importance of decentralized implementation.[1] This is linked to the fact that the possibility offered to developing countries to devise legal frameworks in this field provides them with an opportunity to adopt plant variety protection regimes suited to their specific needs. Thirdly, the case of plant variety protection which is intrinsically linked to agricultural management constitutes an important example of the necessity to involve all concerned actors at every stage from the definition to the implementation of legal regimes given that the agricultural sector in developing countries employs about 60 per cent of the workforce.[2] Fourthly, the question of plant variety protection is both an intellectual property rights issue and an environmental law issue. This chapter

---

[1]   Agreement on Trade-Related Aspects of Intellectual Property Rights, Marrakesh, 15 Apr. 1994, reprinted in 33 *ILM* 1125 (1994) [hereafter TRIPS Agreement].

[2]   Jacques Diouf, 'Vaincre la faim', 579 *Monde diplomatique* 23 (2002) giving figures for 1999.

indirectly indicates that even in recent treaties differential treatment is not necessarily confined to the strict field of international environmental law.[3]

Plant variety protection is significant in the context of this study for other reasons as well. As noted in chapter 4, there is an intrinsic relationship between technology transfers and intellectual property rights. The introduction of plant variety protection in developing countries is therefore likely to have an impact on technology transfer in the field of agricultural biotechnology for instance. Consequently, debates concerning the strengthening of intellectual property rights protection under the TRIPS Agreement should be read in a broader historical context which goes back to the NIEO and the Charter on Economic Rights and Duties of States. Further, plant variety protection being partly an intellectual property rights issue, it is by definition concerned not only with states but also with the farming community and the private sector. This case study therefore demonstrates the need for the progressive transformation of international legal structures towards recognizing the importance of different kinds of non-state actors alongside states. In fact, plant variety protection provides a telling example of the progressive blurring of boundaries between public and private law, and international and national concerns, both of which have tremendous implications for the international legal order. The case of India which is of central importance among developing countries is taken to exemplify the issues highlighted in a concrete situation.

Plant Variety Management and Protection

All forms of agriculture depend fundamentally on the existence of agricultural biodiversity. Seeds are one of the most common forms through which conservation and production is ensured from one season to the next. Agricultural management remains central to meeting the basic food needs of all humankind and is particularly important in most developing countries where a majority of the workforce works in the agricultural sector. Further, the agricultural sector is one of the economic mainstays of a majority of developing countries. This section first sketches the relevant aspects of the management of plant varieties at the international and national levels and then outlines the relevant forms of property rights in this field.

Plant Variety Management

The management of plant varieties bears a number of distinguishing characteristics, which give it special relevance in the context of this study. Firstly, plant varieties are managed by a wide array of actors, including subsistence farmers, governments, international organizations and multinational companies. Further, work on seed

---

[3]   For further detail on the question of differential treatment in other areas of international, see Chapter 6 at pp. 175 ff.

enhancement is carried out at all levels from the village level to centres of the Consultative Group on International Agricultural Research (CGIAR) to private sector research laboratories. Another important element is the fact that plant varieties are under different management systems in different regions and countries.

With regard to the actors involved in plant variety management activities, one may distinguish between the domestic and international levels. At the international level, a significant part of the research on plant varieties is carried out within the International Agricultural Research Centres (IARCs) of the CGIAR.[4] The IARCs hold considerable *ex situ* germplasm collections and have played a significant role in the development of a number of varieties, which have a direct impact on food security in many countries. Even though the CGIAR's *ex situ* germplasm collections constitute only about 15 per cent of an estimated 3.8 million samples stored *ex situ* worldwide, these accessions represent about 40 per cent of unique food crop germplasm.[5]

Despite the CGIAR's importance linked to its food-related germplasm collections, most of the research today is carried out by the private sector, in particular multinational companies, whose involvement in plant variety development has increased manifold in the last two decades with the advent of genetic engineering. The involvement of the private sector in plant variety management is premised on the existence of intellectual property rights, such as patents, which provide the necessary incentives for private actors to undertake work in this area.[6]

At the national level, government agricultural policies often play an important role. Forms of intervention vary significantly between developed and developing countries. While research on plant variety enhancement is largely carried out by private actors in the North, developing country governments have a more direct hand in the development of new varieties. Thus, in India, the government has historically had an important role in the development of new seeds.[7] Besides the establishment of a National Seeds Corporation and a State Farms Corporation of India, the government set up a Department of Agricultural Research and Education responsible for coordinating research and educational activities in agriculture, within which the Indian Council for Agricultural Research has played a key role in developing agricultural technologies. The prominent role of the government in this field has, however, been declining in the last 15 years. Indeed, the introduction of the New Seed Policy and more generally the introduction of the new economic

---

4   William B. Lacy, 'The Global Plant Genetic Resources System: A Competition-Cooperation Paradox', 35 *Crop Science* 335 (1995).

5   Gigi Manicad, 'CGIAR and the Private Sector: Public Good Versus Proprietary Technology in Agricultural Research', 37 *Biotechnology and Dev. Monitor* 8 (1999).

6   In legal terms, the landmark case which led to the rapid development of genetic engineering in the United States and subsequently other countries was Diamond v. Chakrabarty, 447 U.S. 303 (1980).

7   Gurdev Singh and S.R. Asokan, *Seed Replacement Rates – Performance and Problems* 6 (New Delhi: Oxford and IBH, 1994).

policy in 1991 have had significant impacts on the seed sector. Thus, in the case of maize seeds, the market share of private seed companies has risen from 10 per cent in the 1981-85 period to 85 per cent by 1995-97.[8]

In principle, governmental intervention is based on the principle that it is a service to the community at large with the main aim of increasing food security for the country as a whole.[9] Thus, the rationale is not profit and this kind of intervention is not dependent upon monopoly rights such as patents since it is premised on the enhancement of people's overall welfare. The domestic seed sector in developing countries has followed varied fortunes but has often been a secondary actor in plant variety management. In India, the industry developed for a long time mainly in the shadow of government action in this field. While the development of a private seed industry was not banned, it was not strongly promoted, partly because of the perceived need to keep this vital sector premised on the common good rather than on profits. In recent years, there has been a significant expansion of the private sector which now comprises about 140 companies.[10] This new strength has been matched by stronger calls for the development of property rights over plant varieties. In fact, the pressure put on the government to introduce plant breeders' rights is attributable in part to the TRIPS Agreement but also to lobbying from the domestic private industry which saw the lack of legal protection as a major restriction on commercial hybrid seed production.[11]

In most developing countries, farmers remain the most important managers of biological resources such as plant varieties. This is first linked to the fact that rural people account for 60 per cent of the total population in developing countries and 72 per cent in least developed countries.[12] Most rural people are either farmers or working in agricultural production. They are thus closely dependent upon the natural resources in their vicinity for their livelihood and subsistence needs. Overall, the population active in the agricultural sector in developing countries amounts to 86 per cent of the rural population and 52 per cent of the total population in developing countries.[13] This implies that an overwhelming majority of rural people have extremely strong incentives to sustainably manage their resource base. In fact, local communities have often maintained harmonious

---

[8]   R.P. Singh, 'An Interface in Public and Private Maize Research in India', in Roberta V. Gerpacio ed., *Impact of Public- and Private-Sector Maize Breeding Research in Asia, 1966-1997/98* at 44 (Mexico, DF: International Maize and Wheat Improvement Center, 2001).

[9]   Articles 38 and 39 of the Constitution of India.

[10]   Raju Barwale, 'Simple Policy and Legislation Required', in *Survey of Indian Agriculture 2002* 213 (Chennai: Hindu, 2002).

[11]   Biswajit Dhar and Sachin Chaturvedi, 'Introducing Plant Breeders' Rights in India – A Critical Evaluation of the Proposed Legislation', 1 *J. World Intellectual Property* 245 (1998).

[12]   FAOSTAT at http://apps.fao.org and UNCTAD, *The Least Developed Countries 2002 Report* (Geneva: UNCTAD, 2002).

[13]   FAOSTAT at http://apps.fao.org.

relationships with their environment over time and have sustainably managed their resource base even when utilization has been intensive.[14]

Local farmers have traditionally been the main actors involved in saving seeds, selecting specific traits to produce varieties that suit their requirements and generally managing agro-biodiversity. Their importance in seed management at present can, for instance, be ascertained by looking at figures concerning the percentage of seeds sown, which are saved seeds from the previous crop. In India, this is estimated at between 75 per cent and 85 per cent.[15] The percentages of seed supplied by the seed industry vary widely according to the crop. While the industry provides only about 12 per cent of paddy and 8 per cent of wheat seeds, it provides about 29 per cent of maize and 72 per cent of pearl millet.[16] Estimates indicate that inter-farmer sales of seeds account for 60 per cent of seed requirements of agriculture in India.[17] One important characteristic of farmers' seed management is the practice of exchanging seeds with each other. This can take different forms depending on the regions. The transaction can, for instance, involve the obligation for the recipient to give back an equivalent or higher quantity of seeds after the harvest.[18]

This brief review indicates that plant varieties are managed by a variety of actors and that their motivations for engaging in seed enhancement may differ significantly. Further, it is apparent that the different actors operate at different levels and there is no forum that includes them all.

Plant Variety Protection

Plant variety protection refers to the protection by intellectual property rights of innovations in plant breeding. For a long time, plant varieties were excluded from the international intellectual property rights regime. The rationale was that the agricultural sector contributes to the fulfilment of everyone's basic food needs and the development of new plant varieties should not be based on a system seeking individual appropriation of inventions such as the patents system, which was viewed as inappropriate in this context.[19] This was linked to traditional agricultural practices of seed saving and exchange and to the perception that the fulfilment of

[14] Elinor Ostrom, *Governing the Commons – The Evolution of Institutions for Collective Action* 59 (Cambridge: Cambridge University Press, 1990).

[15] Singh and Asokan, supra note 7 concerning Gujarat and Punjab and Suman Sahai, 'What is Bt and what is Terminator?', XXXIV/3-4 *EPW* 84 (1999).

[16] Vandana Shiva and Tom Crompton, 'Monopoly and Monoculture – Trends in Indian Seed Industry', XXXIII/39 *EPW* A-137 (1998).

[17] Suman Sahai, 'Indian Patents Act and TRIPS', 28 *EPW* 1495 (1993).

[18] The *Beej Bachao Andolan* (Save the Seeds Movement) in the state of Uttaranchal, India constitutes an organized attempt by farmers to provide seed exchanges with other farmers. Indira Khurana, 'The Seed Supremo', 7/15 *Down to Earth* (1998).

[19] Jean-Pierre Clavier, *Les catégories de la propriété intellectuelle à l'épreuve des créations génétiques* (Paris: L'Harmattan, 1998).

food needs should not be primarily a profit-making enterprise.[20] This hampered the development of a seed industry and more generally of agricultural businesses. Over time, the development of a form of legal protection of plant varieties was achieved in the North. At the domestic level, the United States was the first country to enact a specific Plant Patent Act in 1930 which provides protection for certain asexually reproduced plants.[21] European countries remained more hesitant and decided to adopt a specific international instrument to cover plant varieties, striking a balance between the absence of protection and the full monopolistic protection offered by patents.[22] It is significant that for a long time, industry was also opposed to the introduction of plant patents on the basis that the innovation lacked the inventiveness requirement of patents because a new plant variety was seen more as an improvement on an existing product of nature than as a 'scientific' invention.[23] At the international level, it remained generally accepted until the 1980s that plant genetic resources should not be the subject of intellectual property rights protection but should instead remain in the public domain as part of the common heritage of humankind.[24] This also constituted the premise on which the CGIAR operated. A dramatic policy shift occurred in the ten years following the adoption of International Undertaking on Plant Genetic Resources which led the international community to accept in principle the introduction of plant variety protection through intellectual property rights. As a result, the TRIPS Agreement imposes the introduction of a form of plant variety protection on all member states. In practice, since most developed countries had already introduced plant variety protection and most developing countries had not, the effect of the TRIPS Agreement is generally to foster the introduction of plant variety protection in the latter countries.

    This section outlines the relevant international legal framework for plant variety protection found in different legal instruments and then turns on to examine the implications of the differential provision found in the TRIPS Agreement concerning plant variety protection.

International legal frameworks for plant variety protection   The legal and policy framework for plant variety protection is scattered in a number of legal instruments which must be considered successively. There are now three main treaties, the

---

20   Commission on Genetic Resources for Food and Agriculture, Possible Formulas for the Sharing of Benefits Based on Different Benefit-Indicators, Rome, 8th Sess., 19-23 Apr. 1999, Doc. CGRFA-8/99/8.

21   Plant Patent Act of 1930, 35 *US Code* 161 et seq.

22   International Convention for the Protection of New Varieties of Plants, Paris, 2 Dec. 1961, as Revised at Geneva on 10 Nov. 1972, 23 Oct. 1978 and 19 Mar. 1991 (UPOV Doc. 221(E), 1996) [hereafter UPOV-1991].

23   Dwijen Rangnekar, Intellectual Property Rights and Agriculture: An Analysis of the Economic Impact of Plant Breeders' Rights (Actionaid UK, 2000).

24   International Undertaking on Plant Genetic Resources, Res. 8/83, Report of the Conference of FAO, 22nd Sess., Rome, 5-23 Nov. 1983, Doc. C83/REP [hereafter International Undertaking].

TRIPS Agreement, the International Convention for the Protection of New Varieties of Plants (UPOV Convention) and the International Treaty on Plant Genetic Resources for Food and Agriculture (PGRFA Treaty) which specifically govern the protection of plant varieties at the international level. Further, the Convention on Biological Diversity is also important.

The TRIPS Agreement The TRIPS Agreement is today of central importance for all WTO member states. The basic principle is that all states should apply similar minimum standards of intellectual protection. In practice, this has the effect of extending the application of intellectual property rights standards already in use in most OECD countries to all WTO member states and thus imposes a significant burden of adjustment on developing country member states. In particular, it provides that patents must be available for inventions, whether products or processes, in all fields of technology.[25] Some general exceptions are granted and states can, for instance, exclude from patentability plants and animals other than micro-organisms.[26]

The question of plant variety protection is the object of a separate provision framed as an exception to the general rule of Article 27.1. It provides that all member states 'shall provide for the protection of plant varieties either by patents or by an effective *sui generis* system or by any combination thereof'.[27] This reflects the continuing debates concerning the appropriateness of imposing patents on plant varieties and constitutes one of relatively few cases in TRIPS where protection is required but not necessarily through patents.[28] In other words, all states must introduce some form of intellectual property protection but are given a certain margin of appreciation to implement this obligation. The significance of this provision is that in the case of plant variety protection, member states which do not wish to introduce patent rights have the choice to provide an alternative protection regime. In effect, Article 27.3.b is a differential provision. This is linked to the fact that while most OECD countries had already introduced either patents or plant breeders' rights before 1994, this was not the case of most developing countries for whom this constitutes a novelty imposed by the WTO. Article 27.3.b, by authorizing developing countries to adopt a *sui generis* system instead of a specified internationally recognized system, thus acknowledges that developing countries which had not introduced any form of plant variety protection until 1994 may need to evolve their own model of protection, suited to their development policies.

---

25   Article 27.1 of the TRIPS Agreement, supra note 1.
26   Article 27.2-3 of the TRIPS Agreement, supra note 1.
27   Article 27.3.b of the TRIPS Agreement, supra note 1.
28   Cf. Susan H. Bragdon and David R. Downes, *Recent Policy Trends and Developments Related to the Conservation, Use and Development of Genetic Resources* (Rome: International Plant Genetic Resources Institute, 1998).

The UPOV Convention The UPOV Convention was first signed in 1961 to provide a form of legal protection of plant varieties for western European countries. It seeks to protect new varieties of plants both in the interest of agricultural development and of plant breeders. Though it did not introduce patents, UPOV sought from the outset to provide incentives to the private sector to engage in commercial plant breeding by introducing so-called Plant Breeders' Rights (PBRs). Despite the distinction between patents and PBRs, the two share several basic characteristics: they provide exclusive commercial rights to holders, reward an inventive process, and are granted for a limited period of time after which they pass into the public domain.

More specifically, UPOV recognizes the exclusive rights of individual plant breeders to produce or reproduce protected varieties, to condition them for the purpose of propagation, to offer them for sale, to commercialize them, including exporting and importing them, and to stock them in view of production or commercialization.[29] Protection under UPOV is granted for developed or discovered plant varieties which are new, distinct, uniform and stable.[30] The concept of novelty under UPOV is noteworthy because it differs from the approach taken under patent law. Under UPOV, a variety is novel if it has not been sold or otherwise disposed of for purposes of exploitation of the variety. Novelty is thus defined in relation to commercialization and not by the fact that the variety did not previously exist. UPOV gives a specific time frame for the application of novelty. To be novel, a variety must not have been commercialized in the country where the application is filed for more than a year before the application and in other member countries for more than 4 years.[31] The criterion of distinctness requires that the protected variety should be clearly distinguishable from any other variety whose existence is a matter of common knowledge at the time of the filing of the application. Stability is obtained if the variety remains true to its description after repeated reproduction or propagation. Finally, uniformity implies that the variety remains true to the original in its relevant characteristics when propagated.

The latest revision of the Convention adopted in 1991 has further strengthened PBRs. It extends, for instance, breeders' rights to all production and reproduction of their varieties and to species as well as general and specific plant varieties. This now also includes so-called 'essentially derived varieties'.[32] Protection of an essentially derived variety is obtained if the variety is predominantly derived from the initial variety and retains its essential characteristics. It must also be clearly distinguishable from the initial variety while confirming to the initial variety in the expression of the essential characteristics.

---

29   Article 14.1 of UPOV-1991, supra note 22.
30   Article 5 of UPOV-1991, supra note 22.
31   Article 6 of UPOV-1991, supra note 22. In the case of other member countries, the relevant timeline is six years for trees and vines.
32   Article 14.5 of UPOV-1991, supra note 22.

One of the main distinguishing features of the original UPOV regime is that the recognition of PBRs is circumscribed by two main exceptions. Firstly, under the 1978 version of the Convention, the so-called 'farmer's privilege' allows farmers to re-use propagating material from the previous year's harvest and to freely exchange seeds of protected varieties with other farmers. Secondly, PBRs do not extend to acts done privately and for non-commercial purposes or for experimental purposes and do not extend to the use of the protected variety for the purpose of breeding other varieties and the right to commercialize such other varieties. The 1991 version of the Convention by strengthening PBRs has conversely limited existing exceptions. The remaining exceptions include acts done privately and for non-commercial purposes, experiments, and for the breeding and exploitation of other varieties. Breeders are now granted exclusive rights to harvested materials and the distinction between discovery and development of varieties has been eliminated.[33] Further, the right to save seed is no longer guaranteed as the farmer's privilege has been made optional.

As noted, PBRs were first conceived as an alternative to patent rights. As a result, UPOV originally provided that the two kinds of intellectual property rights should be kept separate. Under UPOV-1978, member states can, for instance, only offer protection through one form of intellectual property rights. The grant of a PBR on a given variety implies that no other intellectual property right can be granted to the same variety. This restriction has been eliminated under UPOV-1991 and double protection is now allowed.

The UPOV Convention was first negotiated and ratified mostly by developed countries. It is only since the adoption of the TRIPS Agreement that more developing countries have progressively joined the Convention.[34] Even though developing countries did not participate in the development of this legal regime which is designed for the conditions and needs of the North, the rationale for joining it is that the UPOV regime is generally held to fulfil the conditions of a *sui generis* system as required under the TRIPS Agreement.[35]

The International Treaty on Plant Genetic Resources for Food and Agriculture
The International Treaty on Plant Genetic Resources for Food and Agriculture (PGRFA Treaty) is a multi-faceted treaty generally addressing the conservation and

---

33   Gurdial Singh Nijar and Chee Yoke Ling, 'The Implications of the Intellectual Property Rights Regime of the Convention on Biological Diversity and GATT on Biodiversity Conservation: A Third World Perspective', in Anatole F. Krattiger et al. eds, *Widening Perspectives on Biodiversity* 277 (Geneva: International Academy of the Environment, 1994).

34   Overall, as of July 2002, out of 51 member states, there were 16 developing country members, an overwhelming majority of them Latin American countries, with only four developing country members altogether from Africa and Asia.

35   WTO, Review of Article 27.3(b): The View of Switzerland, WTO Doc. IP/C/W/284 (2001).

use of plant genetic resources for food and agriculture.[36] Even though it deals with plant genetic resources and not plant varieties, it is particularly important in the context of plant variety protection because it is the only binding international instrument which directly addresses the question of farmers' rights and because it provides a specific benefit-sharing regime.

The PGRFA Treaty must be read together with the instrument that preceded it, the International Undertaking on Plant Genetic Resources (Undertaking). This instrument, adopted in the form of a non-binding resolution of the FAO Conference in 1983 sought to ensure the conservation and availability of plant genetic resources for plant breeding and scientific purposes.[37] While both instruments can be said to have generally similar objectives, the Undertaking was based on a philosophy which is more or less opposed to the PGRFA Treaty. Where the latter is firmly based on the principle of states' sovereign rights over the plant genetic resources, the guiding principle of the former was that plant genetic resources are a heritage of humankind available to all without restriction.[38] The Undertaking's position constituted an important policy statement at the time when genetic engineering was just beginning to develop since free availability was meant to include not only traditional cultivars, wild species or accessions found in CGIAR gene banks but also varieties developed by scientists in the North. As a result, some developed countries could not adhere to the Undertaking and within a few years, interpretative resolutions were passed by the Conference of the FAO.[39] These resolutions affirmed the sovereign rights of countries over their plant genetic resources and qualified the principle of free availability by recognizing plant breeders' rights and farmers' rights. The adoption of the Biodiversity Convention provided one further impetus to rethink the instrument in its entirety.[40]

The PGRFA Treaty as adopted reflects this convoluted genesis.[41] At its core, the Treaty addresses a limited number of issues pertaining to plant genetic

---

[36]   International Treaty on Plant Genetic Resources for Food and Agriculture, Rome, 3 Nov. 2001 [hereafter PGRFA Treaty].
[37]   Article 1 of the International Undertaking, supra note 24.
[38]   Preamble of the PGRFA Treaty, supra note 36 and article 1 of the International Undertaking, supra note 24.
[39]   Agreed Interpretation of the International Undertaking, Res. 4/89, Report of the Conference of the FAO, 25th Session, Rome, 29 Nov. 1989, Doc. C89/REP and Annex 3 to the International Undertaking on Plant Genetic Resources, Res. 3/91, Report of the Conference of the FAO, 26th Session, Rome, 25 Nov. 1991, Doc. C91/REP.
[40]   Preamble to Resolution 7/93, Revision of the International Undertaking on Plant Genetic Resources, Report of the Conference of FAO, 27th Sess., Rome 6-24 Nov. 1993, Doc. C93/REP, emphasizing the need to revise the Undertaking in harmony with the Biodiversity Convention.
[41]   See generally Kerry ten Kate and Carolina Lasén Diaz, 'The Undertaking Revisited – A Commentary on the Revision of the International Undertaking on Plant Genetic Resources for Food and Agriculture', 6 *Rev. Eur. Community and Int'l Envtl. L.* 284

resources conservation and use. In other words, the Treaty focuses on issues not addressed in other international treaties such as farmers' rights but it does not address directly patents or plant breeders' rights covered in the TRIPS Agreement and the UPOV Convention respectively.[42] From the point of view of plant variety protection, the PGRFA Treaty has a number of significant characteristics. Firstly, it is the first treaty providing a legal framework which not only recognizes the need for conservation and sustainable use of plant genetic resources for food and agriculture but also delineates a regime for access and benefit sharing,[43] and in this process provides direct and indirect links to intellectual property rights instruments. Secondly, it directly links plant genetic resource conservation, intellectual property rights, sustainable agriculture and food security. This is a novel approach in international law which could potentially have significant repercussions if applied to the management of all plant genetic resources for food and agriculture. Thirdly, the element which remains the distinguishing feature of the PGRFA Treaty in the field of plant variety protection is its focus on farmers' rights. In fact, the term farmers' rights is slightly misleading. The PGRFA Treaty gives recognition to farmers' contribution to conserving and enhancing plant genetic resources for food and agriculture. It further gives broad guidelines to states concerning the scope of the rights to be protected under this heading. This includes the protection of traditional knowledge, farmers' entitlement to a part of benefit-sharing arrangements and the right to participate in decision-making regarding the management of plant genetic resources. However, the treaty is silent with regard to farmers' rights over their landraces. In fact, the 'recognition' of farmers' contribution to plant genetic resource conservation and enhancement does not include any property rights. In this context, the only rights that are recognized are the residual rights to save, use, exchange and sell farm-saved seeds.

An important consequence of the Treaty is that guidance concerning the management of CGIAR collections will in the future come from the Treaty's Governing Body.[44] This is significant because the CGIAR has historically worked on the basis of the sharing of resources and knowledge, following in this respect the principle of common heritage of humankind embodied in the 1983 Undertaking. In recent years, following the adoption of the TRIPS Agreement in particular, the CGIAR has progressively modified its position with regard to the grant of intellectual property rights.[45] New guiding principles on intellectual property were adopted to harmonize CGIAR's core principle that designated germplasm is held in trust for the world community with the recognition of various forms of property

---

(1997) and H. David Cooper, 'The International Treaty on Plant Genetic Resources for Food and Agriculture', 11 *Rev. Eur. Community and Int'l Envtl. L.* 1 (2002).

[42]   On the relationship between the Treaty and intellectual property rights instruments, article 12.3.f of the PGRFA Treaty, supra note 36.

[43]   On access and benefit sharing, see infra at p. 158.

[44]   Article 15 of the PGRFA Treaty, supra note 36.

[45]   CGIAR, Progress Report on IPR Matters and Proposal for Review of Plant Breeding, Mid-Term Meeting, 1999, Beijing, CGIAR Doc. MTM/99/20.

rights, including sovereign rights, farmers' rights and private rights.[46] In principle, the IARCs do not apply intellectual property protection to their designated germplasm and require recipients to observe the same conditions. They also refrain from asserting intellectual property rights over the products of their research. An exception to this rule is made in case the assertion of intellectual property rights facilitates technology transfer or otherwise protects developing countries' interests. The CGIAR also requires that any intellectual property rights on the IARCs' output should be assigned to the Centre and not an individual. While the guiding principles generally seek to contain the monopoly elements of intellectual property rights such as patents, plant breeders' rights are specifically welcomed. Recipients of germplasm can apply for plant breeders' rights as long as this does not prevent others from using the original materials in their own breeding programmes.

The Convention on Biological Diversity The Biodiversity Convention is not as closely focused on plant variety protection as the other treaties discussed above but it is nevertheless of great importance in this field for two main reasons. Firstly, it is the main international legal instrument delimiting the rights of states and other relevant actors over biological resources. Secondly, it provides a broad framework for understanding links between biodiversity management and intellectual property rights over biotechnology inventions and the Conference of the Parties has progressively developed the lineaments of an access and benefit-sharing regime.

Generally, the Convention affirms the sovereign rights of states to exploit their resources pursuant to their own environmental policies.[47] This includes the authority to determine access to genetic resources found within their boundaries, with a duty to facilitate access to those resources for environmentally sound uses by other contracting parties. These sovereign rights are limited by states' responsibility to ensure that activities within their jurisdiction do not cause damage to the environment. More generally, the sovereign rights of states over their biological resources are limited by the recognition that these resources are a common concern of humankind.

The Convention also recognizes the rights of other actors. In the context of biodiversity-related technologies, it thus emphasizes the importance of the private sector and of intellectual property rights. It delineates both the duties of the private sector with regard to access, development and transfer of technologies and the necessity for all parties to recognize and protect intellectual property rights in this field. The Convention's attempt to provide an acceptable framework concerning the relationship between its objectives and intellectual property rights proved to be one

---

46   CGIAR, CGIAR Center Statements on Genetic Resources, Intellectual Property Rights, and Biotechnology (Washington, DC: CGIAR, 1999). Individual IARCs have also adopted intellectual property rights policies. International Maize and Wheat Improvement Center, Policy on Intellectual Property (2000).

47   Article 3 of the of the Convention on Biological Diversity, Rio de Janeiro, 5 June 1992, reprinted in 31 *ILM* 818 (1992) [hereafter Biodiversity Convention].

of the stumbling blocks during the negotiations and constituted one of the areas which caused the United States to strongly object to the final text of the treaty.[48]

The Convention also alludes to the contribution of local people and local communities in the sustainable management of biological resources. It does not, however, speak of their rights but mainly of the need for member states to preserve their knowledge and practices and to promote the application of such knowledge with the consent of the holders while providing for an equitable sharing of the benefits arising from the use of such knowledge.

Sui generis *plant variety protection*   The question of *sui generis* plant variety protection has become an issue of international significance in the context of article 27.3.b of the TRIPS Agreement. There remains significant uncertainty as to the exact margin of appreciation that developing countries have in implementing this provision since the only criterion expressed by the TRIPS Agreement is that *sui generis* systems must be 'effective'. The reason for the introduction of an undefined term in the Agreement is due to the fact that a number of countries in the North and the South rejected the compulsory introduction of plant patents and that negotiators did not manage to agree on one specific alternative to patents.[49] As a result, TRIPS gives member states a wide margin of appreciation in determining how to implement their obligation to introduce plant variety protection.

As noted, the question of the introduction of plant variety protection is one that concerns mostly developing countries. In fact, most developed countries had already introduced either plant patents or plant breeders' rights before the adoption of TRIPS. Developing countries that are members of the WTO were left with the choice of either adopting the existing regime proposed in UPOV or devising their own plant variety protection system adapted to their specific situation. A few countries have joined UPOV since 1994 but the majority has decided to adopt their own plant variety protection laws. In a number of cases, these laws draw directly and significantly from the UPOV regime and generally most existing proposals introduce plant breeders' rights. In cases where plant breeders' rights are adopted only as part of the regime, the regime is completed by the introduction of a form of farmers' rights. In fact, existing *sui generis* options can be generally defined as regimes introducing both plant breeders' rights and farmers' rights.

The prominence of the UPOV Convention in the debates concerning sui generis plant variety protection is in part linked to the fact that the interpretation of the concept of 'effective' sui generis system in Article 27.3.b TRIPS remains problematic. The only generally agreed upon interpretation is that UPOV is an

---

[48]   Declaration of the United States of America Made at the Time of Adoption of the Agreed Text of the Convention on Biological Diversity, 22 May 1992.

[49]   On the negotiating positions in this area, GATT – Negotiating Group on Trade-Related Aspects of Intellectual Property Rights, including Trade in Counterfeit Goods, Meeting of Negotiating Group of 30 October-2 November 1989, Doc. MTN.GNG/NG11/16.

effective *sui generis* protection regime under TRIPS. This has led some countries like the member states of the African Intellectual Property Organization to simply adopt a regime modelled after UPOV-1991 while simultaneously committing themselves to join the UPOV Convention.[50]

While a number of countries have attempted to draw up their own sui generis plant variety protection regimes, African states have taken a unique initiative in adopting a Model Legislation for the Protection of the Rights of Local Communities, Farmers and Breeders, and for the Regulation of Access to Biological Resources.[51] The model legislation is premised on the rejection of patents on life or the exclusive appropriation of any life form, including derivatives. Its provisions on access to biological resources make it clear that the recipients of biological resources or related knowledge cannot apply for any intellectual property right of exclusionary nature. The model legislation focuses mainly on the definition of the rights of communities, farmers and breeders. Community rights that are recognized include rights over their biological resources and the right to collectively benefit from their use, rights to their innovations, practices, knowledge and technology and the right to collectively benefit from their utilization. In practice, communities have the right to prohibit access to their resources and knowledge but only in cases where access would be detrimental to the integrity of their natural or cultural heritage. Further, the state is to ensure that at least 50 per cent of the benefits derived from the utilization of their resources or knowledge is channelled back to the communities. The rights of farmers are slightly more precisely defined. These include the protection of their traditional knowledge relevant to plant and animal genetic resources, the right to an equitable share of benefits arising from the use of plant and animal genetic resources, the right to participate in decision making on matters related to the conservation and sustainable use of plant and animal genetic resources, the right to save, use, exchange and sell farm-saved seed or propagating material, and the right to use a commercial breeder's variety to develop other varieties. Breeders' rights defined under the model legislation generally follow the definition given in the UPOV convention and the duration of the rights, is for instance, modelled after UPOV 1991. One feature of the plant breeders' rights regime under the model legislation is the rather broad scope of the exemptions granted. Exemptions to the rights of breeders include the right to use a protected variety for purposes other than commerce, the right to sell plant or propagating material as food, the right to sell within the place where the variety is grown and the use of the variety as an initial source of variation for developing another variety.

---

[50]   Agreement to Revise the Bangui Agreement on the Creation of an African Intellectual Property Organization of 2 March 1977, Bangui, 24 Feb. 1999.

[51]   African Model Legislation for the Protection of the Rights of Local Communities, Farmers and Breeders, and for the Regulation of Access to Biological Resources (2000).

The development of sui generis plant variety protection is still in its infancy. Until now, efforts have been made by developing countries to balance their obligations under Article 27.3.b of TRIPS with their specific needs and conditions. Since UPOV is the only model which is generally recognized as fulfilling the criteria of an 'effective' sui generis plant variety protection regime, a number of states that have not had the time, resources or inclination to devise a completely separate *sui generis* protection regime have decided to take plant breeders' rights as a basis for a plant variety protection regime. In addition to the PBR system, there seems to be a growing trend towards recognizing farmers' rights alongside the provision of different compensation mechanisms (benefit-sharing).

Plant Variety Protection in Practice: The Case of India

India is an interesting case study for a number of reasons. Firstly, while patents were introduced in India long before independence, patent law was overhauled in the decades following independence in an attempt to make it fit the developmental priorities of the country.[52] The resulting Patents Act, 1970 thus provided a number of exceptions to the western model of intellectual property in order to foster the fulfilment of basic needs. Secondly, there have been significant public debates in India at every stage of the development of the new international intellectual property rights framework embodied in the TRIPS Agreement and its implementation. Thirdly, the Indian government's efforts to implement its TRIPS Agreement obligations have been supplemented by proposals from diverse individuals and groups taking an active interest in law and policy-making in this field.

The Patents Act, 1970 provides a starting point to understand the current legal regime. This Act was the result of a long period of deliberation in post-independence India on the need to reform the 1911 Patents and Designs Act inherited from colonization, which was thought inappropriate because it had failed to stimulate invention by Indians and to encourage the development and exploitation of new inventions for industrial purposes in the country so as to secure benefits to the largest section of the people.[53] The resulting Act as adopted in 1970 recognized the basic principles of patent law but also sought to contain and discipline it.[54] The scope of patentability under the Act was particularly noteworthy. The Act excluded the patentability of life forms and specifically precluded the

---

[52]   See generally Justice N. Rajagopala Ayyangar, Report on the Revision of the Patents Law (September 1959).

[53]   Rajeev Dhavan et al. 'Power Without Responsibility on Aspects of the Indian Patents Legislation', 33 *J. Indian L. Institute* 1 (1991).

[54]   Rajeev Dhavan and Maya Prabhu, 'Patent Monopolies and Free Trade: Basic Contradiction in Dunkel Draft', 37 *J. Indian L. Institute* 194 (1995).

patentability of methods of agriculture or horticulture.[55] Further, while allowing process patents on substances intended for use as food, medicine or drug, the Act rejected the possibility of granting patents in respect of the substances themselves.[56] Insofar as the duration of the rights conferred is concerned, the normal 14-year term was reduced to 7 years with respect to processes of manufacture for substances intended for use as food, medicine or drug.[57] The Patents Act, 1970 also introduced a series of measures restricting the rights of patent holders, in particular to encourage use of the invention in India.[58] The rationale for the introduction of limiting clauses in the Act was in part to foster the growth of local industries and in part to foster the availability of essential items such as food and medicine by keeping the prices as low as possible in areas related to the fulfilment of basic needs.[59]

The TRIPS Agreement adopts a different philosophy which generally makes it more difficult for countries to provide the kind of exceptions to patentability adopted by the Patents Act, 1970. In fact, the TRIPS Agreement has been the trigger for a fundamental reform of the 1970 Act. This included a series of changes to the Act and the adoption of a new act concerning the protection of plant varieties. Further, the Biodiversity Act which seeks to implement the Biodiversity Convention is also relevant here as it addresses several intellectual property rights related issues. These three legislative developments are examined in turn.

The Protection of Plant Varieties and Farmers' Rights Act

Historically, the protection of plant varieties through intellectual property rights was disallowed in India, as reflected in the Patents Act, 1970. The introduction of plant variety protection thus constitutes a step in a completely different direction. As noted, TRIPS imposes the introduction of plant variety protection but leaves member states to choose the specific form of protection they want to adopt (*sui generis* option). It does not privilege plant breeders' rights (or in other words, the UPOV Convention) over alternatives such as farmers' rights.

---

[55] Section 3 of the Patents Act, 1970, Act 39 of 1970. [hereafter, reference to the Patents Act, 1970 indicates a reference to the Act as it was until the adoption of the 2002 amendments]. See also, C.S. Srinivasan, 'Current Status of Plant Variety Protection in India', in M.S. Swaminathan ed., *Agrobiodiversity and Farmers' Rights* 77 (Delhi: Konark, 1996).

[56] Section 5 of the Patents Act, 1970, supra note 55. Under the 1970 Act, drugs included insecticides, germicides, fungicides, weedicides and herbicides and all other substance intended to be used for the protection or preservation of plants. Section 2 of the Patents Act, 1970, supra note 55.

[57] Section 53 of the Patents Act, 1970, supra note 55.

[58] Chapter XVI of the Patents Act, 1970, supra note 55 concerning compulsory licences and licences of right.

[59] Sahai, supra note 17 at 1495.

The Indian legislation was first introduced in Parliament in December 1999, just before the TRIPS Agreement's compliance deadline. The main characteristic of the first draft was to propose a plant variety protection model largely fashioned after the UPOV Convention even though India officially sought to propose an alternative framework. This first draft was referred to a Parliamentary Committee which conducted further hearings in 2000 and put forward a substantially revised Bill.[60] This second draft was adopted by Parliament in 2001 and is now known as the Protection of Plant Varieties and Farmers' Rights Act (Plant Variety Act).[61]

Generally, the Act differs from the first draft of the Bill insofar as it clearly seeks to establish both plant breeders' rights and farmers' rights. The proposed regime for plant breeders' rights largely follows the model provided by the UPOV Convention. It introduces rights which are meant to provide incentives for the further development of a commercial seed industry in the country. The criteria for registration are thus the same as those found in UPOV, namely novelty, distinctiveness, uniformity and stability.[62] The Act incorporates a number of elements from the 1978 version of UPOV and also includes some elements of the much more stringent 1991 version, like the possibility of registering essentially derived varieties. The section on farmers' rights constitutes the most interesting part of the legislation from the point of view of the development of *sui generis* regimes. This part was completely changed by the Parliamentary Committee which added a whole chapter on farmers' rights where the first draft dealt with the issue in a single short provision.[63] The Act now seeks to put farmers' rights on a par with breeders' rights. It provides, for instance, that farmers are entitled, like commercial breeders, to apply to have a variety registered.[64] Farmers are generally to be treated like commercial breeders and are to receive the same kind of protection for the varieties they develop. However, it is unsure whether these provisions will have a significant impact in practice since the Act accepts the registration criteria of the UPOV Convention which cannot easily be used for the registration of farmers' varieties.

The Act further seeks to foster benefit sharing in the interest of farmers in cases where registered plant varieties are commercialized. Two different channels for claiming financial compensation are provided for under Section 26 and Section 41. The main difference between the two is that Section 41 specifically targets village communities and provides less stringent procedural conditions. Thus, it neither provides a time frame nor specifies that claimants should pay a fee. In both cases, it

60 Joint Committee on the Protection of Plant Varieties and Farmers' Rights Bill, 1999, Report of the Joint Committee (2000).
61 Protection of Plant Varieties and Farmers' Rights Act, 2001, Act No. 53 of 2001 [hereafter PPVFR Act].
62 Section 15.1 of the PPVFR Act, supra note 61.
63 The Committee specifically indicated that it felt the first bill had very inadequate provisions for protecting the interests of farmers. Joint Committee, supra note 60 at p.x.
64 Section 16.1.d of the PPVFR Act, supra note 61.

is significant that the Plant Varieties and Farmers' Rights Authority has significant discretion in disposing of the benefit sharing claims. Interestingly, Section 41 comes closer to recognizing the intellectual contribution of the benefit claimers than Section 26. The former provides that claims can be made concerning the contribution to the evolution of a variety by a group while the latter only mentions the use of genetic material from the claimant variety as a basis for a claim. Further, while Section 26 requires the commercial utility and the demand for the variety in the market to be taken into account in the assessment of the claims, there is no such requirement under Section 41. The last major distinction is that Section 41 only provides for compensation to a community of individuals whereas a single person may benefit under Section 26. Overall, the existence of two partly overlapping, partly different regimes for benefit sharing is likely to be the cause of much confusion on the part of benefit-claimers and is unlikely to foster their claims for compensation.

Overall, the Act is noteworthy for making a real attempt at balancing breeders' and farmers' rights. However, two main facts are likely to hamper the effectiveness of the provisions for farmers' rights. Firstly, since farmers' rights were only added as an afterthought without changing the criteria for registration of varieties, the existing regime exclusively reflects the registration needs of commercial breeders and is therefore heavily tilted against farmers. Secondly, even though India intended to provide a *sui generis* response to the need to provide plant variety protection under the TRIPS Agreement, it is now in the process of formally joining UPOV, a move which will tilt the balance further away from farmers.[65]

The Patents (Amendment) Act, 2002 and the Biodiversity Act, 2002

As noted, the TRIPS Agreement imposed on India the obligation to substantially modify its patent law. The introduction of a plant variety protection act constituted only one specific element of a wider series of required changes. Other amendments are not strictly related to plant variety protection, for which patents are not allowed in India, however it is difficult to completely separate plant variety protection from patents on microorganisms or, more generally, patents in the field of genetic engineering, which are mandated by TRIPS.

Fulfilling TRIPS obligations has resulted in the dismantling of most of the specificities that were introduced by the 1970 Act in view of the explicit recommendations concerning the working of the earlier colonial patent act.[66] Among the major changes required is an increase in the general patent term from 14 years to 20 years, and from 7 years to 20 years in the case of process patents on food and drugs. Certain control mechanisms restricting the scope of the rights

---

[65]   Anonymous, 'India to Accede to Plants Convention', *The Hindu,* 1 June 2002, available at www.hindu.com.
[66]   Patents Act, 1970 as amended by the Patents (Amendment) Act, 2002 [hereafter Patents Act, 1970/2002].

granted to patent holders such as the existence of licences of right, and more specifically automatic licences of right in the case of process patents relating to substances used as food, have been removed from the Act.[67]

The general consequence of the 2002 amendments in the field of biotechnology will be to promote the development of genetic engineering in the private sector. The Amendment Act takes into account some of the concerns that have been voiced in recent times, in particular with regard to 'biopiracy' or the unwarranted use of traditional knowledge. The Act now obliges inventors to disclose the geographical origin of any biological material used in an invention. Further, there is a specific exclusion on patents that are anticipated in traditional knowledge.[68]

The Biodiversity Act follows on with some more specific provisions concerning intellectual property and benefit sharing. In general, it constitutes a direct response to India's ratification of the Biodiversity Convention in 1994. In fact, the Act does not provide a comprehensive legal regime for the conservation and sustainable use of biological resources but rather focuses on questions of access to biological resources and is in large part indirectly influenced by the TRIPS Agreement.

The core substantive part of the Act focuses on re-asserting India's sovereign rights over its biological resources and their use.[69] The Act also addresses the question of intellectual property rights over inventions based on biological resources found in India. Its position with respect to intellectual property rights is quite ambivalent. Implicitly, it takes the position that India cannot do more than regulating access by foreigners to its knowledge base. It, however, attempts to discipline the intellectual property rights system in some respects. It requires inventors who want to apply for intellectual property rights to seek the National Biodiversity Authority's permission.[70] It also authorizes the Authority to allocate a monopoly right to more than one actor. Further the Authority is entitled to oppose the grant of intellectual property rights outside India.[71]

The Act also seeks to address the question of the rights of holders of local knowledge by setting up a system of benefit sharing. The benefit sharing scheme is innovative insofar as it provides that the Authority can decide to grant joint ownership of a monopoly intellectual right to the inventor and the Authority or the actual contributors if they can be identified.[72] However, the sharing of intellectual property rights is only one of the various avenues that the Authority can choose to give effect to benefit sharing. It is also in the Authority's power to allocate

---

[67] On licences of right, sections 86-88 of the Patents Act, 1970, supra note 55.
[68] Note however that these two provisions only constitute grounds for opposing the grant of a patent or for revocation of a patent. Sections 25.1.j and k and 64.1 p and q of the Patents Act, 1970/2002, supra note 66.
[69] Chapter II of the Biological Diversity Act, 2002.
[70] Section 6 of the Biological Diversity Act, 2002. Note however, that an application for a plant breeder's or farmer's right is not covered by this provision. Section 6.3 of the Biological Diversity Act, 2002.
[71] Section 18.4 of the Biological Diversity Act, 2002.
[72] Section 21.2.a of the Biological Diversity Act, 2002.

intellectual property rights to itself or to a contributor, such as a farmer contributor, where the latter has no right to demand the allocation of property rights. The other forms of benefit sharing are also noteworthy insofar as the Act prioritizes non-financial benefits such as transfer of technology which are more long lasting than financial compensation.[73]

On the whole, the Act provides a property rights framework which seeks to be very firm on the question of access to bioresources for outsiders even though the practical impacts of this stand will be limited because the law cannot be applied extraterritorially. The Act effectively condones the introduction of intellectual property rights in the management of biological resources provided for in the TRIPS Agreement but does not directly seek to ensure that intellectual property rights are supportive of the goals of the Biodiversity Convention.[74]

Alternative Proposals

Controversies surrounding the ratification of the TRIPS Agreement by India ensured that a number of researchers and organizations got directly involved in the search for ways to make the most of the new situation brought about by the creation of the WTO. Alternative proposals in the field of plant variety protection centred mainly around ways to adapt to the new system and to fight the system from within.

Firstly, proposals have been made to alter the patent system so that it recognizes the informal and communal system of innovation which characterize the way farmers and indigenous communities produce, select and breed diverse crops and livestock varieties.[75] In practice, this implies the recognition of collective intellectual property rights. These proposals do not question the patents system itself but seek to broaden its scope to new actors. The rationale for doing so is to stop conventional patentees such as multinational companies from acquiring monopoly rights on inventions realized partly by others. One such proposal was the privately proposed Biodiversity (Rights and Protection) Bill, 1998 which recommended the establishment of biodiversity-related community intellectual rights.[76] It proposed the exclusion of current holders of monopoly rights and the allocation of similar monopoly rights to local communities. It, therefore, sought to 'recognize the more informal, communal system of innovation through which Southern farmers and indigenous communities produce, select, improve and breed a diversity of crop and livestock varieties'.[77] Under this proposal, local communities would be granted collective intellectual property rights to their knowledge but they

---

73   Section 21.2 of the Biological Diversity Act, 2002.
74   As directed in Article 16 of the Biodiversity Convention, supra note 47.
75   Vandana Shiva, *Future of our Seeds, Future of our Farmers – Agricultural Biodiversity, Intellectual Property Rights and Farmers' Rights* (New Delhi: Research Foundation for Science, Technology and Natural Resource Policy, 1996).
76   Biodiversity (Rights and Protection) Bill, 1998 (New Delhi: Research Foundation for Science, Technology and Ecology and Lawyers Collective, 1998).
77   Shiva, supra note 75 at 29.

share their property rights with the Indian government.[78] This is meant to prevent piracy of genetic material to ensure just returns for allowing access to biological resources, and by having state sovereignty backed by people's sovereignty, to strengthen the countries' negotiating capacity. Article 18 thus tries to prevent direct negotiations between a major company and a local community by giving a role to the Indian government in any negotiations pertaining to the exploitation of knowledge of a biological resource.

Secondly, a number of individuals, villages and institutions have organized the process of documenting biological resources and traditional knowledge related to these resources. The rationale for creating biodiversity registers is generally to document existing knowledge to stop patent claims from being accepted in other jurisdictions because of a lack of written description and to levy charges on bioprospecting or royalties on the commercial use of the materials or knowledge. Registers gained prominence after it became public that applications for patents based on biodiversity-related traditional knowledge were being filed abroad.[79] Most registers focus on documentation to stop patent applications and make the knowledge available to researchers everywhere. One noteworthy exception to this trend is the biodiversity register of Pattuvam village in Kerala. The People's Biodiversity Declaration which accompanies the register asserts that no monopoly claims on life forms will be accepted by people living in this area. It also provides the conditions under which experiments on life forms collected from the village territory can be undertaken.[80] The register and its accompanying declaration are thus used not only as a defensive mechanism but also to assert local people's rights over resources found in their territory and the knowledge concerning the management of these resources. Interestingly, this register is generally secret and information sharing is only allowed in exceptional cases. The purpose of the register is not to foster the commercial exploitation of local resources by outsiders but rather to assert property rights and provide a written proof of traditional knowledge to circumvent property rights claims over existing knowledge by outsiders.

Plant Variety Protection and Differential Treatment

The issue of plant variety protection is multi-faceted and can be analyzed from various angles. This section focuses on the differential aspects of intellectual

---

78   Under the assumption that the Government is co-owner of biological resources together with the 'people of India'. Article 6 of the Biodiversity (Rights and Protection) Bill, 1998, supra note 76.

79   US Patent No. 5,401,504, *Use of Turmeric in Wound Healing*, issued 28 Mar. 1995 (after reexamination, expiring 28 March 1999) which claimed an invention related to the use of turmeric to augment the healing process of chronic and acute wounds.

80   This description is based on an English translation of the original Malayalam text by Mohan Kumar.

property law in general and more specifically on that of plant variety protection. It examines some general issues relating to differentiation in fields where intellectual property relates to basic needs. It further examines the specific question of access and benefit sharing and provides some general considerations for the further development of alternative property rights regimes that would be more differential in effect.

Intellectual Property, Differential Treatment and Article 27.3.b TRIPS

The issue of differential treatment in the field of intellectual property is a good example of the significant linkages that can exist between international and domestic law, as well as the impact of inter-state agreements on non-state actors. At the international level, intellectual property gives rise to differential treatment concerns similar to those articulated through international environmental law, including a similar focus on technology transfer. Other concerns are linked to the fact that intellectual property law is specifically interested in the promotion of the private sector which becomes a central actor in this field. Further, in the field of agricultural biotechnology, there is a direct link between differentiation at the international level and the use of foodstuffs directly or indirectly protected by intellectual property rights. In this way, intellectual property has direct links with the realization of basic food needs or in other words the human right to food.

Differential treatment relating to international intellectual property has been a long-standing concern, particularly in the context of the role of patents in fostering the diffusion of technologies in developing countries. These concerns crystallized during the promotion of the NIEO with called for changes in the patent system. A study by UNCTAD in the mid-1970s indicated that the distribution of patents between developed and developing countries had not changed significantly between 1920 and 1970.[81] Further, of the 6 per cent share of patents held by developing countries, five sixths were held by foreigners, 90 per cent of which were not used at all in production processes in these countries.[82] UNCTAD reached the conclusion that the application of the patent system in its present form had 'come to act as a reverse system of preferences granted to foreign patent holders in the market of developing countries' and should be reformed to allow it to effectively contribute to national development policies of developing countries.[83] The reform of the patent system called for by UNCTAD never took place. Moreover, the international patent system has been significantly strengthened with the adoption of the TRIPS Agreement. It is, therefore, not surprising that concerns similar to those raised in the 1970s still surface with regard to the effectiveness of provisions regarding technology transfer to developing countries. Thus, the UN Committee on

---

[81]   UNCTAD, The Role of the Patent System in the Transfer of Technology to Developing Countries, UN Doc. TD/B/AC.11/19/Rev.1 (1975).

[82]   UNCTAD, supra note 81 at 63.

[83]   UNCTAD, supra note 81 at 64.

Economic, Social and Cultural Rights clearly states that the North has a duty to develop international intellectual property regimes that enable developing states to fulfil at least the core obligations they owe to individuals and groups within their jurisdictions.[84] This has now been echoed in the WTO Doha Declaration on health which, though not proposing any change in the TRIPS Agreement, has recognized the need for flexible implementation in situations of epidemics to foster better access to drugs.[85]

Returning to the TRIPS Agreement, the central provisions of the treaty do not provide for a system which includes differential treatment. Notable exceptions include the provision of grace periods for developing and least developed countries.[86] These grace periods notwithstanding, substantive standards are on the whole the same for all countries. The plant variety protection provision constitutes one of the few exceptions where states can choose different levels of intellectual property protection according to their needs. On the surface, Article 27.3.b of the TRIPS Agreement is an unremarkable provision which simply provides a special regime for the protection of plant varieties. However, it has much wider significance of the specific context in which the WTO operates. It is clearly differential in effect because the beneficiaries are the overwhelming majority of developing country member states, which had not introduced plant variety protection before 1994.

The implementation of Article 27.3.b tells a different story from what earlier chapters indicated with regard to international environmental law. It is a well understood matter that TRIPS was one of the most significant achievements of the Uruguay Round for developed countries.[87] Developing countries have never understood TRIPS as being favourable to their own interests but they saw it as part of the broader package deal comprising all the GATT 1994 Agreements. In this context, it might have been expected that developing countries would take full advantage of differential provisions to exploit the limited scope given by the treaty to implement it in a way which suited their needs and specific situation. In practice, however, a number of countries have either decided to join the UPOV convention or adopt plant variety protection regimes based upon the UPOV regime. This is surprising in view of the fact that the private sector seed sector remains marginal in most developing countries, while a very high percentage of the population works in the agricultural sector and is directly dependent on its own production for meeting its food needs.[88] Further, while UPOV and TRIPS focus on the protection of formal

---

84   Statement by the Committee on Economic, Social and Cultural Rights on Human Rights and Intellectual Property, in Committee on Economic, Social and Cultural Rights, Report on the Twenty-Fifth, Twenty-Sixth and Twenty-Seventh Sessions, UN Doc. E/2002/22-E/C.12/2001/17, Annex XIII.

85   WTO, Declaration on the TRIPS Agreement and Public Health, Ministerial Conference – Fourth Session, WTO Doc. WT/MIN(01)/DEC/2 (2001).

86   Articles 65 and 66 of the TRIPS Agreement, supra note 1.

87   United States Trade Representative, *2001 Special 301 Report* at 4 (2001).

88   Diouf, supra note 2.

breeders, the international legal system now also provides, at least in part, for the protection of farmers' rights via the recently adopted PGRFA Treaty. The Indian example is on the whole very interesting because it constitutes one of the few national statutes which at least attempts to provide a comprehensive answer to the requirements of the international legal system.

Plant variety protection in TRIPS is of particular interest because it affects, at one level or the other, international institutions, states, the private sector, farming communities and individual farmers around the world, and indirectly all end-users of foodstuffs. These direct links between an intellectual property rights treaty and the fulfilment of the human right to food are significant for a variety of reasons. Firstly, the links which are apparent at the local level should also be taken into account in the course of further development of international law. Secondly, it is becoming increasingly difficult to dissociate 'technical' areas of international and national law like intellectual property from other areas such as environmental law or human rights. In this sense, the differential treatment content of Article 27.3.b TRIPS has implications beyond the strict field of intellectual property rights. Developing countries cannot implement their differential obligations in this field without taking into account their other domestic and international commitments. Thirdly, differentiation which fosters decentralization can be an effective tool to give more scope to countries to implement their international obligations in a manner which suits their needs and situations. At the same time, it also implies that states have a duty to make sure that they implement all their international obligations in a coherent manner. The introduction of plant variety protection should thus be undertaken with specific regard for environmental considerations embodied, for instance, in the Biosafety Protocol and for socio-economic considerations reflected, for instance, in human rights provisions.[89]

Access and Benefit Sharing in Plant Variety Protection

The question of access and benefit sharing has received more and more importance in international policy debates in different arenas. The issue of access refers generally to the conditions under which states or entities can get hold of biological resources or traditional knowledge. States have traditionally had control over their natural resources according to the principle of permanent sovereignty over natural resources and this has recently been extended to plant genetic resources as well.[90] The direct or indirect appropriation of resources or knowledge through the assertion of intellectual property rights in nations other than the country of origin have prompted concerns regarding the actual control of states over their biological

---

[89]   Cartagena Protocol on Biosafety to the Convention on Biological Diversity, Montreal, 20 Jan. 2000, reprinted in 39 *ILM* 1027 (2000). For the human right to food, International Covenant on Economic, Social and Cultural Rights, New York, 16 Dec. 1966, reprinted in 6 *ILM* 360 (1967).

[90]   Biodiversity Convention, supra note 47 and PGRFA Treaty, supra note 36.

resources and traditional knowledge. Benefit sharing is a notion which follows directly from discussions concerning access. Recent treaties, while reiterating the sovereign rights of states over their biological resources, have also promoted access to these resources for outsiders. In response, source states have requested the establishment of compensation schemes in cases where knowledge or resources are accessed for commercial purposes or appropriated through intellectual property rights.

Access and benefit sharing is of specific interest in the context of differential treatment for several reasons. Firstly, concerns regarding benefit sharing are a direct consequence of the introduction of intellectual property rights over inventions derived from traditional knowledge on biological resources or the resources themselves. In this sense, benefit sharing constitutes one of the specific ways in which the international community provides differentiated mechanisms in the field of intellectual property rights. Secondly, benefit sharing is a specific mechanism instituted to bridge the divide between holders of intellectual property rights and original holders of biological resources and traditional knowledge, seeking to provide a form of compensation to the latter for direct or indirect appropriation by the former. Thirdly, benefit sharing is a tool used, for instance, in the Indian Plant Variety Act to implement in part the commitment to recognize farmers' rights.

At the international level, two main regimes deal with access and benefit sharing. These are the Biodiversity Convention and the PGRFA Treaty. In the context of the former, the Bonn guidelines on access to genetic resources and equitable sharing of the benefits have been adopted by the Conference of the Parties, and member states are encouraged to use these to develop their own legal frameworks in this area.[91] The guidelines emphasize the central need for prior informed consent and provide examples of monetary and non-monetary benefits that should be considered by states. The benefit-sharing regime proposed by the PGRFA Treaty embodied in a binding instrument is more specific than the Bonn guidelines. The PGRFA Treaty first imposes an obligation on source states to facilitate access to all the crops covered by the Multilateral System.[92] Conditions for access may include limits or prescriptions on the uses that can be made of accessions, such as a focus on enhancing food security; procedural requirements such as the need to make all available passport data accessible and a prohibition on claiming intellectual property rights over accessions in the form received. The benefit-sharing provisions provide fairly detailed descriptions of the types of benefits that are to be shared. These include exchange of information, access to and

91   Bonn Guidelines on Access to Genetic Resources and Fair and Equitable Sharing of the Benefits Arising out of their Utilization, in Dec. VI/24, Access and Benefit-Sharing as Related to Genetic Resources, *Report of the Sixth Meeting of the Conference of the Parties to the Convention on Biological Diversity*, The Hague, 7-19 April 2002, UN Doc. UNEP/CBD/COP/6/20.
92   On the Multilateral System, Articles 11 and 12 of the PGRFA Treaty, supra note 36.

transfer of technology, capacity building, and the sharing of the benefits arising from commercialization. The technology transfer provision is particularly interesting. It commits member states to promote partnerships in research and development and to foster access to improved varieties and genetic material developed through the use of accessions from the Multilateral System. At the same time, the treaty indicates that access is intrinsically limited by intellectual property rights but a special provision is made for the benefit of developing countries, for instance, in the case of technologies that benefit farmers. With regard to the sharing of monetary benefits, the treaty provides that recipients who commercialize a product incorporating an accession from the Multilateral System must pay an 'equitable' share of the benefits.[93] These benefits must primarily reach farmers who sustainably manage agro-biodiversity in developing countries.

A number of countries have developed or are in the process of developing benefit-sharing regimes. In India, two different systems are proposed in the Plant Variety Act and the Biodiversity Act. In the former, benefit sharing is clearly associated with a form of financial compensation. These monetary benefits are to be channelled through a National Gene Fund.[94] In this legislation, benefit sharing is clearly proposed as an alternative to the allocation of intellectual or other property rights to holders of traditional knowledge and biological resources in general. In the Biodiversity Act as well, benefit sharing is through monetary benefits which can be either channelled to the benefit claimers or used generally for biodiversity management activities. In this case, the potential claimants do not have automatic access to a share of the benefits since the decision resides with the National Biodiversity Authority. As noted earlier, under the Biodiversity Act, benefit sharing can also imply the sharing of intellectual property rights. In this case too, it is the Authority which takes a decision concerning the sharing of property rights.

Plant Variety Management and Local Actors: Towards Sui Generis *Systems*

The preceding analysis can be summarized as follows. Firstly, the TRIPS Agreement obliges all states to introduce plant variety protection but gives member states the freedom to design their own protection regime. Secondly, the emphasis on plant breeders' rights as defined in the UPOV Convention as a model for developing countries in their attempts to introduce plant variety protection provides at best a partial response to the needs of most developing countries. Thirdly, the proposed and adopted Indian legal framework shows that despite significant attention being provided at the governmental and non-governmental levels to the question of the introduction of intellectual property rights in agriculture, there still remains significant gaps in the attempt to introduce farmers' rights as a counterweight to the introduction of plant breeders' rights.

---

[93]   On the sharing of monetary and other benefits of commercialization, Article 13.2.d of the PGRFA Treaty, supra note 36.

[94]   Section 45 of the PPVFR Act, supra note 61.

The debate over plant variety protection has been constrained to a large extent by the fact that it is taking place within the narrow context of the TRIPS Agreement. As indicated, the introduction of plant variety protection in developing countries may be triggered by the TRIPS Agreement but it is impossible to understand it only from this perspective. The importance of the TRIPS Agreement in the context of differentiation is in the end not so much the fact that it includes a differential treatment provision with respect to plant variety protection but the fact that it does so in an area where differentiation cannot stop at the level of states.

The example of states like India which have tried to provide a plant variety protection regime going beyond plant breeders' rights indicate the direction in which *sui generis* systems might go as well as the limits of recent attempts. The legal framework in India reflects some of the problems of lack of coherence between different international treaties dealing with overlapping issues and the way in which this is carried over at the national level. In fact, there is very little coordination between the Biodiversity Act, the Plant Variety Act and the 2002 amendments to the Patents Act. The regime for benefit sharing in the Plant Variety and Biodiversity Acts illustrates the kinds of overlaps and inconsistencies that affect the legal framework. On the one hand, the Biodiversity Act offers a broad definition of benefit sharing which encompasses various forms of benefits, from monetary compensation to transfer of technology and the grant of joint ownership of intellectual property rights. In contrast, in the Plant Variety Act benefit sharing is conceived only as a form of monetary compensation. However, the procedure for allocating benefits is much more clearly outlined in the Plant Variety Act. Instead, a generic benefit sharing mechanism ought to be outlined in the Biodiversity Act and the plant variety protection statute should only include elements which differ from the common regime. The lack of statutory relationship between the Biodiversity Act and the Patents Act is also strange in the context of benefit sharing. The sharing of benefits is a direct consequence of the introduction of intellectual property rights in agro-biotechnology. As a result, without express links between the two Acts, there is a possibility that in practice the provisions with regard to benefit-sharing contained in the Biodiversity Act, such as the possibility to allocate joint ownership of intellectual property rights, may on the whole remain inoperative.

While the legal framework for plant variety management and protection in India suffers to an extent from the lack of coordination between the proposed and adopted statutes, it is otherwise rather comprehensive with regard to the coverage of issues related to intellectual property rights and environmental management. Socio-economic concerns, however, are clearly sidelined in the current framework. In fact, concerns regarding the fulfilment of basic food needs and the realization of the human right to food are virtually absent. This is quite surprising given that the introduction of intellectual property rights over plant varieties has significant socio-economic and human rights implications. Though until recently there has been comparatively little discussion concerning the relationship between intellectual property rights and human rights, this has now become an area of significant concern at the international level.[95] Given that the allocation of intellectual property rights in areas such as agro-biotechnology can have impacts on the fulfilment of basic needs, this implies, at the very least, that in implementing intellectual property rights treaties, states must take into account their human rights obligations.[96] This is indirectly acknowledged by the TRIPS Agreement which specifically requires that there should be a balance of rights and obligations for holders of intellectual property rights.[97] The Indian legal framework does not really incorporate this dimension insofar as it fails to even fully take into account the international recognition of health and nutrition as essential sectors and that states are entitled to adopt measures to promote the public interest in sectors of vital importance to their socio-economic development.[98] The need to incorporate a human rights perspective in the introduction of intellectual property rights for plant variety protection was, for instance, recognized by the Indian Law Commission in its own draft Biodiversity Bill, where it provided that no intellectual property right should be granted on species used for alimentary or medicinal purposes.[99]

The shortcomings of the reviewed Indian legislation, which is itself among the most progressive existing frameworks, necessitates further analysis to examine ways of framing a differential *sui generis* system which takes into account the various concerns outlined above. The rest of this section outlines some of the conceptual issues that need to be tackled in the process of defining alternative legal frameworks in the field of plant variety protection.

Impact of plant variety protection on farming practices   The first difficulty in trying to devise an appropriate basis for alternative plant variety protection systems is that it is difficult to analyze the impacts of plant variety protection on farmers' agricultural practices. This is due to several factors. Firstly, while a patent on a plant variety does not directly restrict the rights of farmers to save seeds per se, it forms part of a wider web of relationships which are closely interrelated. Secondly, in countries where property rights on plant varieties are only in the process of being introduced, impacts on agricultural management are difficult to measure. To assess these impacts, one must first examine briefly the context in which they fall. In India, agriculture still represents a fundamental economic activity. Though its share of GDP has declined to 25 per cent, it still employs 60 per cent of the working population. Further, a number of industries, such as the cotton and jute textile

---

[95]   Sub-Commission on Human Rights Resolution 2001/21, Intellectual Property and Human Rights, UN Doc. E/CN.4/SUB.2/RES/2001/21.

[96]   Sub-Commission on the Promotion and Protection of Human Rights, The Impact of the Agreement on Trade-Related Aspects of Intellectual Property Rights on Human Rights, UN Doc. E/CN.4/Sub.2/2001/13.

[97]   Article 7 of the TRIPS Agreement, supra note 1.

[98]   Article 8 of the TRIPS Agreement, supra note 1.

[99]   Section 9.i.c of the Law Commission of India, Biodiversity Bill (One Hundred Seventy First Report on Biodiversity Bill, January 2000).

industries or the sugar industry, are directly based on agricultural goods.[100] Agricultural products still constitute an important source of exports.[101] It is noteworthy that agriculture is a large-scale commercial activity only in some small pockets but the livelihood of a large section of the rural community.[102]

Two main kinds of agricultural management can be identified. The first is generally known as traditional agriculture. It implies agricultural practices which see soil management as a comprehensive activity and which take into account not only yields but also other elements such as the long-term productivity of the soil and the management of pests. The second is chemical agriculture: it emphasizes high yields and soil management and is geared mainly towards this aim. It includes, for instance, the use of chemical fertilizers and pesticides. In India, chemical agriculture spread with the introduction of the green revolution which heralded the introduction of new agricultural management techniques in the late 1960s. It included primarily high-yielding varieties which require the application of a number of external inputs, from irrigation to chemical fertilizers and chemicals. The introduction of these new varieties had a significant impact on yields.[103]

Despite increases in yields, the green revolution has been increasingly criticized.[104] Firstly, it is now associated with significant long-term environmental costs. These include falling water tables due to the overuse of tubewells, waterlogged and saline soils from many large irrigation schemes, declining soil fertility with excessive chemical fertilizer use and water pollution with pesticides.[105] Secondly, the sustainability of the yield increases has been questioned in view of evidence of diminishing returns on intensive production with high-yielding varieties.[106] Thirdly, the application of the new technique necessitates important investments in seeds, fertilizers, pesticides and irrigation which are beyond the

[100] Abha Lakshmi Singh and Shahab Fazal, *Agriculture and Rural Development* (New Delhi: B.R. Publishing, 1998).
[101] The share of agricultural products in total exports is declining but still accounted for 13.5% of all exports in 2000-2001. *Indian Economic Survey 2001-2002* (Delhi: Akalank, 2002).
[102] Suman Sahai, 'Government Legislation on Plant Breeders' Rights', 29 *EPW* 1573 (1994).
[103] Rita Sharma and Thomas T. Poleman, *The New Economics of India's Green Revolution – Income and Employment Diffusion in Uttar Pradesh* (New Delhi: Vikas, 1994).
[104] Vandana Shiva, *The Violence of the Green Revolution* (London: Zed, 1991)
[105] Bina Agarwal, *Gender, Environment and Poverty Interlinks in Rural India* 7 (Geneva: UNRISD, 1995) and G.S. Dhaliwal and V.K. Dilawari, 'Impact of Green Revolution on Environment', in B.S. Hansra and A.N. Shukla eds, *Social, Economic and Political Implications of Green Revolution in India* (New Delhi: Classical Publishing, 1991).
[106] Gordon R. Conway and Edward B. Barbier, *After the Green Revolution – Sustainable Agriculture for Development* (London: Earthscan, 1990).

means of all but the biggest farmers.[107] Finally, skewed distribution of food remains a significant problem to date despite the overall increase in production.

The introduction of monopoly rights is likely to have a number of impacts on small farmers' agricultural practices and farmers' lives. Firstly, the two have the potential to be in conflict due to the fact that they rely on and promote different knowledge systems, identify innovations differently and reward inventors in different ways. More generally, while the reward system established by patents and plant breeders' rights is mainly financial, established agricultural management practices do not concentrate exclusively on financial incentives for innovation. Secondly, farmers' knowledge is often less individual oriented than scientific knowledge produced in laboratories. Even if it is usually possible to identify one specific individual as having provided a specific contribution to a given technical or scientific development, s/he will often not be the exclusive inventor. This is one reason why monopoly rights which channel all the benefits to a single inventor may not be adequate since they marginalize or even negate the contribution of the different actors present and will inevitably limit or stop free access to the invention by other users. Further, even when local knowledge is protected, for instance, by being restricted or secret, this is usually not done exclusively for commercial reasons.[108] Thirdly, patents in agriculture generally foster the commercialization of a number of major agricultural inputs. One of the most direct impacts of patents is to raise the price of patented seeds compared to other seeds. Further, while patents on seeds only give patentees rights over the invented seeds, impacts are in practice more wide-ranging. Farmers tend to become dependent on private firms for their seeds and for other inputs, such as pesticides and fertilizers.[109] As demonstrated in some countries, patenting in agriculture may eventually lead to the integration of a majority of steps in the food production system.[110] Fourthly, patents on plant varieties may have significant indirect impacts on the preservation of biodiversity. In general, patented varieties have the tendency to displace local varieties and to foster monocultures.[111] This leads in turn to a loss of agro-biodiversity in cases where farmers stop maintaining existing local varieties.

The potential impacts of monopoly rights mirror some of the problems apparent in the case of the green revolution. The introduction of the green revolution was premised on principles which differ completely from the rationale for the

---

[107]   B.H. Joshi, *An Analytical Approach to Problems of Indian Agriculture: A Theoretical and System Approach* (New Delhi: B.R. Publishing, 1992).

[108]   Naomi Roht-Arriaza, 'Of Seeds and Shamans: The Appropriation of the Scientific and Technological Knowledge of Indigenous and Local Communities', 17 *Michigan J. Int'l L.* 919 (1996).

[109]   Cf. C. Shambu Prasad, 'Suicide Death and Quality of Indian Cotton', XXXIV *EPW* PE-12 (1999).

[110]   Neil D. Hamilton, 'Why own the Farm if you can Own the Farmer (and the Crop)? - Contract Production and Intellectual Property Protection of Grain Crops', 73 *Nebraska L. Rev.* 48 (1994).

[111]   Sahai, supra note 15.

introduction of patents on plant varieties. Indeed, high-yielding varieties were the outcome of public research efforts based on the principle of free exchange of germplasm with a view to foster food security across the world. The promoters of the green revolution did not specifically promote commercial exploitation for profit. In the case of the introduction of patented varieties, in contrast, one the major incentives for the participation of the private sector is the availability of patents or plant breeders' rights. Despite the different premises, a number of lessons can be learnt from the experience accumulated over the past three decades due to the similarity of impacts.[112] The green revolution package, like the introduction of patented varieties, tends to lead to a loss of seed diversity. Further, they both lead to the diminution of the farmer's ability to save seeds. In the case of high yielding seeds, farmers are not technically bound to purchase new seeds each year but the yield of saved seeds is much lower even in the second year. This thus constitutes a very strong incentive for yearly purchases. In the case of patented varieties, farmers are not supposed to replant saved seeds.[113]

Overall, while a system of monopoly rights may be appropriate in countries where agriculture has become mainly an industrial activity on a fairly large-scale, monopoly rights do not seem to provide an effective answer to the multiplicity of factors and needs of the actors which are present in Indian agriculture and by extension in a majority of developing countries. Further, monopoly rights seem to be associated with negative environmental side effects. These include the displacement of local seeds and the attendant loss of agro-biodiversity.

Characteristics of an alternative a sui generis *system* The development of a *sui generis* system for the protection of plant varieties can fulfil several goals at the same time. Firstly, it allows WTO member states to fulfil their TRIPS obligations under Article 27.3.b. Secondly, it can provide property rights which are based on the recognition that agricultural innovation is carried out by a variety of actors in a variety of contexts. Thirdly, it constitutes an appropriate avenue to devise a property rights system which takes into account not only TRIPS obligations but also the other international obligations of WTO member states, in particular in the field of environmental law.

A *sui generis* system for the protection of property rights in plant varieties should aim at fulfilling a number of objectives. Firstly, it should seek to foster food

---

[112] Cf. Robert B. Horsch and Robert T. Fraley, 'Agricultural Industrialization and the Loss of Biodiversity', in Lakshman D. Guruswamy and Jeffrey A. McNeely eds, *Protection of Global Biodiversity – Converging Strategies* 66 (Durham, NC: Duke University Press, 1998).

[113] In practice, however, in a country like India, most small farmers will be able to carry on the practice of saving seeds because, unlike in the US where agriculture is mostly a large-scale activity, litigation against millions of small farmers by seed companies is simply not feasible. This loophole may disappear if patented seeds that cannot reproduce are marketed. US Patent 5,723,765, *Control of Plant Gene Expression*, issued 3 Mar. 1998.

security for all individuals. Aggregate increases in food production brought about by advances, such as the green revolution have helped countries such as India to become self-sufficient but this quantitative increase has not been associated with similar improvements in the distribution of existing food supplies. The introduction of plant variety protection should not contribute to the same lopsided results; rather it should promote the fulfilment of basic needs for all. Secondly, a *sui generis* system should contribute to sustainable agricultural management and should promote types of agricultural management which do not lead to the erosion of the genetic base and which are compatible with local climatic conditions.[114] Thirdly, it should generally contribute to the development of crops which do not harm the environment. This implies a need to include biosafety provisions in plant variety protection regimes.[115]

The mandatory features of *sui generis* systems envisaged under Article 27.3.b were not defined during the negotiations. Some elements can nevertheless be derived from the text. Firstly, it implies the allocation of property rights. Forms of financial compensation which are being proposed under the guise of benefit sharing as a substitute to property rights do not directly contribute to the definition of a *sui generis* system.[116] Secondly, the text indicates that the drafters meant the *sui generis* system to be an alternative to patents. This alternative is by definition an intellectual property rights system because it is knowledge which must be protected; however it is an alternative to monopoly rights. A number of developing states have already taken advantage of the proposition that the patentability of plant varieties can be excluded but they have been less successful in devising alternatives.[117] As a result, a central characteristic of a *sui generis* system would be to recognize non-monopoly rights. This is the only means of providing rights or entitlements to all the actors engaged in plant breeding and development. In practice, a *sui generis* system could replicate a solution proposed in the interpretative resolutions to the International Undertaking, by recognizing concurrently and equally the rights of farmers and the rights of commercial breeders. The fundamental element here is that the two sets of rights should both have the same importance. Legislations, such as the Indian Plant Variety Act, which put farmers and breeders on the same level go in this direction. However, the

---

114   Cf. Article 1 of the Biodiversity Convention, supra note 47. See also, World Trade Organization, The TRIPS Agreement: Communication from Kenya on behalf of the African Group, WTO Doc. WT/GC/W/302 (1999) in which the African Group calls for the harmonization of Article 27.3.b TRIPS with the provisions of the Biodiversity Convention and the International Undertaking.

115   The Indian Plant Variety Act is noteworthy in this regard since it includes a provision banning the registration of varieties containing genes or gene sequences involving technologies that are injurious to the life or health of human beings, plants or animals. Section 29 of the PPVFR Act, supra note 61.

116   Cf. M. Geetha Rani, 'Community Gene Banks Sustain Food Security and Farmers' Rights', 41 *Biotechnology and Dev. Monitor* 19 (2000).

117   African Model Legislation, supra note 51.

rights provided to farmers and local communities must be as strict as the rights offered to breeders if these statements are to go beyond mere rhetoric. In the case of the African Model Law, the substance of the law does not match the principles enunciated at the outset. Local communities can, for instance, only prohibit access to their biological resources and related knowledge where this is detrimental to the integrity of their natural or cultural heritage.[118] A balance between the property rights of farmer breeders and commercial breeders is also not attained if the only right farmers have is to charge commercial breeders a fee when their varieties are used.[119]

A more evolved property rights system would define the entitlements of all actors in plant breeding and agricultural management. This would include not only farmers and commercial breeders, but also local communities, indigenous peoples and national agricultural research institutes. Entitlements should be provided to each actor and they should generally not be exclusionary since most of the knowledge and resources which are used are derived from other resources maintained by human beings.[120] In this situation, none of the entitlements should stop other actors from carrying out their activities.

The development of a *sui generis* system must also take into account the importance and relevance of sub-national entities in agricultural management. The move away from monopoly rights with regard to private actors should also be promoted at this level. Indeed, in many cases, the assertion of permanent sovereignty over natural resources has only served as a vehicle for the appropriation of resources at the centre to the detriment of the regions. This has been the case in a number of post-colonial states in particular. Decentralization is thus another area which should be tackled if the benefits of a non-monopoly intellectual property rights system are to be fully realized.

Generally, one of the major issues which need to be tackled in developing a *sui generis* system is the designation of the holders of the rights. The difficulties associated with this explain in part why states and international instruments have focused on individual rights such as patents or plant breeders' rights. As noted, innovation in agriculture cannot always be ascribed to a particular individual or even a single community. It is, therefore, necessary to devise schemes which take into account the collective nature of agricultural management in many localities. One option is to focus on the recognition of the collective rights of local communities or farming communities.[121] The distrust which surrounds all forms of collective rights in domestic and international discourses constitutes an argument

---

[118] Article 20 of the African Model Legislation, supra note 51.

[119] Article 5 of the proposed Convention of Farmers and Breeders (New Delhi: Gene Campaign, 1998).

[120] Commission on Genetic Resources for Food and Agriculture/Ximena Flores Palacios, Contribution to the Estimation of Countries' Interdependence in the Area of Plant Genetic Resources (Background Study Paper No.7 Rev.1, 1997).

[121] Cf. J.S. Fingleton, *Legal Recognition of Indigenous Groups* (Rome: FAO, 1998).

against pursuing this avenue. Further, the focus on the community tends to overlook existing inequalities within communities.[122]

Another option is to follow the model adopted by the European Union at the international level and by all the federal states which devolve substantial authority to lower bodies. In this manner, the definition of a *sui generis* system can be part of a broader attempt to foster both the decentralization and the democratization of decision-making. In the case of India, even though the Constitution refers to a 'union of states', the practice indicates that States are weak compared to other federal states such as the United States. Attempts at providing more decentralized decision-making have included the 73rd and 74th amendments to the Constitution in 1992 which aimed to strengthen the role of local institutions of democratic governance (panchayats).[123] The panchayats constitute a good starting point in the search for a local body capable of holding rights where it is not possible or feasible to ascribe them to one or more identifiable individuals. Focusing on a local elected body constitutes one of the best ways to realize democratic decentralization which is being called for in many areas and which is especially needed in the case of plant variety protection.

Another strategy which can be used to influence the practical outcomes of a given property rights regime is to allocate different durations for different rights. In a situation where plant breeders' rights and farmers' rights are accorded equal value, it is possible to foster broader development policy goals by reducing the duration of commercial breeders' rights and extending farmers' rights as far as possible.[124]

As noted, the development of plant variety protection in compliance with TRIPS obligations does not occur in a vacuum. Most countries have other international obligations in this field. The Biodiversity Convention is central in this regard since it constitutes the main instrument concerned with biological resources. Further, it acknowledges the potential impacts of intellectual property rights on biodiversity management and even provides specific guidance to member states to ensure that such intellectual property rights are supportive of and do not run counter to the objectives of the Convention.[125] Since states must concurrently comply with all their international obligations and since most WTO member states are also parties to the Biodiversity Convention, it is imperative that a plant variety protection regime should also comply with the latter. It is thus of the utmost importance that member states adopt legislations concerning the management of

---

[122]   Robert Chambers, *Whose Reality Counts? – Putting the Last First* (London: IT Publications, 1997).

[123]   Constitution of India (Seventy-third Amendment) Act, 1992 and Constitution of India (Seventy-fourth Amendment) Act, 1992.

[124]   This had been successfully implemented, for instance, in the Indian Patents Act, 1970 which provided that the duration of patents on processes of manufacture for substances intended for use as food would be half the normal term. Section 53 of the Patents Act, 1970, supra note 55.

[125]   Article 16.5 of the Biodiversity Convention, supra note 47.

biological resources which cover all the relevant aspects. This implies that a plant variety protection regime should not normally be a separate piece of legislation. Plant varieties are only a subset of all biological resources which should be covered under an Act implementing obligations under the Biodiversity Convention. Situations where different national authorities are set up for plant variety protection and for biodiversity with varying and/or overlapping mandates, as in the case of India, should be avoided. In principle, there should be a generic regime for the management of biological resources which may include a sub-section concerning plant varieties to deal with the specific elements which may arise in this case, either because of the characteristics of the subject matter involved or because of the requirements of the TRIPS agreement.

Sui Generis Systems and the Future of Differential Treatment

The significance of Article 27.3.b may well not be limited to the field of plant variety protection and has broader lessons to offer. Firstly, it indicates that in cases where a multiplicity of actors have a stake in the concerned area, a legal regime channelling all the benefits to only one type of actor may not be entirely appropriate in terms of equity and, in the case of biological resources, in terms of the sustainable management of these resources. The opportunity offered by Article 27.3.b to develop a legal regime which takes into account all international obligations in this field is also significant. Indeed, the non-existence of a hierarchy among the various areas of international law implies that states should implement each treaty in the light of their other obligations, even if the treaty in question is not explicitly linked with the other. In principle, it would be more appropriate if international law were more centralized and had fully evolved mechanisms to deal with overlaps and conflicts between different instruments. In the present situation where such centralization does not exist, a form of differentiation which allows states sufficient latitude to implement their obligations in one treaty without contradicting their other obligations constitutes a positive alternative.

Finally, the case of plant variety protection under TRIPS clearly indicates the existence of a new link between differentiation and decentralization. While chapter 4 demonstrated the linkages at the international level, this chapter has highlighted the importance of involving all the relevant actors to enhance the fairness of the regime and to foster a more sustainable use of the resources. The emphasis on local institutions is in fact very important. It is imperative to recognize the potential of democratically elected bodies to foster the democratization of international law by bringing international rules and their implementation closer to the people than is the case at present in a number of countries.

While the previous chapters focused mainly on differentiation at the inter-state level, this chapter shows that differentiation cannot be fully understood if the analysis stops at the international level. The implementation of international norms, in many cases, goes right down to the local level. It is imperative to recognize that in many cases, a sharp distinction between the domestic and international spheres does not exist in practice. The case of financial mechanisms set up to provide implementation aid reflects this. Further, this chapter also indicates that the sharp distinction between private and public law is not necessarily upheld in practice. The web of interrelationships between intellectual property and environmental law testifies to the impossibility to deal with these issues in completely isolated settings.

Chapter 6

The Future of Differential Treatment

Over the course of the twentieth century, international relations have undergone fundamental changes, in particular after the Second World War. International law has, however, remained surprisingly immune to these changes. Thus, the basic principle of equal sovereignty which has constituted the basis of international relations for several centuries has remained a cornerstone of international law. While sovereign equality has been consistently upheld in principle, a number of exceptions to its application have been noted over time. States establishing the UN decided, for instance, that while sovereign equality would hold in the context of the relatively toothless General Assembly, representation would be biased towards a few militarily and politically powerful states in the Security Council. Generally, the principle of sovereign equality, which implies that states are to a large extent free to pursue their own interests and take unilateral decisions, has been increasingly qualified, at least in some specific areas.[1]

The broadening of the international community through the accession to statehood of numerous nations and the proliferation of international problems, such as those relating to the international environment, have further tested the validity of strict reliance on equal sovereignty to manage inter-state relations. International law has evolved to an extent in response to these changes and new challenges. The development of differential treatment constitutes one of the ways in which a solution has been sought to adapt international law to the new realities of the time.

Since the traditional system, which relies mainly on the fiction of legal equality, has for a large part been favourable to bigger and economically more developed states, differentiation provides not only a conceptual tool to analyze international law in theory but also a mechanism to foster more benefits for disadvantaged states. The role of public international law in maintaining world order is often disregarded because some of its basic principles are often not upheld in times of crises. However, on a day-to-day basis, international law plays an essential role in facilitating smooth relations between states in a number of different fields. It is therefore essential for the international legal system, as well as for most national legal systems, to acknowledge the limitations of the rule of legal equality and to provide measures to remedy results which are deemed undesirable either from a broader moral perspective or in the context of the implementation of existing

---

[1] Cf. Edith Brown Weiss, 'The Emerging Structure of International Environmental Law', in Norman J. Vig and Regna S. Axelrod eds, *The Global Environment: Institutions, Law And Policy* 98 (Washington, DC: Congressional Quarterly, 1999).

norms. In fact, while this book has focused mostly on the situation of developing countries as a group to bring out some general trends, the rationale for differential treatment goes beyond North-South issues and is as relevant even in the case of relations between Germany and Albania or India and the Maldives. As the preceding chapters show, a compelling case can be made for the use of differentiation in international environmental law. In practice, differential treatment has been used in a number of contexts in this field, but there remains significant scope for further development.

Differential Treatment in Perspective

Differential treatment is, in essence, related to considerations of justice. It is thus concerned with questions of equity in international law. Beyond this ethical dimension, differentiation also constitutes a very pragmatic approach to solving certain international problems. In this sense, it constitutes an acknowledgment of the limitations of a system which does not take into account a state's capacity to implement specific international obligations and does not provide decentralized implementation in recognition of the different needs and situations of individual states. Further, differentiation also brings out the fact that the distinction between national and international law can be extremely artificial. For instance, in the case of international environmental issues it is impossible to address most of these problems without taking an integrated approach which includes both national and international concerns as well as all the interests of relevant non-state actors.

Differentiation, Substantive Equality and Solidarity

Differential treatment first constituted a response to the increasing difficulty in providing fair rules for all states in an international community where inequalities, such as economic inequalities, had become more obvious with the accession to statehood of former colonial territories. This led to a search for rules fostering substantive equality rather than formal equality. It did not result in a rejection of formal equality as much as an addition to the set of legal tools available to produce fair rules. Formal equality is in fact only sidelined in cases where inequalities are too significant to allow all states to benefit equally from a legal regime which provides all states exactly the same rights and duties.

  The first phase of the development of differential treatment in the context of the international law of development ultimately failed to achieve any significant change in the international legal structure as it was premised on principles which forced confrontation between developed and developing countries. More recently, differentiation has been undertaken in a much more conciliatory atmosphere which sees nearly all states finding an advantage in the development of differentiation.

  International environmental law is the area where differentiation has developed most significantly in the past two decades. This is due both to the fact that it has been one of the fastest developing branches of international law in recent years and to the fact that a number of international environmental problems have forced states to find new ways to foster cooperation among themselves. While the existence of environmental problems of global significance has not really impacted the definition of sovereignty, it has led states to adopt new forms of partnership to solve common problems. These have included, for instance, the provision of non-reciprocal norms, as well as the development of regimes for the exploitation of natural resources based on principles acknowledging the cooperative nature of the activity, such as the principle of common heritage of humankind. It is remarkable that the special situation of developing countries and that of developing countries with specific environmental concerns and needs have been acknowledged in a rather consistent manner. Even more significant is the fact that, unlike in the NIEO era, steps have actually been taken to implement differential norms and regimes.

Differentiation in environmental agreements has been closely associated with the broader notion of solidarity. This is reflected in the fact that differential treatment has been most successfully implemented where the solution to common problems necessitates the cooperation of all states. Solidarity is strongly present in actions against a number of environmental problems, where states which have contributed more to the creation of the concerned problem end up partially bearing the costs incurred by states which have contributed comparatively less and lack the capacity to tackle the problem. This form of solidarity has come to be more widely accepted than the solidarity promoted in the NIEO era and implies a stronger partnership among states to solve common problems, reflected in legal terms in the development of the principle of common but differentiated responsibility.

The progress made in realizing substantive equality at the international level should not hide the significant gaps and limitations of the current approach. Firstly, even though states appear to have become more responsive to calls for equity at the international level, differential concerns have not been systematically applied and a general binding legal principle in this area is yet to emerge. Indeed, while differential concerns have increased in some areas, they have definitely receded in others, such as in trade law. Secondly, the development of differential treatment in recent years is to an extent linked to the specificities of the problems considered. In fact, while differential regimes in environmental law foster the realization of substantive equality, it is significant that the effective application of differentiation has only been possible in areas where a specific convergence of interests has emerged. In practice, this implies that differentiation has been effective mainly in cases where developed countries have found it to be in their interest. Thirdly, differential treatment suffers from a certain lack of clarity insofar as it constitutes an exception to the normal rule of formal equality. Since the concept of differentiation is still relatively novel, general principles concerning its use and the limits of its application have not emerged. This tends to reinforce the view that it threatens the certainty of the legal order even though in principle, differentiation does nothing more than equity does in its judicial application.

Differentiation and the Implementation of International Law

Differential treatment has been mostly associated with equity considerations at the conceptual level, partly because of the link with preferential treatment. While this constituted the thrust of the international law of development, in recent years differentiation has been used in a much more practical way at the level of the implementation of international treaties. If the conceptual premises for granting implementation aid or technology transfer come from the broader idea of fostering substantive equality, the main motive in practice is to foster more effective implementation of international norms. Differential treatment at the implementation level has been most successfully applied in cases where the states lacking the capacity to fully implement international norms were reluctant to enter into an agreement altogether. The provision of implementation aid or technology transfer has thus been used as a bargaining chip by states interested in reaching an agreement on a given topic while having the capacity to solve it or to help other states to solve it. The case of the Indian and Chinese ratifications of the Montreal Protocol illustrate this well.

Providing measures to foster more effective implementation of international norms has become increasingly important. Indeed, one of the frequent complaints about international law in general has been the lack of compliance on the one hand and the lack of implementation on the other. The latter quite often depends on the availability of sufficient resources. Again, environmental problems have provided an interesting background for the development of differential implementation measures since the technological or financial capacity to solve a given environmental problem often exists in the world but is likely to be beyond the reach of a majority of developing countries. The interests of countries seeking to solve an environmental problem but unable to achieve their goal without the collaboration of all states seems to have been sufficient to engender new dynamics.

The positive contribution of differential measures at the implementation level must, however, be qualified to an extent. Recent international environmental agreements in particular have all provided for some form of implementation aid or technology transfers. These provisions, unlike the ones negotiated in the heyday of the NIEO, have been implemented. However, commitments made in terms of technology transfer are much more restricted than they were a decade or two ago. Further, while aid has been forthcoming, this is in a context where the relative importance of public aid is rapidly diminishing. The overall influence of implementation measures may thus not be as striking as it appears at first sight.

Differentiation and Decentralization

The third main feature of differential treatment highlighted in this study is the link between differentiation and the search for means of opening up the international legal field to non-state actors. The process of defining differential treatment has in fact led to a rethinking of some of the structures which give the state a central and monopolistic place in international affairs. This is in fact a logical consequence of the search for substantive equality both at the broad level of states and at the level of individual citizens. The democratic shortcomings evident in a number of states constitute some of the reasons for attempting to give other actors a more important role right from the constitution of legal regimes to their implementation.

Environmental issues have provided an interesting background for the development of new ideas in this field. Indeed, in many cases, environmental problems are not caused by governments and the management of environmental resources is carried out mainly by non-state actors. In this situation, the involvement of the private sector, civil society and individuals becomes much more important to the overall success of the legal regime than in the case of some traditional areas of international law, such as international peace.

The link between differentiation and decentralization is so strong that the aim of substantive equality can probably not be realized without involving non-state actors in the process. To date, piecemeal changes can be observed. These include the growing role of the civil society in international forums and the formalization of the presence of the private sector at the negotiating table. The decentralization of decision-making probably constitutes, as it does at the domestic level, a good strategy to foster the progressive democratization of international law. In this sense, the involvement of the various actors contributes to the realization of substantive equality.

The link between differential treatment and decentralization illustrates one of the main lessons to be learnt from the development of differentiation: differential treatment may not necessarily contribute directly to changes in international law, but it is part of a wider process aiming to adapt international law to the new realities of today's world.

Avenues for Further Development

The need for differential treatment has been felt strongly at least since the end of the decolonization process. The conditions that prevailed in the 1960s and 1970s which warranted the first calls for differentiation in international law still obtain to a large extent in today's world. The development of differentiation in international environmental law in a relatively consistent manner has been possible due to the specificities of global environmental problems. In fact, the growth of differentiation in the environmental context has been accompanied by a rapid decline in differentiation in the economic and trade context. There are, however, signs that acceptance of differential treatment beyond the environmental field might be on the rise again in other fields. In this sense, the Kyoto Protocol which is largely informed by differential concerns is a remarkable treaty since it is not just a major environmental treaty but also a major economic treaty. The importance of the Kyoto Protocol notwithstanding, the most significant institution in the field of trade relations is without doubt the WTO and recent developments in this regime are indicative of possible future trends. Beyond trade law, it is also interesting to examine how differential treatment informs or can inform other areas of international law. International human rights are particularly interesting where differentiation has been a long-standing concern, especially in the context of economic and social rights.

Revival of Differential Treatment in the WTO?

As noted, differential treatment in the context of trade agreements constituted a major feature of trade law until the 1980s. Landmark developments in the GATT context included the introduction of an additional section to the treaty on trade and development in the mid-1960s. The 1971 decision on a Generalized System of Preferences confirmed the validity of derogations from the most favoured nation clause and the 1979 decision gave preferential treatment a permanent legal basis in the GATT context (Enabling Clause).[2] The rationale for differentiation in trade law was to facilitate and promote international trade for developing countries by giving them better market access for exports while allowing them enough flexibility to pursue policies aimed at fostering economic development.

Differential treatment in the GATT context has gone through a phase of significant changes over the past two decades and has been viewed with increasing suspicion during the Uruguay Round trade negotiations. In fact, the results of the Uruguay Round are partly premised on the idea that differential treatment for developing countries has not worked and that developing countries would be better served if they were to implement all relevant WTO disciplines. Differential treatment in the Uruguay Round agreements is thus mostly conceived as a tool for recognizing the special problems that developing countries may face in implementing commitments which are generally common for all WTO member states. It includes in particular transition periods for implementation and technical assistance. Even though there does not exist a focus on differentiation any longer, there remain a number of differential treatment provisions within the WTO framework by virtue of the fact that the Uruguay Round package includes previous agreements, including, for instance, the Enabling Clause.[3] However, differential treatment provisions such as the Enabling Clause which aim to enhance trading opportunities for developing countries, tend to remain non-binding commitments.

---

[2]   Differential and More Favourable Treatment, Reciprocity and Fuller Participation of Developing Countries (Enabling Clause), Decision of 28 Nov. 1979 (L/4903). See also, Ndiva Kofele-Kale, 'The Principle of Preferential Treatment in the Law of GATT: Toward Achieving the Objective of an Equitable World Trading System', 18 *California Western Int'l L.J.* 291 (1987/88).

[3]   *Cf.* Hesham Youssef, *Special and Differential Treatment for Developing Countries in the WTO* (Geneva: South Centre, 1999).

In fact, a large number of differential treatment provisions in WTO suffer from the shortcoming that they are unenforceable.[4]

While the decreasing use of differential treatment characterizes the Uruguay Round agreements, this has not been universally accepted by developing countries. The South does not accept, for instance, that differential treatment is to be faulted for its inability to increase exports but rather blames existing constraints on the supply-side.[5] The decrease in importance given to differential treatment in the WTO has persisted for a number of years but there are signs that changes are in the offing. In fact, the ministerial declaration adopted at the Doha conference clearly states that 'all special and differential treatment provisions shall be reviewed with a view to strengthening them and making them more precise, effective and operational'.[6] Further, in the context of the new negotiations on the agricultural sector, the ministerial declaration agreed that differential treatment would be an integral part of the negotiations and specifically mentioned that the development needs of developing countries, including food security and rural development must be taken into account.[7] This falls short of the 'development box' requested by some developing countries which would enable them to pursue policies for achieving food security and protecting the livelihoods of small farmers, whether or not such measures are compatible with the existing Agreement on Agriculture.[8] The existing statement, however, definitely goes in the direction of giving differential treatment enhanced standing in trade matters.

The Doha ministerial conference entrusted the Committee on Trade and Development with the task of reviewing existing differential treatment provisions with a view to strengthen the framework for differentiation within the WTO context.[9] In this context, states have made specific proposals for strengthening differentiation and there are ongoing discussions within the WTO on these issues.[10] Current WTO debates indicate that there is scope for stronger differential treatment provisions in the future. While development in the WTO context may take time to materialize, other UN agencies have started to address some of the relevant

---

[4]   Edwini Kessie, 'Enforceability of the Legal Provisions Relating to Special and Differential Treatment under the WTO Agreements', 3 *J. World Intellectual Property* 955, 957 (2000).

[5]   Constantine Michalopoulos, Role of Special and Differential Treatment for Developing Countries in GATT and the World Trade Organization (Washington, DC: World Bank, Working Paper #2388, 2000). See also, Kessie, supra note 4 at 974.

[6]   WTO, Ministerial Declaration, Ministerial Conference – Fourth Session, WTO Doc. WT/MIN(01)/DEC/1 (2001) at § 44.

[7]   *Id.* at § 13.

[8]   Non-Governmental Liaison Service, 'New Trade Negotiations Launched at Doha', 89 *Go Between* 30 (Dec. 2001-Jan. 2002).

[9]   WTO, Implementation-Related Issues and Concerns, Ministerial Conference – Fourth Session, WTO Doc. WT/MIN(01)/17 (2001).

[10]   Committee on Trade and Development, Report to the General Council, WTO Doc. TN/CTD/3 (2002).

conceptual issues. Thus, in the context of a recent discussion on the WTO Agreement on Agriculture, the UN High Commissioner for Human Rights specifically recalled the need for differential treatment. She emphasized that where unequals are treated as equals this may be problematic for the promotion and protection of human rights and could result in the institutionalization of discrimination against the poor and marginalized. She thus advocates the need for special measures to protect vulnerable people and groups.[11]

Human Rights, Environment and Differential Treatment

Human rights and differential treatment have a lot in common. Firstly, some of differential treatment's conceptual bases analyzed in chapter 2 are closely related to human rights. These include, for instance, the focus on solidarity and the focus on basic needs which are related to a number of fundamental human rights such as the right to food and health. Secondly, international human rights law is the only branch of international law which predominantly recognizes rights, not of states but of individuals and groups. This ties in closely with the broader reach of differential treatment as outlined in chapter 5, which goes beyond the inter-state level to examine consequences for individuals in specific countries. Thirdly, debates concerning a human right to environment, or to use another term environmental justice, have shown that there are significant equity dimensions to the issues involved.

Both differential treatment and human rights recognize that the successful implementation of fair legal standards often requires cooperation and solidarity among states and between the various state and non-state actors. The notion of solidarity leads to a considerable broadening of the scope of human rights and is therefore controversial. 'Solidarity rights', such as the right to development or the right to environment, have been particularly contentious because their realization requires not only measures at the national level but also solidarity from the international community as a whole and solidarity among the various actors involved in their realization.[12] In fact, at some level differential treatment and solidarity rights are broadly similar. Thus, the right to development was closely associated with the new international economic order and this contributed to making its establishment very controversial.[13] Similarly, the right to environment has an important solidarity dimension insofar as it has strong links with inter- and intra-generational equity and goes beyond the traditional human rights focus on the

---

[11]   Report of the High Commissioner for Human Rights, Globalization and its Impact on the Full Enjoyment of Human Rights, UN Doc. E/CN.4/2002/54 (2002).

[12]   UNGA Res. 41/128, Declaration on the Right to Development, 4 Dec. 1986, in Resolutions and Decisions Adopted by the General Assembly During its 41st Session, UN Doc. A/41/53.

[13]   K. Vasak, 'Pour une troisième génération des droits de l'homme', in Christophe Swinarski ed., *Studies and Essays on International Humanitarian Law and Red Cross Principles in Honour of Jean Pictet* 837 (The Hague: Nijhoff, 1984).

relationship between the state and the individual. While the notion of solidarity in the context of human rights remains controversial,[14] some links between solidarity, differentiation and human rights are clearly apparent. Thus, the recognition that exposure to environmental degradation is often a consequence of economic and political inequalities could lead to the conclusion that positive discrimination measures are required to foster the realization of certain standards of environmental quality for all.[15]

International human rights are generally concerned with the rights of individuals. This constitutes another level at which there are strong links between differential treatment and human rights since both deal with inter-state relations as well as the relations between states and non-state actors. Human rights have, for instance, traditionally focused on the power imbalance between individuals or groups and states. Human rights are especially relevant since it is with their development that international law first took steps towards giving non-state actors a much more prominent role in some areas, for instance, by awarding individuals enforceable rights against states. One of the major contributions of human rights law is thus to have made it possible for some categories of non-state actors to have legal standing in some international adjudicative forums.[16] These synergies between differentiation and human rights have generally not been acknowledged even though this would contribute to the development of both simultaneously.

There is no recognized human right to environment at the international level even though a great number of national constitutions have enshrined some form of right to the environment.[17] However, significant attention has been accorded to the relationship between environmental quality and human rights and different ways to integrate environmental concerns in human rights law have been identified.[18] Firstly, environmental protection may be used as a means to uphold human rights standards. A degraded physical environment contributes directly to infringements of rights, such as the right to life or health, and therefore acts leading to environmental degradation may constitute immediate violations of internationally recognized human rights. Secondly, the legal protection of human rights constitutes an effective means to foster environmental conservation. The realization of human rights could bring about conditions in which claims for environmental protection

---

[14]   Cf. Alan Boyle, 'The Role of International Human Rights Law in the Protection of the Environment', in Alan E. Boyle and Michael R. Anderson eds, *Human Rights Approaches to Environmental Protection* 43 (Oxford: Clarendon, 1996).

[15]   Cf. Michael R. Anderson, 'Human Rights Approaches to Environmental Protection', in Alan E. Boyle and Michael R. Anderson eds, *Human Rights Approaches to Environmental Protection* 1 (Oxford: Clarendon, 1996).

[16]   Convention for the Protection of Human Rights and Fundamental Freedoms, Rome, 4 Nov. 1950, *European Treaty Series*, N° 5 et al.

[17]   Fatma Zohra Ksentini-Special Rapporteur, Human Rights and the Environment – Final Report, Sub-Commission on Prevention of Discrimination and Protection of Minorities, UN Doc. E/CN.4/Sub.2/1994/9.

[18]   See generally, Anderson, supra note 15.

are more likely to be respected. Thirdly, new procedural environmental rights, such as a right to environmental impact assessment as well as a substantive right to environment have also been proposed. Some procedural rights already exist while the adoption of a substantive right at the international level remains a distant goal.[19]

The link between human rights and environmental protection has sometimes been made in terms of 'environmental justice'. Environmental justice has received particular attention in the United States where its development was closely linked to concerns over racial discrimination.[20] The significance of environmental justice lies, however, not in its focus on race but in other elements. It has served to highlight the equity and fairness dimensions of environmental policies at the domestic level and can be applied similarly at the international level. It is based upon the recognition that environmental costs and benefits have not been distributed in a fair and equitable manner and that traditional environmentalism has not been sufficiently concerned with divergent local situations and the plight of minorities.[21] Thus environmental justice concerns centre mainly on the side effects of industrial activity, such as the location of waste disposal facilities,[22] the proximity of industrial pollution, workplace exposure to industrial toxins and in-house lead exposure, in particular for children. Overall, the environmental justice movement has sought to redefine the traditional environmental movement by incorporating the concerns of minorities within environmental policy making.[23] The major thrust of the environmental justice movement is to shift the focus of attention from the environment to people, specifically to identified communities. It seeks to show that environmental protection should not be planned in a vacuum and that environmental goals should take into account social, political and economic realities. In other words, environmental justice is about positive discrimination: it seeks to achieve a redistribution of the costs of environmental justice so as to lower the disproportionately high burden borne by some segments of society. Further, environmental justice shifts the focus away from the conservation of nature in a

---

[19]   Concerning debates at the level of the UN Human Rights Commission, Ksentini, supra note 17. See also, Neil A.F. Popovic, 'In Pursuit of Environmental Human Rights: Commentary on the Draft Declaration of Principles on Human Rights and the Environment', 27 *Columbia Hum. Rts. L. Rev.* 487 (1996).

[20]   Commission for Racial Justice United Church of Christ, *Toxic Wastes and Race in the United States – A National Report on the Racial and Socio-Economic Characteristics of Communities with Hazardous Waste Sites* (New York: United Church of Christ, 1987).

[21]   Robert D. Bullard, 'Introduction', in Robert D. Bullard ed., *Confronting Environmental Racism – Voices from the Grassroots* 7 (Boston: South End Press, 1993).

[22]   Charles J. McDermott, 'Balancing the Scales of Environmental Justice', 21 *Fordham Urban L.J.* 689 (1995).

[23]   Gerald Torres, 'Changing the Way Government Views Environmental Justice', C981 *American Law Institute – American Bar Association* 561 (1995).

pristine condition, for instance, through the setting up of nature reserves, to the impact of the environment on people's lives.

Overall, human rights have integrated a number of differential concerns, such as the recognition that implementation of economic and social rights is partly dependent on a state's levels of economic development, as well as the acknowledgement that the realization of the right to equality may imply positive discrimination measures. Some human rights are also, like differential treatment, directly dependent on solidarity among states and between different actors. Additionally, debates concerning the recognition of a right to environment point to further similarities between the two fields. This indicates that there are levels at which differential treatment is already being mainstreamed into other areas of international law even if this is done in the guise of a different discourse.

Concluding Remarks

Differential treatment has proved to be an interesting instrument to foster the adaptation of international law to the new and changing nature of both the international community and international problems. It achieves this by extending the use of equity, already extensively used at the judicial level, to other areas of law, in particular in the farming of norms and at the implementation level. In other words, it is part of a broader realization that international law should adapt itself to reflect more effectively the reality within which it evolves.

The preceding analysis of differential treatment shows that its application is not confined to international environmental law but that it exists in different forms in other areas of international law. It must be noted that there are usually no linkages between these different forms of differentiation as they arise in separate areas of international law which generally evolve independently of each other. Further, it is apparent that differentiation in international law is in some way the extension of a phenomenon that has received considerable attention at the national level in the form of affirmative action programmes.

The widespread use of differentiation at the national and international levels notwithstanding, equity considerations in both domestic law and international law remain controversial. This is especially the case whether differential treatment implies a redistribution of resources or the allocation of rights in a manner more favourable to the disadvantaged members of the community. In international law, two main considerations seem to influence the development of differential treatment. Firstly, power relations among states vary over time and are influenced by the specific circumstances under which negotiations take place. Thus, developing countries found themselves in a relatively strong bargaining position at the time the proposals for a new international economic order were being put forth as this was linked in part to the global energy crisis. Similarly, developing countries were recognized as necessary members of the community of states in attempts to tackle some of today's significant global environmental problems such as climate change and biodiversity management. Secondly, differential treatment is largely influenced by the willingness of the state from whom something is extracted. Thus, the relatively successful development of certain differential environmental regimes is undeniably linked to the fact that developed countries took a lead on some issues like the protection of the ozone layer and that it was in their own interest to make developing countries sign up to the proposed international legal regime.

Developments in international environmental law indicate that differentiation has only been successfully implemented where the North also finds an interest in its application. Self-interest, not solidarity may thus be the main motives for successfully implementing differentiation in practice. However, even if the self-interest of the parties on whom redistributive measures are imposed is an important consideration, it cannot explain differential treatment in its totality. Part of it is also linked to the other motives outlined in chapter 2. Thus, in some of the preferential trading arrangements such as the Lomé IV convention between the European Community and ACP states, the rationale for the preferential regime was both mutual interest and solidarity.[24]

In practice, some countries have been less willing to accept differentiation than others. Thus, in the case of the climate change regime, the United States has been at the forefront of calls for developing countries to take on emission reduction commitments while other OECD countries have been more amenable to the development of a legal regime which is fundamentally based on differential treatment. In this case, a remarkable feature is that the United States' reservations with regard to several aspects of the Kyoto Protocol, including the question of differentiation, has not stopped the regime from progressing towards implementation despite the vital importance of having the United States as a full partner in this regime. The position of the United States can be explained by the fact that it is not sufficiently within its self-interest to promote differential treatment in this regime. This is partly linked to the perception that the implementation of differential treatment will impose significant costs to the United States in terms of the financial commitments that are required from developed countries and that the country may lose some of its competitive advantage vis-à-vis some developing countries in the case of an agreement like the Kyoto Protocol where there are also high economic stakes besides the central environmental issues.[25]

In conclusion, while the future of differential treatment is fraught with uncertainty, its further development seems probable. Indeed, if positive

24   Article 1 of the Fourth ACP-EEC Convention, Lomé, 15 Dec. 1989, reprinted in 29 *ILM* 783 (1990).
25   Cf. Mark A. Drumbl, 'Poverty, Wealth, and Obligation in International Environmental Law', 76 *Tulane L. Rev.* 843, 957 (2002).

developments in differential treatment can occur in the difficult context of international trade law, it is likely that progress in the field of international environmental law will be forthcoming.

Bibliography

Recurring references

Abi-Saab, G., 'Whither the International Community?', 9 *Eur. J. Int'l L.* 248 (1998).

Agarwal, B., *Gender, Environment and Poverty Interlinks in Rural India* (Geneva: UNRISD, 1995).

Anderson, M.R., 'Human Rights Approaches to Environmental Protection', in Alan E. Boyle and Michael R. Anderson eds, *Human Rights Approaches to Environmental Protection* 1 (Oxford: Clarendon, 1996).

Biermann, F., '"Common Concern of Humankind": The Emergence of a New Concept of International Environmental Law', 34 *Archiv des Völkerrechts* 426 (1996).

Birnie, P.W. and Alan E. Boyle, *International Law and the Environment* (Oxford: Oxford University Press, 2002).

Brownlie, I., 'Legal Status of Natural Resources in International Law (Some Aspects)', 162 *RCADI* 245 (1979-I).

Brownlie, I., *Principles of Public International Law* (Oxford: Clarendon, 5th ed. 1998).

Brown Weiss, E., 'Environmental Equity and International Law', in Sun Lin ed., *UNEP's New Way Forward: Environmental Law and Sustainable Development* 7 (Nairobi: UNEP, 1995).

Brown Weiss, E., 'The Emerging Structure of International Environmental Law', in Norman J. Vig and Regna S. Axelrod eds, *The Global Environment: Institutions, Law And Policy* 98 (Washington, DC: Congressional Quarterly, 1999).

Brunnée, J. and André Nollkaemper, 'Between the Forests and the Trees – An Emerging International Forest Law', 23 *Envtl. Conservation* 307 (1996).

Cassese, A., *International Law in a Divided World* (Oxford: Clarendon, 1986).

Chinkin, C., 'Normative Development in the International Legal System', in Dinah Shelton ed., *Commitment and Compliance – The Role of Non-binding Norms in the International Legal System* 21 (Oxford: Oxford University Press, 2000).

Decaux, E., *La réciprocité en droit international* (Paris: Librairie générale de droit et de jurisprudence, 1980).

Dolzer, R., 'The Global Environment Facility – Towards a New Concept of the Common Heritage of Mankind', in Gudmundur Alfredsson and Peter McAlister-Smith eds, *The Living Law of Nations – Essays on Refugees, Minorities, Indigenous Peoples and the Human Rights of Other Vulnerable Groups* 331 (Kehl: N.P. Engel, 1996).

Drumbl, M.A., 'Poverty, Wealth, and Obligation in International Environmental Law', 76 *Tulane L. Rev.* 843 (2002).

Dupuy, P.-M., 'Où en est le droit international de l'environnement à la fin du siècle?', 101 *Revue générale de droit international public* 873 (1997).

Dupuy, R.-J., *La communauté internationale entre le mythe et l'histoire* (Paris: Economica, 1986).

Feuer, G. and Hervé Cassan, *Droit international du développement* (Paris: Dalloz, 2nd ed. 1991).

Franck, T.M., *Fairness in International Law and Institutions* (Oxford: Clarendon, 1995).

Halvorssen, A., *Equality Among Unequals in International Environmental Law – Differential Treatment for Developing Countries* (Colorado: Westview Press, 1999).

Handl, G., 'Environmental Security and Global Change: The Challenge to International Law', 1 *Yb. Int'l Envtl. L.* 3 (1990).

Higgins, R., *Problems and Process – International Law and How we Use it* (Oxford: Clarendon, 1994).

Janis, M.W., 'The Ambiguity of Equity in International Law', 9 *Brooklyn J. Int'l L.* 7 (1983).

Jordan, A. and Jacob Werksman, 'Incrementality and Additionality: A New Dimension to North-South Resource Transfers?', 6 *World Resource Rev.* 178 (1994).

Kessie, E., 'Enforceability of the Legal Provisions Relating to Special and Differential Treatment under the WTO Agreements', 3 *J. World Intellectual Property* 955 (2000).

Kofele-Kale, N., 'The Principle of Preferential Treatment in the Law of GATT: Toward Achieving the Objective of an Equitable World Trading System', 18 *California Western Int'l L.J.* 291 (1987/88).

McDonald, R.St.J., 'Solidarity in the Practice and Discourse of Public International Law', 8 *Pace Int'l L. Rev.* 259 (1996).

Magraw, D.B., 'Legal Treatment of Developing Countries: Differential, Contextual and Absolute Norms', 1 *Colorado J. Int'l Envtl. L. & Pol'y* 69 (1990).

Miller, M.A.L., 'Sovereignty Reconfigured: Environmental Regimes and Third World States', in Karen T. Litfin ed., *The Greening of Sovereignty in World Politics* 173 (Cambridge, Mass: MIT Press, 1998).

O'Connell, D.P., *International Law* (London: Stevens, vol. 1, 2nd ed. 1970).

Reinicke, W.H. and Jan Martin Witte, 'Interdependence, Globalization, and Sovereignty: The Role of Non-binding International Legal Accords', in Dinah Shelton ed., *Commitment and Compliance – The Role of Non-binding Norms in the International Legal System* 75 (Oxford: Oxford University Press, 2000).

Schachter, O., *Sharing the World's Resources* (New York: Columbia University Press, 1977).

Schermers, H.G. and Niels M. Blokker, *International Institutional Law – Unity Within Diversity* (The Hague: Nijhoff, 1995).

Schrijver, N., *Sovereignty over Natural Resources – Balancing Rights and Duties* (Cambridge: Cambridge University Press, 1997).

Shaw, M.N., *International Law* (Cambridge: Cambridge University Press, 4th ed. 1997).

Shearer, I.A., *Starke's International Law* (London: Butterworths, 11th ed. 1994).

Shelton, D. ed., *Commitment and Compliance – The Role of Non-binding Norms in the International Legal System* (Oxford: Oxford University Press, 2000).

Shue, H., 'Global Environment and International Inequality', 75 *Int'l Aff.* 531 (1999).

Simma, B., 'From Bilateralism to Community Interest in International Law', 250 *Recueil des cours – Académie de droit international* 217 (1994).

Sinha, S.P., *Legal Polycentricity and International Law* (Durham, North Carolina: Carolina Academic Press, 1996).

Verhoosel, G., 'International Transfer of Environmentally Sound Technology: The new Dimension of an old Stumbling Block', 27 *Envtl. Pol'y and L.* 470 (1997).

Verwey, W.D., 'The Principle of Preferential Treatment for Developing Countries', 23 *Indian J. Int'l L.* 343 (1983).

World Commission on Environment and Development, *Our Common Future* (Oxford: Oxford University Press, 1987).

Chapter 1

Allott, P., *Eunomia – New Order for a New World* (Oxford: Oxford University Press, 1990).

Byers, M., *Custom, Power, and the Power of Rules – International Relations and Customary International Law* (Cambridge: Cambridge University Press, 1999).

Carrillo-Salcedo, J.-A., 'Droit international et souveraineté des Etats', 257 *RCADI* 35 (1996).

Delbruck, J., 'The Role of the United Nations in Dealing with Global Problems', 4 *Indiana J. Global Legal Studies* 277 (1997).

Do Nascimento E Silva, G.E., 'Pending Problems on International Environmental Law of the Environment', in René-Jean Dupuy ed., *The Future of the International Law of the Environment* 217 (Dordrecht: Nijhoff, 1985).

Ehrlich, P.R. et al., *The Stork and the Plow – The Equity Answer to the Human Dilemma* (New York: Putman's Sons, 1995).

Evans, T., 'International Environmental Law and the Challenge of Globalization', in Tim Jewell and Jenny Steele eds, *Law in Environmental Decision-Making – National, European, and International Perspectives* 207 (Oxford: Clarendon, 1998).

Gelber, H.G., *Sovereignty through Interdependence* (London: Kluwer Law International, 1997).

Keohane, R.O. et al., 'The Effectiveness of International Environmental Institutions', in Peter M. Haas et al. eds, *Institutions for the Earth – Sources of Effective International Environmental Protection* 3 (Cambridge, Mass: MIT Press, 1993).

Kornicker, E., *Ius Cogens und Umweltvölkerrecht* (Basel: Helbing, 1997).

Lorimer, J., *The Institutes of the Law of Nations* (Edinburgh: William Blackwood and Sons, 1883).

Mathews, J.T., 'Power Shift (Changing Role of Central Government)', 76 *Foreign Aff.* 50 (1997).

Meadows, D.H./Club of Rome, *The Limits to Growth* (London: Earth Island, 1972).

Oppenheim, L., *International Law – A Treatise* (Ronald F. Roxburgh ed., 3rd ed. vol. 1, London: Longmans, 1920).

Rao, P.S., 'Environment as a Common Heritage of Mankind: A Policy Perspective', in *International Law on the Eve of the 21st Century – Views from the International Law Commission* 201 (New York: UN, 1997).

Rossi, C.R., *Equity and International Law – A Legal Realist Approach to the Legal Process of International Decisionmaking* (Irvington, NY: Transnational Publishers, 1993).

Sands, P., 'International Law in the Field of Sustainable Development', 65 *British Yb. Int'l L.* 303 (1994).

Singh, N., 'The Distinguishable Characteristics of the Concept of Law as it Developed in Ancient India', in Marten Bos and Ian Brownlie eds, *Liber Amicorum for the Rt. Hon. Lord Wilberforce* 91 (Oxford: Clarendon, 1987).

Waters, M., *Globalization* (London: Routledge, 2nd ed. 2001).

Westlake, J., *Chapters on the Principles of International Law* (Cambridge: University Press, 1894).

Yaker, L., 'Joint Implementation from a Southern Perspective', in Catrinus J. Jepma ed., *The Feasibility of Joint Implementation* 87 (Dordrecht: Kluwer, 1995).

Chapter 2

Abi-Saab, G., 'The Legal Formulation of a Right to Development (Subjects and Content)', in René-Jean Dupuy ed., *The Right to Development at the International Level* 159 (Alphen aan den Rijn: Sijthoff and Noordhoff, 1980).

Akehurst, M., 'Equity and General Principles of Law', 25 *Int'l and Comp. L.Q.* 801 (1976).

Anaya, S.J., 'On Justifying Special Ethnic Group Rights', in Will Kymlicka and Ian Shapiro eds, *Ethnicity and Group Rights – Nomos XXXIX* 222 (New York: New York University Press, 1997).

Aristotle, *The Nicomachean Ethics* (trans. David Ross, revised by J.L Ackrill and J.O. Urmson, Oxford: Oxford University Press, 1991).

Banuri, T. et al., 'Equity and Social Considerations', in James P. Bruce et al. eds, *Climate Change 1995 – Economic and Social Dimensions of Climate Change – Contributions of Working Group III to the Second Assessment Report of the IPCC* (Cambridge: Cambridge University Press, 1996).

Barry, B., *The Liberal Theory of Justice: A Critical Examination of the Principal Doctrines in A Theory of Justice by John Rawls* (Oxford: Clarendon, 1973).

Barry, B., 'Humanity and Justice in Global Perspective', in J. Roland Pennock and John W. Chapman eds, *Ethics, Economics and the Law – Nomos XXIV* 219 (New York: New York University Press, 1982).

Bedjaoui, M., 'Pour un nouveau droit social international', 39 *Yb. Association Attenders and Alumni* 17 (1969).

Bedjaoui, M., 'Some Unorthodox Reflections on the "Right to Development"', in Francis Snyder and Peter Slinn eds, *International Law of Development: Comparative Approaches* 87 (Abingdon: Professional Books, 1987).

Beitz, C.R., 'Justice and International Relations', in Charles R. Beitz et al. eds, *International Ethics* 286 (Princeton, NJ: Princeton University Press, 1985).

Benedek, W., 'The Lomé Convention and the International Law of Development: A Concretisation of the New International Economic Order?', 26 *J. African L.* 74 (1982).

Bhaskar, V., 'Distributive Justice and the Control of Global Warming', in V. Bhaskar and Andrew Glyn eds, *The North, the South and the Environment – Ecological Constraints and the Global Environment* 102 (London: Earthscan, 1995).

Brown Weiss, E., *In Fairness to Future Generations: International Law, Common Patrimony and Intergenerational Equity* (Tokyo: UN University, 1989).

Brown Weiss, E., 'International Environmental Law: Contemporary Issues and the Emergence of a New World Order', 81 *Georgetown L.J.* 675 (1993).

Caflish, L., 'Unequal Treaties', 35 *German Yb. Int'l L.* 52 (1992).

Calabresi, G. and A. Douglas Melamed, 'Property Rules, Liability Rules, and Inalienability: One View of the Cathedral', 85 *Harvard L. Rev.* 1089 (1972).

Chemillier-Gendreau, M., 'La signification des principes équitables dans le droit international contemporain', 16 *Belgian Rev. Int'l L.* 509 (1981).

Chowdhury, S.R., 'Common but Differentiated State Responsibility in International Environmental Law: From Stockholm (1972) to Rio (1992)', in Konrad Ginther et al. eds, *Sustainable Development and Good Governance* 322 (Dordrecht: Nijhoff, 1995).

Dobson, A., *Justice and the Environment* (Oxford: Oxford University Press, 1998).

Douglas, M. et al., 'Human Needs and Wants', in Steve Rayner and Elizabeth L. Malone eds, *Human Choice and Climate Change – Volume One – The Societal Framework* 195 (Columbus, Ohio: Battelle Press, 1998).

Faundez, J., *Affirmative Action – International Perspectives* (Geneva: International Labour Office, 1994).

Ferguson, C.C., 'Redressing Global Injustices: The Role of Law', in Frederik E. Snyder and Surakiart Sathirathai eds, *Third World Attitudes Toward International Law: An Introduction* 365 (Dordrecht: Nijhoff, 1987).

Flory, M., *Droit international du développement* (Paris: Presses universitaires de France, 1977).

Galanter, M., *Competing Equalities – Law and the Backward Classes in India* (Berkeley: UC Press, 1984).

Galenkamp, M., 'Collective Rights: Much Ado About Nothing? – A Review Essay', 9 *Netherlands Q. Hum. Rts.* 291 (1991).

Gündling, L., 'Compliance Assistance in International Environmental Law: Capacity-Building Through Financial and Technology Transfer', 56 *Zeitschrift für ausländisches öffentliches Recht und Völkerrecht* 796 (1996).

Haq, I., 'From Charity to Obligation: A Third World Perspective on Concessional Resource Transfers', 14 *Texas Int'l L.J.* 389 (1979).

Hardin, G., 'Living on a Lifeboat', 24 *Bioscience* 561 (1974).

Hart, H.L.A., *The Concept of Law* (Oxford: Clarendon, 2nd ed. 1994).

Inkster, I., 'Colonial and Neo-Colonial Transfers of Technology: Perspectives on India Before 1914', in Roy McLeod and Deepak Kumar eds, *Technology and the Raj – Western Technology and Technical Transfers to India 1700-1947* at 25 (New Delhi: Sage, 1995).

Kahlenberg, R.D., 'Class-Based Affirmative Action', 84 *California L. Rev.* 1037 (1996).

Khurshid, S., 'Justice and the New International Economic Order', in Kamal Hossain ed., *Legal Aspects of the New International Economic Order* 108 (London: Pinter, 1980).

Kwiatkowska, B., 'Equitable Maritime Boundary Delimitation, as Exemplified in the Work of the International Court of Justice During the Presidency of Sir Robert Yewdall Jennings and Beyond', 28 *Ocean Development and Int'l L.* 91 (1997).

Kymlicka, W., 'Concepts of Community and Social Justice', in Fen Osler Hampson and Judith Reppy eds, *Earthly Goods – Environmental Change and Social Justice* 30 (Ithaca, NY: Cornell University Press, 1996).

Lauterpacht, Sir Hersch, *The Development of International Law by the International Court* (London: Stevens and Sons, 1958).

McDonald, R.St.J., 'The Principle of Solidarity in Public International Law', in Christian Dominicé et al. eds, *Etudes de droit international en l'honneur de Pierre Lalive* 275 (Basel: Helbing, 1993).

Makarczyk, J., *Principles of a New International Economic Order* (Dordrecht: Nijhoff, 1988).

Naqvi, F.H., 'People's Rights or Victim's Rights: Reexamining the Conceptualization of Indigenous Rights in International Law', 71 *Indiana L.J.* 673 (1996).

Nesiah, D., *Discrimination with Reason – The Policy of Reservations in the United States, India and Malaysia* (New Delhi: Oxford University Press, 1999).

Newman, R.A., 'The General Principles of Equity', in Ralph A. Newman ed., *Equity in the World's Legal Systems* 589 (Brussels: Bruylant, 1973).

Nielsen, K., 'Global Justice, Capitalism and the Third World', in Robin Attfield and Barry Wilkins eds, *International Justice and the Third World – Studies in the Philosophy of Development* 17 (London: Routledge, 1992).

Nozick, R., *Anarchy, State and Utopia* (New York: Basic Books, 1974).

O'Manique, J., 'Development, Human Rights and Law', 14 *Hum. Rts. Q.* 383 (1992).

Parijs, P. van, *Real Freedom for All* (Oxford: Clarendon, 1995).

Rakowski, E., *Equal Justice* (Oxford: Clarendon, 1991).

Rawls, J., *A Theory of Justice* (Oxford: Clarendon, 1972).

Rawls, J., 'The Law of Peoples', in Steven Shute and Susan Hurley eds, *On Human Rights – The Oxford Amnesty Lectures* 1993 (New York: Basic Books, 1993).

Rossi, C.R., *Equity and International Law – A Legal Realist Approach to the Legal Process of International Decisionmaking* (Irvington, NY: Transnational Publishers, 1993).

Schrijver, N., 'The Dynamics of Sovereignty in a Changing World', in Konrad Ginther et al. eds, *Sustainable Development and Good Governance* 80 (Dordrecht: Nijhoff, 1995).

Schütz, R., *Solidarität im Wirtschaftsvölkerrecht – eine Bestandsaufnahme zentraler entwicklungsspezifischer Solidarrechte und Solidarpflichten im Völkerrecht* (Berlin: Duncker and Humblot, 1994).

Sen, A., *Inequality Reexamined* (Cambridge, Mass: Harvard University Press, 1992).

Shue, H., *Basic rights – Subsistence, Affluence, and U.S. Foreign Policy* (Princeton: Princeton University Press, 2nd ed. 1996).

Shukla, P.R., 'Justice, Equity and Efficiency in Climate Change: A Developing Country Perspective', in Ferenc L. Tóth ed., *Fair Weather? Equity Concerns in Climate Change* 145 (London: Earthscan 1999).

Singer, P., 'Famine, Affluence, and Morality', in Charles R. Beitz et al. eds, *International Ethics* 247 (Princeton, NJ: Princeton University Press, 1985).

Snyder, R.N., 'Natural Law and Equity', in Ralph A. Newman ed., *Equity in the World's Legal Systems* 34 (Brussels: Bruylant, 1973).

Sowell, T., *Preferential Policies – An International Perspective* (New York: W. Morrow, 1990).

Vasciannie, S.C., *Land-Locked and Geographically Disadvantaged States in the International Law of the Sea* (Oxford: Clarendon, 1990).

Wallerstein, I., 'The Present State of the Debate on World Inequality', in Mitchell A. Seligson and John T. Passé-Smith eds, *Development and Underdevelopment: The Political Economy of Inequality* 217 (Boulder, CO: L. Rienner, 1993).

Werksman, J., 'Compliance and the Kyoto Protocol: Building a Backbone into a 'Flexible' Regime', 9 *Yb. Int'l Envtl. L.* 48 (1998).

Wolfrum, R., 'Means of Ensuring Compliance with and Enforcement of International Environmental Law', 272 *RCADI* 9 (1998).

Young, H.P., *Equity in Theory and Practice* (Princeton, NJ: Princeton University Press, 1994).

Chapter 3

Anand, R.P., 'Attitude of the Asian-African States Toward Certain Problems of International Law', 15 *Int'l and Comp. L.Q.* 55 (1966).

Anand, R.P., 'A New International Economic Order for Sustainable Development?', in Najeeb Al-Nauimi and Richard Meese eds, *International Legal Issues Arising Under the United Nations Decade of International Law* 1209 (The Hague: Nijhoff, 1995).

Attard, D.J., *The Exclusive Economic Zone in International Law* (Oxford: Clarendon, 1987).

Barsh, R.L., 'A Special Session of the UN General Assembly Rethinks the Economic Rights and Duties of States', 85 *Am. J. Int'l L.* 192 (1991).

Baslar, K., *The Concept of the Common Heritage of Mankind in International Law* (The Hague: Kluwer Law International, 1998).

Beck, H., *Die Differenzierung von Rechtspflichten in den Beziehungen zwischen Industrie- und Entwicklungsländern – Eine völkerrechtliche Untersuchung für die Bereiche des internationalen Wirtschafts-, Arbeits- und Umweltrechts* (Frankfurt: Peter Lang, 1994).

Bekhechi, M.A., 'Une nouvelle étape dans le développement du droit international de l'environnement: La Convention sur la désertification', 101 *Revue Générale de droit international public* 5 (1997).

Benedek, W., 'Implications of the Principle of Sustainable Development, Human Rights and Good Governance for the GATT/WTO', in Konrad Ginther et al. eds, *Sustainable Development and Good Governance* 274 (Dordrecht: Nijhoff, 1995).

Biermann, F., 'Financing Environmental Policies in the South – Experiences from the Multilateral Ozone Fund', 9 *Int'l Envtl. Aff.* 179 (1997).

Biermann, F., 'Justice in the Greenhouse: Perspectives from International Law', in F.L. Tóth ed., *Fair Weather? Equity Concerns in Climate Change* 160 (London: Earthscan, 1999).

Bodansky, D., 'The Legitimacy of International Governance: A Coming Challenge for International Environmental Law?', 93 *Am. J. Int'l L.* 614 (1999).

Boyle, A., 'Comment on the Paper by Diana Ponce-Nava', in Winfried Lang ed., *Sustainable Development and International Law* 137 (London: Graham and Trotman, 1995).

Cain, P.J. and A.G. Hopkins, *British Imperialism – Crisis and Deconstruction 1914-1990* (London: Longman, 1993).

Carreau, D., 'Rapport du directeur d'études de la section de langue française du Centre', in Dominique Carreau and Malcolm N. Shaw eds, *The External Debt* 3 (London: Kluwer Law International, 1995).

Corea, G., *Taming Commodity Markets – The Integrated Programme and the Common Fund in UNCTAD* (Manchester: Manchester University Press, 1992).

Dupuy, P.-M., 'Soft Law and the International Law of the Environment', 12 *Michigan J. Int'l L.* 420 (1991).

Fatouros, A.A., 'The International Law of the New International Economic Order: Emerging Patterns of Norms', XII *Thesaurus Acroasium* 445 (1981).

Flory, M., 'Mondialisation et droit international du développement', 101 *Revue générale de droit international public* 609 (1997).

French, D., 'Developing States and International Environmental Law: The Importance of Differentiated Responsibilities', 49 *Int'l and Comp. L.Q.* 35 (2000).

Gavouneli, M., 'Compliance With International Environmental Treaties: The Empirical Evidence', 91 *Am. Society Int'l L. Proceedings* 234 (1997).

Gianaris, W.N., 'Weighted Voting in the International Monetary Fund and the World Bank', 14 *Fordham Int'l L.J.* 910 (1990-91).

Griffin, K., *International Inequality and National Poverty* (London: Macmillan, 1978).

Grossman, C. and Daniel Bradlow, 'Are we Being Propelled Towards a People-Centered Transnational Legal Order?', 9 *Am. University J. Int'l L. and Pol'y* 1 (1993).

Harris, P.G., 'Common but Differentiated Responsibility: The Kyoto Protocol and United States Policy', 7 *New York University Envtl. L.J.* 27 (1999).

Hossain, K., 'Sustainable Development: A Normative Framework for Evolving a More Just and Humane International Economic Order', in Subrata Roy Chowdhury et al. eds, *The Right to Development in International Law* 259 (Dordrecht: Nijhoff, 1992).

Iles, A., 'The Desertification Convention: A Deeper Focus on Social Aspects of Environmental Degradation', 36 *Harvard Int'l L.J.* 207 (1995).

Jaenicke, G., 'The United Nations Convention on the Law of the Sea and the Agreement Relating to the Implementation of Part XI of the Convention', in Ulrich Beyerlin et al. eds, *Recht zwischen Umbruch und Bewahrung* 121 (Berlin: Springer, 1995).

Kellersmann, B., *Die gemeinsame, aber differenzierte Verantwortlichkeit von Industriestaaten und Entwicklungsländern für den Schutz der globalen Umwelt* (Berlin: Springer, 2000).

Kenen, P.B., 'Debt Relief as Development Assistance', in Jagdish N. Bhagwati ed., *The New International Economic Order: The North-South Debate* 50 (Cambridge, Mass: MIT Press, 1977).

Kiss, A., 'Conserving the Common Heritage of Mankind', 59 *Revista Juridica de la Universidad de Puerto Rico* 773 (1990).

Koskenniemi, M. and Marja Lehto, 'The Privilege of Universality – International Law, Economic Ideology and Seabed Resources', 65 *Nordic J. Int'l L.* 533 (1996).

Lee, S., 'A Puzzle of Sovereignty', 27 *California Western Int'l L.J.* 241 (1997).

Lewis, A., 'The Evolving Process of Swapping Debt for Nature', 10 *Colorado J. Int'l Envtl. L. and Pol'y* 431 (1999).

McDonald, R.St.J., 'The Common Heritage of Mankind', in Ulrich Beyerlin et al. eds, *Recht zwischen Umbruch und Bewahrung* 153 (Berlin: Springer, 1995).

McGoldrick, D., 'Sustainable Development and Human Rights: An Integrated Conception', 45 *Int'l and Comp. L.Q.* 796 (1996).

Mahiou, A., 'Le droit au développement', in *International Law on the Eve of the 21st Century – Views from the International Law Commission* 217 (New York: United Nations, 1997).

Makarczyk, J., *Principles of a New International Economic Order* (Dordrecht: Nijhoff, 1988).

Mercure, P.-F., 'Le choix du concept de développement durable plutôt que celui du patrimoine commun de l'humanité afin d'assurer la protection de l'atmosphère', 41 *McGill L.J.* 595 (1996).

Mindaoudou, D.A., 'La notion de majorité comme preuve de démocratie à l'Assemblée générale des Nations Unies', 8 *African J. Int'l and Comp. L.* 447 (1996).

Moomaw, W.R., 'International Environmental Policy and the Softening of Sovereignty', 21 *Fletcher F. World Aff.* 7 (1997).

O'Neill, C.A. and Cass R. Sunstein, 'Economics and the Environment: Trading Debt and Technology for Nature', 17 *Columbia J. Envtl. L.* 93 (1992).

Oxman, B.H., 'The 1994 Agreement and the Convention', 88 *Am. J. Int'l L.* 687 (1994).

Paolillo, F., 'Final Report', 67/1 *Yb. Institute Int'l L.* 437 (1997).

Parikh, J.K., 'North-South Cooperation for Joint Implementation', in J.K. Parikh et al. eds, *Climate Change and North-South Cooperation – Indo-Canadian Cooperation in Joint Implementation* 192 (New Delhi: Tata McGraw-Hill, 1997).

Patlis, J.M., 'The Multilateral Fund of the Montreal Protocol: A Prototype for Financial Mechanisms in Protecting the Global Environment', 25 *Cornell Int'l L.J.* 181 (1992).

Payer, C., *Lent and Lost – Foreign Credit and Third World Development* (London: Zed Books, 1991).

Quesada Mateo, C.A. ed., *Debt-For-Nature Swaps to Promote Natural Resource Conservation* (Rome: FAO, 1993).

Raghavan, C., *Recolonization – GATT, the Uruguay Round and the Third World* (London: Zed, 1990).

Ratner, S.R., 'Drawing a Better Line: Uti Possidetis and the Borders of New States', 90 *Am. J. Int'l L.* 590 (1996).

Redgwell, C., 'The Law of Reservations in Respect of Multilateral Conventions', in J.P. Gardner ed., *Human Rights as General Norms and a State's Right to Opt Out – Reservations and Objections to Human Rights Conventions* 3 (London: British Institute of International and Comparative Law, 1997).

Reinisch, A., *State Responsibility for Debts – International Law Aspects of External Debts and Debt Restructuring* (Vienna: Böhlau Verlag, 1995).

Sell, S.K., *Power and Ideas – North-South Politics of Intellectual Property and Antitrust* (Albany: State University of New York Press, 1998).

South Commission, *The Challenge to the South* (Oxford: Oxford University Press, 1990).

Subedi, S.P., 'The Doctrine of Objective Regimes in International Law and the Competence of the United Nations to Impose Territorial or Peace Settlements on States', 37 *German Yb. Int'l L.* 162 (1994).

Vasciannie, S.C., *Land-Locked and Geographically Disadvantaged States in the International Law of the Sea* (Oxford: Clarendon, 1990).

Verwey, W.D., 'The Principles of a New International Economic Order and the Law of the General Agreement on Tariffs and Trade (GATT)', 3 *Leiden J. Int'l L.* 117 (1990).

Virally, M., 'Panorama du droit international contemporain', 183 *RCADI* 9 (1983/V).

Wälde, T.W., 'A Requiem for the "New International Economic Order" - The Rise and Fall of Paradigms in International Law', in Najeeb Al-Nauimi and Richard Meese eds, *International Legal Issues Arising under the United Nations Decade of International Law* 1301 (The Hague: Nijhoff, 1995).

Weston, A., 'The Uruguay Round: Unravelling the Implications for the Least Developed and Low-Income Countries', in UNCTAD, *International Monetary and Financial Issues for the 1990s – Volume VI* at 61 (New York: UNCTAD, 1995).

Wilkins, B., 'Debt and Underdevelopment: The Case for Cancelling Third World Debts', in Robin Attfield and Barry Wilkins eds, *International Justice and the Third World – Studies in the Philosophy of Development* 169 (London: Routledge, 1992).

Woods, N., 'The Challenge of Good Governance for the IMF and the World Bank Themselves', 28 *World Development* 823 (2000).

Woods, N., 'Making the IMF and the World Bank more Accountable', 77 *Int'l Aff.* 83 (2001).

Young, O.R., 'Environmental Ethics in International Society', in Jean-Marc Coicaud and Daniel Warner eds, *Ethics and International Affairs – Extent and Limits* 161 (Tokyo: UNU Press, 2001).

Young, R., 'The Legal Regime of the Deep-Sea Floor', 62 *Am. J. Int'l L.* 641 (1968).

Chapter 4

Achanta, A. and Prodipto Ghosh, 'Technology Transfer and Environment', in Vicente Sanchez and Calestous Juma eds, *Biodiplomacy – Genetic Resources and International Relations* 157 (Nairobi: African Centre for Technology Studies, 1994).

Barton, J.H., 'The Economic and Legal Context of Contemporary Technology Transfer', in Edgardo Buscaglia et al. eds, *The Law and Economics of Development* 83 (Greenwich, Conn: JAI Press, 1997).

Benedick, R.E., *Ozone Diplomacy – New Directions in Safeguarding the Planet* (Cambridge, Mass: Harvard University Press, enlarged ed. 1998).

Benestad, O., 'Energy Needs and CO_2 Emissions – Constructing a Formula for Just Distributions', 22 *Energy Pol'y* 725 (1994).

Biermann, F., *Saving the Atmosphere – International Law, Developing Countries and Air Pollution* (Frankfurt am Main: Peter Lang, 1995).

Blakeney, M., *Legal Aspects of the Transfer of Technology to Developing Countries* (Oxford: ESC Publishing, 1989).

Bowman, M.J., 'The Ramsar Convention Comes of Age', 42 *Netherlands Int'l L. Rev.* 1 (1995).

Brown Weiss, E. and Harold K. Jacobson eds, *Engaging Countries – Strengthening Compliance with International Accords* (Cambridge, Mass: MIT Press, 1998).

Brown Weiss, E., 'The Five International Treaties: A Living History', in Edith Brown Weiss and Harold K. Jacobson eds, *Engaging Countries: Strengthening Compliance with International Accords* 89 (Cambridge, Mass: MIT Press, 1998).

Brunnee, J., 'A Fine Balance: Facilitation and Enforcement in the Design of a Compliance Regime for the Kyoto Protocol', 13 *Tulane Envtl. L.J.* 223 (2000).

Bush, E.J. and L.D. Danny Harvey, 'Joint Implementation and the Ultimate Objective of the United Nations Framework Convention on Climate Change', 7 *Global Envtl. Change* 265 (1997).

Campbell, L.B., 'The Role of the Private Sector and other Non-state Actors in Implementation of the Kyoto Protocol', in W. Bradnee Chambers ed., *Inter-linkages – The Kyoto Protocol and the International Trade and Investment Regimes* 17 (Tokyo: UN University, 2001).

Charney, J.I., 'Transnational Corporations and Developing Public International Law', 1983 *Duke L.J.* 748 (1983).

Coldiron, B.M., 'Thinning of the Ozone Layer: Facts and Consequences', 27 *J. Am. Academy Dermatology* 653 (1992).

Cullet, P. and Patricia Kameri-Mbote, 'Joint Implementation and Forestry Projects – Conceptual and Operational Fallacies', 74 *Int'l Aff.* 393 (1998).

Cullet, P., 'Desertification', in UNESCO, *Knowledge for Sustainable Development* (Oxford: EOLSS Publishers, 2002).

Emmanuel, A., *Technologie appropriée ou technologie sous-développée* (Paris: Presses universitaires de France, 2nd ed. 1982).

Gallagher, A., 'The "New" Montreal Protocol and the Future of International Law for the Protection of the Global Environment', 14 *Houston J. Int'l L.* 267 (1992).

Ghosh, J. et al., 'Privatising Natural Resources', XXX/38 *EPW* 2351 (1995).

Ghosh, P. and Jyotsna Puri eds, *Joint Implementation of Climate Change Commitments – Opportunities and Apprehensions* (New Delhi: Tata Energy Research Institute, 1994).

Grubb, M. et al., *Greenhouse Gas Emissions Trading* (Geneva: UNCTAD, 1998).

Gupta, J., *The Climate Change Convention and Developing Countries: From Conflict to Consensus?* (Dordrecht: Kluwer, 1997).

Guruswamy, L., 'Climate Change: The Next Dimension', 15 *J. Land Use and Envtl. L.* 341 (2000).

Heller, T., Joint Implementation and the Path to a Climate Change Regime (Jean Monnet Chair Paper, The Robert Schuman Centre at the European University Institute, 1995).

Hurlbut, D., 'Beyond the Montreal Protocol: Impact on Nonparty States and Lessons for Future Environmental Protection Regimes', 4 *Colorado J. Int'l Envtl. L. and Pol'y* 344 (1993).

Johnston, S., 'Financial Aid, Biodiversity and International Law', in Michael Bowman and Catherine Redgwell eds, *International Law and the Conservation of Biological Diversity* 271 (London: Kluwer Law International, 1996).

Kameri-Mbote, P., *Property Rights and Biodiversity Management in Kenya – The Case of Land Tenure and Wildlife* (Nairobi: ACTS Press, 2002).

Kete, N. et al., Should Development Aid be Used to Finance the Clean Development Mechanism? 5 (Washington, DC: World Resources Institute, 2001).

Kohona, P.T.B., 'The Environment: An Opportunity for North/South Cooperation', *Third World Legal Studies* 71 (1993).

Korobkin, R.B. and Thomas S. Ulen, 'Efficiency and Equity: What can be Gained by Combining Coase and Rawls?', 73 *Washington L. Rev.* 329 (1998).

Kwakwa, E., 'Emerging International Development Law and Traditional International Law – Congruence or Cleavage?', in Anthony Carty ed., *Law and Development* 407 (Aldershot: Dartmouth, 1992).

Linklater, A., *Beyond Realism and Marxism – Critical Theory and International Relations* (Basingstoke: Macmillan, 1990).

Litfin, K.T., *Ozone Discourses – Science and Politics in Global Environmental Cooperation* (New York: Columbia University Press, 1994).

Mascarenhas, R.C., *Technology Transfer and Development – India's Hindustan Machine Tool Company* (Boulder, CO: Westview Press, 1982).

Mertens, S.K., 'Towards Accountability in the Restructured Global Environment Facility', 3 *Rev. Eur. Community and Int'l Envtl. L.* 105 (1994).

Missfeldt, F., 'Flexibility Mechanisms: Which Path to Take after Kyoto?', 7 *Rev. Eur. Community and Int'l Envtl. L.* 128 (1998).

Muchlinski, P., *Multinational Enterprises and the Law* (Oxford: Blackwell, 1995).

Mugabe, J. and Norman Clark, *Technology Transfer and the Convention on Biological Diversity – Emerging Policy and Institutional Issues* (Nairobi: African Centre for Technology Studies, 1996).

Müller, B., Ratifying the Kyoto Protocol: The Case for Japanese-Russian Joint Implementation (London: Royal Institute of International Affairs – Energy and Environment Programme, Briefing Paper – New Series N° 21, 2001).

Mumma, A., 'The Poverty of Africa's Position at the Climate Change Convention Negotiations', 19 *UCLA J. Envtl. L. and Pol'y* 181 (2000/2001).

Navid, D., 'Compliance Assistance in International Environmental Law: Capacity-Building, Transfer of Finance and Technology', 56 *Zeitschrift für ausländisches öffentliches Recht und Völkerrecht* 810 (1996).

Papasavva, S. and William R. Moomaw, 'Adverse Implications of the Montreal Protocol Grace Period for Developing Countries', 9 *Int'l Envtl. Aff.* 219 (1997).

Pearce, D., 'Joint Implementation – A General Overview', in Catrinus J. Jepma ed., *The Feasibility of Joint Implementation* 15 (Dordrecht: Kluwer, 1995).

Redclift, M. and Colin Sage, 'Introduction', in Michael Redclift and Colin Sage eds, *Strategies for Sustainable Development – Local Agendas for the Southern Hemisphere* 1 (Chichester: Wiley, 1994).

Riddell, R., *Aid in the 21st Century* (New York: UNDP, 1996).

Rosenzweig, R. et al., *The Emerging International Greenhouse Gas Market* (Arlington, VA: Pew Center on Global Climate Change, 2002).

Rostow, W.W., *The Stages of Economic Growth: A Non-Communist Manifesto* (Cambridge: Cambridge University Press, 3rd ed. 1990).

Sand, P.H., 'Trusts for the Earth: New International Financial Mechanisms for Sustainable Development', in Winfried Lang ed., *Sustainable Development and International Law* 167 (London: Graham and Trotman, 1995).

Sand, P.H., 'International Economic Instruments for Sustainable Development: Sticks, Carrots and Games', 36 *Indian J. Int'l L.* 1 (1996).

Schmidheiny, S. et al., *Financing Change: The Financial Community, Eco-Efficiency, and Sustainable Development* (Cambridge, Mass: MIT Press, 1996).

Schumacher, E.F., *Small is Beautiful: A Study of Economics as if People Mattered* (London: Blond and Briggs, 1973).

Sebenius, J.K., 'Designing Negotiations Towards a New Regime – The Case of Global Warming', 15 *Int'l Security* 110 (1991).

Smith, K.R. et al., 'Who Pays (to Solve the Problem and How Much)?', in Peter Hayes and Kirk Smith eds, *The Global Greenhouse Regime – Who Pays? – Science, Economics and North-South Politics in the Climate Change Convention* 70 (London: Earthscan, 1993).

Stewart, F., *Technology and Underdevelopment* (London: Macmillan, 2nd ed. 1978).

Stone, C.D., *The Gnat is Older than Man – Global Environment and Human Agenda* (Princeton, NJ: Princeton University Press, 1993).

Thompson, M. and Steve Rayner, 'Cultural Discourses', in Steve Rayner and Elizabeth L. Malone eds, *Human Choice and Climate Change – Volume One – The Societal Framework* 265 (Columbus, Ohio: Battelle Press, 1998).

Trebilcock, M.J., 'What Makes Poor Countries Poor? – The Role of Institutional Capital in Economic Development', in Edgardo Buscaglia et al. eds, *The Law and Economics of Development* 15 (Greenwich, Conn: JAI Press, 1997).

Verhoosel, G., 'Beyond the Unsustainable Rhetoric of Sustainable Development: Transferring Environmentally Sound Technologies', 11 *Georgetown Int'l Envtl. L. Rev.* 49 (1998).

Victor, D.G. et al. eds, *The Implementation and Effectiveness of International Environmental Commitments – Theory and Practice* (Cambridge, Mass: MIT Press, 1998).

Wolfrum, R., 'Means of Ensuring Compliance with and Enforcement of International Environmental Law', 272 *RCADI* 9 (1998).

Chapter 5

Ayyangar, Justice N.R., Report on the Revision of the Patents Law (September 1959).

Bragdon, S.H. and David R. Downes, *Recent Policy Trends and Developments Related to the Conservation, Use and Development of Genetic Resources* (Rome: International Plant Genetic Resources Institute, 1998).

Chambers, R., *Whose Reality Counts? – Putting the Last First* (London: IT Publications, 1997).

Clavier, J.-P., *Les catégories de la propriété intellectuelle à l'épreuve des créations génétiques* (Paris: L'Harmattan, 1998).

Conway, G.R. and Edward B. Barbier, *After the Green Revolution – Sustainable Agriculture for Development* (London: Earthscan, 1990).

Cooper, H.D., 'The International Treaty on Plant Genetic Resources for Food and Agriculture', 11 *Rev. Eur. Community and Int'l Envtl. L.* 1 (2002).

Dhaliwal, G.S. and V.K. Dilawari, 'Impact of Green Revolution on Environment', in B.S. Hansra and A.N. Shukla eds, *Social, Economic and Political Implications of Green Revolution in India* (New Delhi: Classical Publishing, 1991).

Dhar, B. and Sachin Chaturvedi, 'Introducing Plant Breeders' Rights in India – A Critical Evaluation of the Proposed Legislation', 1 *J. World Intellectual Property* 245 (1998).

Dhavan, R. et al. 'Power Without Responsibility on Aspects of the Indian Patents Legislation', 33 *J. Indian L. Institute* 1 (1991).

Dhavan, R. and Maya Prabhu, 'Patent Monopolies and Free Trade: Basic Contradiction in Dunkel Draft', 37 *J. Indian L. Institute* 194 (1995).

Fingleton, J.S., *Legal Recognition of Indigenous Groups* (Rome: FAO, 1998).

Hamilton, N.D., 'Why own the Farm if you can Own the Farmer (and the Crop)? - Contract Production and Intellectual Property Protection of Grain Crops', 73 *Nebraska L. Rev.* 48 (1994).

Horsch, R.B. and Robert T. Fraley, 'Agricultural Industrialization and the Loss of Biodiversity', in Lakshman D. Guruswamy and Jeffrey A. McNeely eds, *Protection of Global Biodiversity – Converging Strategies* 66 (Durham, NC: Duke University Press, 1998).

Joshi, B.H., *An Analytical Approach to Problems of Indian Agriculture: A Theoretical and System Approach* (New Delhi: B.R. Publishing, 1992).

Kate, K. ten and Carolina Lasén Diaz, 'The Undertaking Revisited – A Commentary on the Revision of the International Undertaking on Plant Genetic Resources for Food and Agriculture', 6 *Rev. Eur. Community and Int'l Envtl. L.* 284 (1997).

Lacy, W.B., 'The Global Plant Genetic Resources System: A Competition-Cooperation Paradox', 35 *Crop Science* 335 (1995).

Nijar, G.S. and Chee Yoke Ling, 'The Implications of the Intellectual Property Rights Regime of the Convention on Biological Diversity and GATT on Biodiversity Conservation: A Third World Perspective', in Anatole F. Krattiger et al. eds, *Widening Perspectives on Biodiversity* 277 (Geneva: International Academy of the Environment, 1994).

Ostrom, E., *Governing the Commons – The Evolution of Institutions for Collective Action* (Cambridge: Cambridge University Press, 1990).

Prasad, C.S., 'Suicide Death and Quality of Indian Cotton', XXXIV *EPW* PE-12 (1999).

Rangnekar, D., Intellectual Property Rights and Agriculture: An Analysis of the Economic Impact of Plant Breeders' Rights (Actionaid UK, 2000).

Roht-Arriaza, N., 'Of Seeds and Shamans: The Appropriation of the Scientific and Technological Knowledge of Indigenous and Local Communities', 17 *Michigan J. Int'l L.* 919 (1996).

Sahai, S., 'What is Bt and what is Terminator?', XXXIV/3-4 *EPW* 84 (1999).

Sahai, S., 'Indian Patents Act and TRIPS', 28 *EPW* 1495 (1993).

Sahai, S., 'Government Legislation on Plant Breeders' Rights', 29 *EPW* 1573 (1994).

Sharma, R. and Thomas T. Poleman, *The New Economics of India's Green Revolution – Income and Employment Diffusion in Uttar Pradesh* (New Delhi: Vikas, 1994).

Shiva, V., *The Violence of the Green Revolution* (London: Zed, 1991).

Shiva, V., *Future of our Seeds, Future of our Farmers – Agricultural Biodiversity, Intellectual Property Rights and Farmers' Rights* (New Delhi: Research Foundation for Science, Technology and Natural Resource Policy, 1996).

Shiva, V. and Tom Crompton, 'Monopoly and Monoculture – Trends in Indian Seed Industry', XXXIII/39 *EPW* A-137 (1998).

Singh, A.L. and Shahab Fazal, *Agriculture and Rural Development* (New Delhi: B.R. Publishing, 1998).

Singh, R.P., 'An Interface in Public and Private Maize Research in India', in Roberta V. Gerpacio ed., *Impact of Public- and Private-Sector Maize Breeding Research in Asia, 1966-1997/98* at 44 (Mexico, DF: International Maize and Wheat Improvement Center, 2001).

Srinivasan, C.S., 'Current Status of Plant Variety Protection in India', in M.S. Swaminathan ed., *Agrobiodiversity and Farmers' Rights* 77 (Delhi: Konark, 1996).

Chapter 6

Boyle, A., 'The Role of International Human Rights Law in the Protection of the Environment', in Alan E. Boyle and Michael R. Anderson eds, *Human Rights Approaches to Environmental Protection* 43 (Oxford: Clarendon, 1996).

Bullard, R.D., 'Introduction', in Robert D. Bullard ed., *Confronting Environmental Racism – Voices from the Grassroots* 7 (Boston: South End Press, 1993).

Commission for Racial Justice United Church of Christ, *Toxic Wastes and Race in the United States – A National Report on the Racial and Socio-Economic Characteristics of Communities with Hazardous Waste Sites* (New York: United Church of Christ, 1987).

McDermott, C.J., 'Balancing the Scales of Environmental Justice', 21 *Fordham Urban L.J.* 689 (1995).

Michalopoulos, C., Role of Special and Differential Treatment for Developing Countries in GATT and the World Trade Organization (Washington, DC: World Bank, Working Paper #2388, 2000).

Popovic, N.A.F., 'In Pursuit of Environmental Human Rights: Commentary on the Draft Declaration of Principles on Human Rights and the Environment', 27 *Columbia Hum. Rts. L. Rev.* 487 (1996).

Torres, G., 'Changing the Way Government Views Environmental Justice', C981 *American Law Institute – American Bar Association* 561 (1995).

Vasak, K., 'Pour une troisième génération des droits de l'homme', in Christophe Swinarski ed., *Studies and Essays on International Humanitarian Law and Red Cross Principles in Honour of Jean Pictet* 837 (The Hague: Nijhoff, 1984).

Youssef, H., *Special and Differential Treatment for Developing Countries in the WTO* (Geneva: South Centre, 1999).

Documents

Treaties

Agreement Establishing the Common Fund for Commodities, Geneva, 27 June 1980, *reprinted in* 19 *ILM* 896 (1980).

Agreement Establishing the Fund for the Development of the Indigenous Peoples of Latin America and the Caribbean, Madrid, 24 July 1992, *reprinted in* Wolfgang E. Burhenne ed., *International Environmental Law – Multilateral Treaties* 992:55 (1995).

Agreement Establishing the World Trade Organization, Marrakesh, 15 Apr. 1994, *reprinted in* 33 *ILM* 1144 (1994).

Agreement on Agriculture, Marrakesh, 15 Apr. 1994, in World Trade Organization, *The Legal Texts – The Results of the Uruguay Round of Multilateral Trade Negotiations* (Cambridge: Cambridge University Press, 1999).

Agreement on Textiles and Clothing, Marrakesh, 15 Apr. 1994, in World Trade Organization, *The Legal Texts – The Results of the Uruguay Round of Multilateral Trade Negotiations* (Cambridge: Cambridge University Press, 1999).

Agreement on the Global System of Trade Preferences among Developing Countries, Belgrade, 13 Apr. 1988, *reprinted in* 27 *ILM* 1204 (1988).

Agreement on Trade-Related Aspects of Intellectual Property Rights, Marrakesh, 15 Apr. 1994, *reprinted in* 33 *ILM* 1125 (1994).

Agreement Relating to the Implementation of Part XI of the United Nations Convention on the Law of the Sea of 10 December 1982, New York, 28 July 1994, *reprinted in* 33 *ILM* 1309 (1994).

Agreement to Revise the Bangui Agreement on the Creation of an African Intellectual Property Organization of 2 March 1977, Bangui, 24 Feb. 1999.

Articles of Agreement of the International Bank for Reconstruction and Development, 27 Dec. 1945, 2 *UNTS* 134.

Cartagena Protocol on Biosafety to the Convention on Biological Diversity, Montreal, 20 Jan. 2000, *reprinted in* 39 *ILM* 1027 (2000).

Convention Concerning Minimum Standard of Social Security (Convention N° 102), 28 June 1952, *reprinted in* International Labour Organization, *International Labour Conventions and Recommendations – 1952-1976 – Volume II* (Geneva: International Labour Office, 1996).

Convention for the Protection of Human Rights and Fundamental Freedoms, Rome, 4 Nov. 1950, *European Treaty Series*, N° 5 et al.

Convention for the Protection of the World Cultural and Natural Heritage, Paris, 23 Nov. 1972, *reprinted in* 11 *ILM* 1358 (1972).

Convention on Biological Diversity, Rio de Janeiro, 5 June 1992, *reprinted in* 31 *ILM* 818 (1992).

Convention on Persistent Organic Pollutants, Stockholm, 23 May 2001, *reprinted in* 55 *ILM* 531 (2001).

Convention on the Conservation of European Wildlife and Natural Habitats, Berne, 19 Sept. 1979, *European Treaty Series* N° 104.

Convention on the Elimination of All Forms of Discrimination against Women, New York, 18 Dec. 1979, *reprinted in* 19 *ILM* 33 (1980).

Convention on the Law of the Non-navigational Uses of International Watercourses, 12 May 1997, *reprinted in* 36 *ILM* 700 (1997).

Convention on the Law of Treaties, Vienna, 23 May 1969, *reprinted in* 8 *ILM* 679 (1969).

Convention on Wetlands of International Importance Especially as Waterfowl Habitat, Ramsar, 2 Feb. 1971, *reprinted in* 11 *ILM* 963 (1972).

Convention to Combat Desertification in Those Countries Experiencing Serious Drought and/or Desertification, Particularly in Africa, Paris, 17 June 1994, *reprinted in* 33 *ILM* 1328 (1994).

Fourth ACP-EEC Convention, Lomé, 15 Dec. 1989, *reprinted in* 29 *ILM* 783 (1990).

Framework Convention on Climate Change, New York, 9 May 1992, *reprinted in* 31 *ILM* 849 (1992).

General Agreement on Tariffs and Trade, Geneva, 31 Oct. 1947, 55 *UNTS* 187 (1950).

Instrument for the Establishment of the Restructured Global Environment Facility, Geneva, 16 Mar. 1994, *reprinted in* 33 *ILM* 1273 (1994).

International Cocoa Agreement, Geneva, 16 July 1993, UN Doc. TD/COCOA.8/17/Rev.1 (1995).

International Convention for the Protection of New Varieties of Plants, Paris, 2 Dec. 1961, as Revised at Geneva on 10 Nov. 1972, 23 Oct. 1978 and 19 Mar. 1991 (UPOV Doc. 221(E), 1996).

International Covenant on Economic, Social and Cultural Rights, New York, 16 Dec. 1966, *reprinted in* 6 *ILM* 360 (1967).

International Treaty on Plant Genetic Resources for Food and Agriculture, Rome, 3 Nov. 2001.

International Tropical Timber Agreement, Geneva, 26 Jan. 1994, *reprinted in* 33 *ILM* 1014 (1994).

Joint Convention on the Safety of Spent Fuel Management and on the Safety of Radioactive Waste Management, Vienna, 5 Sept. 1997, *reprinted in* 36 *ILM* 1436 (1997).

Kyoto Protocol to the United Nations Framework Convention on Climate Change, Kyoto, 11 Dec. 1997, UN Doc. FCCC/CP/1997/7/Add.1.

Partnership Agreement Between the Members of the African, Caribbean and Pacific Group of States of the one Part, and the European Community and its Member States, of the other Part, Cotonou, 23 June 2000, *Official Journal* L 317, 15/12/2000 p. 3.

Protocol on Substances that Deplete the Ozone Layer, Montreal, 16 Sept. 1987, *reprinted in* Ozone Secretariat – UNEP, *Handbook for the International Treaties for the Protection of the Ozone Layer* (5th ed. 2000).

Protocol to Amend the 1963 Vienna Convention on Civil Liability for Nuclear Damage, Vienna, 12 Sept. 1997, *reprinted in* 36 *ILM* 1462 (1997).

United Nations Convention on the Law of the Sea, Montego Bay, 10 Dec. 1982, *reprinted in* 21 *ILM* 1261 (1982).

Vienna Convention on Succession of States in Respect of Treaties, 22 Aug. 1978, *reprinted in* 17 *ILM* 1488 (1978).

Other Official Documents and Documents of International Organizations

Agenda 21, *Report of the United Nations Conference on Environment and Development*, Rio de Janeiro, 3-14 June 1992, UN Doc. A/CONF.151/26/Rev.1 (Vol. 1), Annex II.

Bonn Guidelines on Access to Genetic Resources and Fair and Equitable Sharing of the Benefits Arising out of their Utilization, in Dec. VI/24, 'Access and Benefit-Sharing as Related to Genetic Resources', *Report of the Sixth Meeting of the Conference of the Parties to the Convention on Biological Diversity*, The Hague, 7-19 April 2002, UN Doc. UNEP/CBD/COP/6/20.

Brussels Declaration, Third United Nations Conference on the Least Developed Countries, 20 May 2001, UN Doc. A/CONF.191/12.

CGIAR, Progress Report on IPR Matters and Proposal for Review of Plant Breeding, Mid-Term Meeting, 1999, Beijing, CGIAR Doc. MTM/99/20.

CGIAR, CGIAR Center Statements on Genetic Resources, Intellectual Property Rights, and Biotechnology (1999).

Code of Conduct for Responsible Fisheries, Report of the Conference of FAO, 28th Sess., Rome 20-31 Oct. 1995, Doc. C 95/REP, Annex I.

Commission on Genetic Resources for Food and Agriculture/Ximena Flores Palacios, Contribution to the Estimation of Countries' Interdependence in the Area of Plant Genetic Resources (Background Study Paper No.7 Rev.1, 1997).

Commission on Genetic Resources for Food and Agriculture, Possible Formulas for the Sharing of Benefits Based on Different Benefit-Indicators, Rome, 8th Sess., 19-23 Apr. 1999, Doc. CGRFA-8/99/8.

Commission on Human Rights, Ways and Means to Carry out a Political Dialogue Between Creditor and Debtor Countries in the United Nations System, based on the Principle of Shared Responsibility, 52nd Session, UN Doc. E/CN.4/1996/22.

Committee on Economic, Social and Cultural Rights, Statement by the Committee on Economic, Social and Cultural Rights on Human Rights and Intellectual Property, UN Doc. E/2002/22-E/C.12/2001/17, Annex XIII.

Declaration of the United Nations Conference on the Human Environment, Stockholm, 16 June 1972, *reprinted in* 11 *ILM* 1416 (1972).

Draft International Code of Conduct on the Transfer of Technology, 5 June 1985, *reprinted in* UNCTAD, International Investment Instruments: A Compendium – Volume I, UN Doc. UNCTAD/DTCI/30(Vol. I) (1996).

FAO, International Undertaking on Plant Genetic Resources, Res. 8/83, Report of the Conference of FAO, 22nd Sess., Rome, 5-23 Nov. 1983, Doc. C83/REP.

FAO, Agreed Interpretation of the International Undertaking, Res. 4/89, Report of the Conference of the FAO, 25th Session, Rome, 29 Nov. 1989, Doc. C89/REP.

FAO, Annex 3 to the International Undertaking on Plant Genetic Resources, Res. 3/91, Report of the Conference of the FAO, 26th Session, Rome, 25 Nov. 1991, Doc. C91/REP.

FAO, Handbook on TCDC (1992).

GATT, Differential and More Favourable Treatment, Reciprocity and Fuller Participation of Developing Countries (Enabling Clause), Decision of 28 Nov. 1979 (L/4903).

GEF/Ken King, The Incremental Costs of Global Environmental Benefits (Washington, DC: GEF, 1993).

GEF/Helen Sjoeberg, From Idea to Reality – The Creation of the Global Environment Facility (Washington, DC: GEF, 1994).

GEF/Gareth Porter et al., Study of GEF's Overall Performance (Washington, DC: GEF, 1998).

GEF, Focusing on the Global Environment – The First Decade of the GEF – Second Overall Performance Study (2002).

Human Rights Committee, General Comment N° 18, Non-discrimination (Thirty-seventh session, 1989), UN Doc. E/C.12/2000/4 (2000).

International Labour Office, *Employment, Growth and Basic Needs* (New York: Praeger, 1976).

Non-Legally Binding Authoritative Statement of Principles for a Global Consensus on the Management, Conservation and Sustainable Development of all Types of Forests, Rio de Janeiro, 14 June 1992, *reprinted in* 31 *ILM* 881 (1992).

Programme of Action for the Least Developed Countries, Third United Nations Conference on the Least Developed Countries, Brussels, Belgium, 20 May 2001, UN Doc. A/CONF.191/11.

Programme for the Further Implementation of Agenda 21, UNGA Res. S-19/2 (Annex), *reprinted in* 36 *ILM* 1639 (1997).

Regulations on Prospecting and Exploration for Polymetallic Nodules in the Area, in International Seabed Authority, Decision of the Assembly Relating to the Regulations on Prospecting and Exploration for Polymetallic Nodules in the Area, 13 July 2000, Doc. ISBA/6/A/18.

Report of the Open-ended Working Group on the Question of Equitable Representation on and Increase in the Membership of the Security Council and Other Matters related to the Security Council, UN Doc. A/55/47 (2001).

Report of the United Nations Conference on the Human Environment, Stockholm, 5-16 June 1972, UN Doc. A/CONF.48/14/Rev.1.

Rio Declaration on Environment and Development, 14 June 1992, Rio de Janeiro, *reprinted in* 31 *ILM* 874 (1992).

Sub-Commission on Prevention of Discrimination and Protection of Minorities/Fatma Zohra Ksentini-Special Rapporteur, Human Rights and the Environment – Final Report, UN Doc. E/CN.4/Sub.2/1994/9.

Sub-Commission on Human Rights Resolution 2001/21, Intellectual Property and Human Rights, UN Doc. E/CN.4/Sub.2/RES/2001/21.

Sub-Commission on the Promotion and Protection of Human Rights, The Impact of the Agreement on Trade-Related Aspects of Intellectual Property Rights on Human Rights, UN Doc. E/CN.4/Sub.2/2001/13.

UNCTAD, Proceedings of the UNCTAD 1, Final Act and Report, UN Doc. E/Conf.46/139-E/Conf.46/141 (Vol. I) at Annex A.I.1.

UNCTAD, The Role of the Patent System in the Transfer of Technology to Developing Countries, UN Doc. TD/B/AC.11/19/Rev.1 (1975).

UNCTAD Res. 93 (IV), Integrated Programme for Commodities, 30 May 1976, in Proceedings of the UNCTAD, Fourth Session, Nairobi, 5-31 May 1976, UN Doc. TD/218 (Vol. I).

UNCTAD, Negotiations on an International Code of Conduct on the Transfer of Technology, UN Doc. TD/CODE TOT/60 (1995).

UNCTAD/Andrew Barnett, Do Environmental Imperatives Present Novel Problems and Opportunities for the International Transfer of Technology?, UN Doc. UNCTAD/DST/4 (1995).

UNCTAD, Fostering Technological Dynamism: Evolution of Thought on Technological Development Processes and Competitiveness, UN Doc. UNCTAD/DST/9 (1996).

UNCTAD, Promoting the Transfer and Use of Environmentally Sound Technologies: A Review of Policies, UN Doc. UNCTAD/DST/12 (1997).

UNCTAD, Statistical Profile of the Least Developed Countries 2001, UN Doc. UNCTAD/LDC/Misc.72 (2001).

UNCTAD, Economic Development in Africa: Policy, Prospects and Policy Issues, UN Doc. UNCTAD/GDS/AFRICA/1-TD/B/48/12 (2002).

UNCTAD, Partnerships and Networking in Science and Technology for Development, UN Doc. UNCTAD/ITE/TEB/11 (2002).

UNCTAD, *The Least Developed Countries Report* (Geneva: UNCTAD, annual).

UNDP, *Human Development Report* (New York: Oxford University Press, annual).

UNDP, UNEP and World Bank, *Global Environment Facility – Independent Evaluation of the Pilot Phase* (Washington, DC: The World Bank, 1994).

UNFCCC, Decision 5/CP.1, Activities Implemented Jointly Under the Pilot Phase, *Report of the Conference of the Parties on its First Session*, Berlin 28 Mar.-7 Apr. 1995, UN Doc. FCCC/CP/1995/7/Add.1.

UNFCCC, Decision 17/CP.7, Modalities and Procedures for a Clean Development Mechanism as Defined in Article 12 of the Kyoto Protocol, *Report of the Conference of the Parties on its Seventh Session*, Marrakesh, 29 Oct.-10 Nov. 2001, UN Doc. FCCC/CP/2001/13/Add.2.

UNFCCC, Draft Decision -/CMP.1 (Mechanisms), in Decision 15/CP.7, Principles, Nature and Scope of the Mechanisms Pursuant to Articles 6, 12 and 17 of the Kyoto Protocol, *Report of the Conference of the Parties on its Seventh Session*, Marrakesh, 29 Oct.-10 Nov. 2001, UN Doc. FCCC/CP/2001/13/Add.2.

UNGA Res. 14 (I), Budgetary and Financial Arrangements, 13 Feb. 1946, in Resolutions Adopted by the General Assembly During the First Part of its First Session from 10 Jan. to 14 Feb. 1946.

UNGA Res. 1803 (XVII), Permanent Sovereignty over Natural Resources, 14 Dec. 1962, *reprinted in* 2 *ILM* 223 (1963).

UNGA Res. 1995 (XIX), Establishment of the United Nations Conference on Trade and Development as an Organ of the General Assembly, 30 Dec. 1964, in Resolutions Adopted by the General Assembly During its 19th Session, 1 Dec. 1964-1 Sept. 1965, UN Doc. A/5815.

UNGA Res. 2625 (XXV), Declaration on Principles of International Law Concerning Friendly Relations and Cooperation Among States in Accordance with the Charter of the United Nations, 24 Oct. 1970, *reprinted in* 9 *ILM* 1292 (1970).

UNGA Res. 2749 (XXV), Declaration of Principles Governing the Sea-Bed and the Ocean floor, and the Subsoil Thereof, Beyond the Limits of National Jurisdiction, 17 Dec. 1970, in Resolutions Adopted by the General Assembly During its 25th Session, UN Doc. A/8028.

UNGA Res. 3201 (S-VI), Declaration on the Establishment of a New International Economic Order, 1 May 1974, *reprinted in* 13 *ILM* 715 (1974).

UNGA Res. 3281 (XXIX), 12 Dec. 1974, Charter of Economic Rights and Duties of States, in Resolutions Adopted by the General Assembly during its 29th Session, 17 Sept.-8 Dec. 1974, UN Doc. A/9631.

UNGA Res. 41/128, Declaration on the Right to Development, 4 Dec. 1986, Resolutions and Decisions Adopted by the General Assembly During its 41st Session, 16 Sept.-19 Dec. 1986, GAOR 41st Session, Supp. 53 (A/41/53).

UNGA Res. S-18/3, Declaration on International Economic Cooperation, in particular the Revitalization of Economic Growth and Development of the Developing Countries, 1 May 1990, General Assembly 18th Special Session, UN Doc. A/S-18/15 (1990).

UNGA Res. 45/212, Protection of Global Climate for Present and Future Generations of Mankind, 21 Dec. 1990, in Resolutions and Decisions Adopted by the General Assembly During its 45th Session, UN Doc. A/45/49.

UNGA Res. 47/188, Establishment of an Intergovernmental Negotiating Committee for the Elaboration of an International Convention to Combat Desertification in those Countries Experiencing Serious Drought and/or Desertification, Particularly in Africa, 22 Dec.

1992, in Resolutions and Decisions Adopted by the General Assembly During its 47th Session, UN Doc. A/47/49.

UNGA Res. 52/185, Enhancing International Cooperation Towards a Durable Solution to the External Debt Problem of Developing Countries, 18 Dec. 1997, UN Doc. A/RES/52/185.

UNGA Res. 55/5, Scale of Assessments for the Apportionment of the Expenses of the United Nations, 22 Jan. 2001, UN Doc. A/RES/55/5 B-F.

UNGA Res. 55/199, 10-year Review of Progress Achieved in the Implementation of the Outcome of the UN Conference on Environment and Development, 20 Dec. 2000, UN Doc. A/RES/55/199.

UNGA Res. 53/30, Question of the Equitable Representation on and Increase in the Membership of the Security Council and Related Matters, 1 Dec. 1998, UN Doc. A/RES/53/30.

UNGA Res. 55/2, United Nations Millenium Declaration, 18 Sept. 2000, UN Doc. A/RES/55/2.

UNGA Res. 56/83, Responsibility of States for Internationally Wrongful Acts, 12 Dec. 2001, UN Doc. A/RES/56/83.

UN High Commissioner for Human Rights, Globalization and its Impact on the Full Enjoyment of Human Rights, UN Doc. E/CN.4/2002/54 (2002).

Universal Declaration of Human Rights, in Human Rights – A Compilation of International Instruments, Volume I (First Part) – Universal Instruments, UN Doc. ST/HR/1/Rev.4 (Vol.I/Part 1, 1993).

Vienna Programme of Action on Science and Technology for Development, in Report of the United Nations Conference on Science and Technology for Development, Vienna, 20-31 Aug. 1979, UN Doc. A/CONF.81/16.

World Bank, Res. N° 91-5, Global Environment Facility, *reprinted in* 30 *ILM* 1735 (1991).

World Bank, Resolution No. 96-9/Resolution No. IDA 96-5, Establishment of the Heavily Indebted Poor Countries (HIPC) Debt Initiative Trust Fund, *reprinted in* 36 *ILM* 990 (1997).

World Bank, The Seed Industry in South Asia (Washington, DC: World Bank, Precis N° 112, 1996).

World Bank, *The World Bank Annual Report* (Washington, DC: World Bank, annual).

World Bank, *World Development Indicators* (Washington, DC: World Bank, annual).

World Bank, *World Development Report* (New York: Oxford University Press, annual).

World Resources Institute et al., *World Resources* (New York: Oxford University Press, annual).

WTO, Preferential Tariff Treatment for Least-developed Countries – Decision on Waiver, 15 June 1999, WTO Doc. WT/L/304.

WTO, Ministerial Declaration, Ministerial Conference – Fourth Session, WTO Doc. WT/MIN(01)/DEC/1 (2001).

WTO, Declaration on the TRIPS Agreement and Public Health, Ministerial Conference – Fourth Session, WTO Doc. WT/MIN(01)/DEC/2 (2001).

WTO, Implementation-Related Issues and Concerns, Ministerial Conference – Fourth Session, WTO Doc. WT/MIN(01)/17 (2001).

Cases

Brown v. Board of Education, 347 U.S. 483 (1953).
Continental Shelf (Tunisia/Libyan Arab Jamahiriya), Judgment, *ICJ Reports 1982*, p.18.
Corfu Channel Case, Judgment, *ICJ Reports 1949*, p. 4.
Delimitation of the Maritime Boundary in the Gulf of Maine Area, Judgment, *ICJ Reports 1984*, p. 246.
Diamond v. Chakrabarty, 447 U.S. 303 (1980).
European Communities – Regime for the Importation, Sale and Distribution of Bananas, Report of the Appellate Body, 22 Aug. 1997, WTO Doc. WT/DS27/AB/R.
Gabčíkovo-Nagymaros Project (Hungary/Slovakia), Judgment, *ICJ Reports 1997*, p. 7.
Island of Palmas Case (Netherlands v. USA), the Hague, April 1928, 2 *Rep. Int'l Arbitral Awards* 829 (1949).
Lujan v. Defender of Wildlife, 112 S. Ct. 2130 (1992).
Maritime Delimitation in the Area between Greenland and Jan Mayen, Judgment, *ICJ Reports 1993*, p. 38.
Minors Oposa v. Secretary of the Department of Environment and Natural Resources, The Philippines Supreme Court, 30 July 1993, *reprinted in* 33 *ILM* 173 (1994).
Reparation for Injuries Suffered in the Service of the United Nations, 11 Apr. 1949, *ICJ Reports 1949*, p. 174.
Request for an Examination of the Situation in Accordance with Paragraph 63 of the Court's Judgment of 20 December 1974 in the Nuclear Tests (New Zealand v. France) Case, *ICJ Reports 1995*, p. 288.
Reservations to the Convention on Genocide, Advisory Opinion, *ICJ Reports 1951*, p. 15.
S.S. 'Lotus', Permanent Court of International Justice, Collection of Judgments, Series A – N° 10, 1927.
South West Africa, Second Phase, Judgment – Dissenting Opinion of Judge Tanaka, *ICJ Reports 1966*, p. 6.
Trail Smelter Case (United States v. Canada), 16 Apr. 1938 and 11 Mar. 1941, 3 *Rep. Int'l Arbitral Awards* 1905.

Other Documents

African Model Legislation for the Protection of the Rights of Local Communities, Farmers and Breeders, and for the Regulation of Access to Biological Resources (2000).
India, Law Commission of India, Biodiversity Bill (One Hundred Seventy First Report on Biodiversity Bill, January 2000).
India, Patents Act, 1970, Act 39 of 1970.
India, Protection of Plant Varieties and Farmers' Rights Act, 2001, Act No. 53 of 2001.
Institute of International Law, Responsibility and Liability under International Law for Environmental Damage, Resolution of 4 Sept. 1997, *reprinted in* 7 *Rev. Eur. Community and Int'l Envtl. L.* 99 (1998).

International Law Association, Declaration on the Progressive Development of Principles of Public International Law relating to a New International Economic Order, *Report of the Sixty-Second Conference* 2 (1987).

International Law Association, Declaration of Principles of International Law Relating to Sustainable Development, New Delhi, 6 April 2002.

United Kingdom, Greenhouse Gas Emissions Trading Scheme 2002, Doc. ETS(01)06.rev1 (2002).

United States, Byrd-Hagel Resolution (S. Res. 98), Expressing Sense of Senate Regarding U.N. Framework Convention on Climate Change, 143 *Congressional Record* S8113-05, S8139 (25 July 1997).

United States, Clean Air Act, 42 U.S.C. §§ 7401 et seq. (1988).

United States, Patent No. 5,401,504, *Use of Turmeric in Wound Healing*, issued 28 Mar. 1995 (after reexamination, expiring 28 March 1999).

United States, Patent 5,723,765, *Control of Plant Gene Expression*, issued 3 Mar. 1998.

United States, Plant Patent Act of 1930, 35 *US Code* 161 et seq.

United States, Tropical Forest Conservation Act of 1998, 22 *US Code* 2431.

United States, United States Trade Representative, *2001 Special 301 Report* at 4 (2001).

Index